More Praise for *Rethinking Gender in Revolutions and Resistance*

'*Rethinking Gender in Revolutions and Resistance* challenges dominant periodizations of revolutions in the region, mapping a new and persuasive historiography of deeply feminist concerns. An important and original contribution to transnational, postcolonial feminist scholarship.'

Chandra Talpade Mohanty, distinguished professor of women's and gender studies, Syracuse University

'If you are interested in Palestinian resistance of Israeli sexual interrogation techniques and/or the post-revolutionary politics of Egypt, Libya and Tunisia and how they have placed the body and sexuality at centre stage, this book offers fresh discussions of new approaches, debates and constructions that will help you appreciate the study of old and new forms of power and their complex relations.'

Mervat F. Hatem, Howard University

About the Editors

Maha El Said is a professor at the English Department, Cairo University. She has more than 22 years of experience teaching at Egyptian universities with a special interest in American studies. She was the first to write a book-length dissertation on Arab-American poetry, in 1997. She has published on Arab-American writings, creative writing, popular culture and the impact of new technologies on literature. In 2003–2004 she was a Fulbright visiting scholar at the University of California, Berkeley, where she researched the development of the spoken word as political expression.

Lena Meari is an assistant professor at the Social and Behavioral Sciences Department and the Institute of Women's Studies at Birzeit University, Palestine. Her teaching, research interests and writing focus on settler colonialism in Palestine and formations of revolutionary movements, subjectivities, gender relations and development.

Nicola Pratt is reader in the international politics of the Middle East at University of Warwick. She has been researching and writing about Middle East politics since the end of the 1990s and is particularly interested in feminist approaches as well as 'politics from below'. Her work has appeared in *International Studies Quarterly*, *Third World Quarterly*,

Review of International Studies and Review of International Political Economy, amongst others. She is author of *Democracy and Authoritarianism in the Arab World*, co-author (with Nadje Al-Ali) of *What Kind of Liberation? Women and the Occupation of Iraq* and co-editor (with Sophie Richter-Devroe) of *Gender, Governance and International Security* and (with Nadje Al-Ali) *Women and War in the Middle East*. Between 2010 and 2013, she was co-director of the 'Reconceptualising Gender: Transnational Perspectives' research network with Birzeit University, Palestine.

Rethinking Gender in Revolutions and Resistance

Lessons from the Arab World

Edited by Maha El Said, Lena Meari and Nicola Pratt

Zed Books

LONDON

Rethinking Gender in Revolutions and Resistance: Lessons from the Arab World was first published in 2015 by Zed Books Ltd, Unit 2.8, The Foundry, 17 Oval Way, London, SE11 5RR, UK

www.zedbooks.co.uk

Typeset in Joanna by Swales & Willis Ltd, Exeter, Devon, UK
Index: Kerry Taylor
Cover designed by Kika Sroka-Miller

A catalogue record for this book is available from the British Library

ISBN 978-1-78360-283-4 hb
ISBN 978-1-78360-282-7 pb
ISBN 978-1-78360-284-1 pdf
ISBN 978-1-78360-285-8 epub
ISBN 978-1-78360-286-5 mobi

Printed and bound by CPI Group (UK) Ltd, Croydon, CR0 4YY

MIX
Paper from
responsible sources
FSC® C013604

Contents

PART II The Body and Resistance

PART III Gender and the Construction of the Secular/Islamic Binary

Acknowledgements

We would like to take this opportunity to thank all those who made this book possible. We begin by thanking the British Academy, as well as the Department of Politics and International Studies and the Centre for the Study of Women and Gender, both at the University of Warwick, for their funding of a workshop in July 2013 entitled 'Rethinking Gender in Revolutions and Resistance: Lessons from the Arab World'. The workshop came at the end of a three-year research partnership, funded by the British Academy, between the Centre for the Study of Women and Gender and Birzeit University's Institute of Women's Studies. The workshop enabled us to invite a number of scholars from the Middle East, North America, Europe and the UK to discuss women's agency, gender politics and the gender dimensions of socio-political transformations in the region. While we were unable to include all workshop participants in this volume, we would like to express our appreciation to everyone for their contributions, papers and stimulating discussions over the course of the workshop, in particular Shereen Abouelnaga, Anoud Abusalim, Sahar Mediha Alnaas, Abeer Al-Najjar, Alessia Belli, Erika Biagini, Frances Hasso, Nadia El

Kholy, Solava Ibrahim, Merve Kutuk, Nof Nasser Eddin, Hala G. Sami, Mounira Soliman and Dina Wahba for their presentations; Nadje Al-Ali, Ruth Pearson, Sophie Richter-Devroe and Khursheed Wadia for chairing; and Lana Tatour for assistance.

We are very grateful to all the contributors to this book, who trusted us to compile this volume and who patiently and graciously worked on revisions to their chapters. Finally, we thank our commissioning editor, Kim Walker, for her support, guidance and patience throughout this project.

Nicola would like to give a special thanks to Professor Ruth Pearson, emeritus professor of development studies at Leeds University, for encouraging her to produce an edited volume based on the workshop, and to her co-editors, Lena Meari and Maha El Said, for their hard work and dedication to seeing this project through. It has been a great pleasure working together.

Lena would like to thank the members of the Institute of Women's Studies at Birzeit University for encouraging her to participate in the project and co-edit this volume. Further, she expresses her deep appreciation to the women whose life experiences, struggles and aspirations for liberation and justice have constituted the subject and material of this volume.

Maha would like to thank her colleagues at the Department of English Language and Literature, Cairo University, who have provided continuous support throughout the process. A special thanks goes to her co-editors, Nicola Pratt and Lena Meari, whose insights and perceptions sustained the intellectual stimulation amongst the editors and the authors until the final production.

INTRODUCTION

Rethinking Gender in Revolutions and Resistance in the Arab World

Maha El Said, Lena Meari and Nicola Pratt

The aim of this volume is to go beyond the dichotomy of the discourses that have emerged since 2011, which either celebrate women's participation in the uprisings and mass protests that occurred across the Arab region or highlight that women's rights are being threatened by newly empowered conservative forces. Such narratives are predicated upon assumptions, rooted in Eurocentric/Orientalist epistemologies, about the essential and fixed patriarchal nature of Arab/Muslim culture and religion and its role in determining the position of women in Arab/Muslim countries. In this way, other factors shaping women's experiences, such as political economies or imperialist geopolitics, are ignored, whilst religion is posited as necessarily oppressive for women, as opposed to secularism, which supposedly guarantees their rights. Within such a framework of assumptions, there is a tendency to treat women's agency in the Arab world as an indication and reflection of liberal/feminist desires.

None of the above assumptions encapsulates or explains the shifts in gender identities, gender relations and gender norms that have occurred both leading up to and since the outbreak of what has problematically come to be known as the Arab Spring. Narratives about gender and the Arab Spring tend to homogenize women's experiences across time and space, ignoring issues of class, nationality and other axes of social difference. Meanwhile, presenting the Arab Spring as the starting point in a discussion of gender in the Arab world erases a long history of women's resistance activities and involvement in civil society dissent and anti-colonial movements in general.

Rethinking the Arab Spring

First of all, we question the term 'Arab Spring', which not only assumes that the Arab world was hibernating through a long winter prior to the end of 2010 but also suggests a teleology of political change, progressing from the green sprouts of political reform in spring to the full blossoms of democracy in summer. Initially, many people from the region disputed the term. Some considered the mass protests and uprisings witnessed from the end of 2010 onwards as revolutions, with the aims of not only political reform towards procedural democracy but radical socio-political transformation. However, others contended that counter-revolutionary forces were re-asserting their power, or argued that events were manipulated by imperialist interests to reshape the Arab region. We believe that all the above apply in different forms and to different degrees when analysing events that swept the Arab world.

It is certainly difficult to select any one term to describe the socio-political upheavals witnessed since the end of 2010, which have included not only peaceful protests and sit-ins, but also armed conflicts, geopolitical proxy wars, state fragmentation, counter-revolution, political repression and authoritarian renewal. Even amongst the writers contributing to this book, there is no consensus over how to describe events since 2010. One example is Libya, where a grassroots uprising against Muammar Gaddafi's regime developed into armed conflict, with anti-government rebels supported by NATO military intervention, which divided Arab public opinion over whether events in Libya constituted a popular revolution against a dictatorship or an imperialist design to secure Libyan oil. Another example of the contestation over the labelling of particular events is the 30 June 2013 popular protests in Egypt that led to the military deposing Muslim Brotherhood president Mohammed Morsi on 3 July. For many Egyptians, including activists who protested against Morsi's conservative economic and socio-political agenda, including his gender agenda, from the end of 2012 onwards, the president's departure was necessary to ensure the continuation of the goals of the 25 January Revolution. However, for others, not only the Muslim Brotherhood and its supporters, the Egyptian army took advantage of popular opposition to stage a coup and launch a counter-revolution. Indeed, since July 2013, we have seen a huge state crackdown not only on the Muslim Brotherhood but on all forms of political dissent within Egypt (Amnesty International 2014). Yet, seemingly paradoxically, many Egyptian women have supported the army (the most masculinist of institutions) and former army general Abdel Fattah El-Sisi, who was elected president in May 2014. Meanwhile, the 2014 constitution, drafted under the watchful eye of the military, includes state-declared guarantees for gender equality.

The movement from revolution to counter-revolution since 2011 has particularly impacted colonized Palestine and, specifically, the Gaza Strip. In 2011 Palestinians in the Gaza Strip, strangled by four years of Israeli-imposed blockade, benefitted from the departure of president Hosni Mubarak, who had been complicit in Israel's siege, when Egyptian authorities finally opened the Rafah crossing.[1] Meanwhile in Egypt popular protests called for not only political change at home but also justice for the Palestinians. In 2012 the coming to power of the Muslim Brotherhood in Egypt was a boon for Hamas, and Morsi successfully negotiated a ceasefire between Hamas and Israel in November 2012. Conversely, the ousting of Mohammed Morsi in 2013 isolated Hamas and the Palestinians of Gaza in general. Undoubtedly, Israel was able to capitalize on the changing balance of power to launch a war against the Gaza Strip in July 2014, even more deadly than any other Israeli war in the previous decade, including Operation Cast Lead in 2008–2009. No Arab leader condemned the Israeli attack, whilst popular protests against Israel's actions in 2014 were almost non-existent, most notably in Egypt, where the national media stirred up anti-Hamas and anti-Palestinian sentiments and the new regime muted any voices of dissent.

A focus only on the political or geopolitical levels may lead us to negatively evaluate the political changes since the end of 2010 as failing to respond to the aspirations of those who went out in their millions to protest against their leaders. However, such an evaluation fails to capture the socio-political transformations that certainly precede the end of 2010 and which have been given new impetus since then. In particular, transformations in gender norms, identities and roles are intrinsic to the political upheavals since 2010, as well as to resistance and dissent before then. Despite the large number of academic books and articles about events in the Arab region since the end of 2010, the majority of scholars have largely ignored or marginalized socio-political change prior to 2010 and women's participation in it. The relatively short time that has elapsed since the onset of the Arab Spring cannot explain this considerable gap in the literature given the not insignificant number of 'gender-blind' books that have already been published about it.[2]

This volume seeks to address the gender deficit in current studies of socio-political transformations in the Arab world and, specifically, women's agency and gender politics within those transformations. We aim not only to rethink gender in relation to changes in the Arab region but also to challenge historicist perceptions[3] and dominant periodizations of socio-political change, particularly the representation of 2011 as being the start of socio-political transformations in the Arab region. In effect, the term 'Arab Spring' marginalizes earlier moments of transformation and other resistance movements in which women have also participated, such as the Algerian Revolution of the 1950s–1960s and the Palestinian Revolution beginning in the mid-1960s, as well as significant popular dissent and civil society mobilizations in several Arab countries many years prior to what commentators and authors often refer to as the Arab Spring.

We believe that an attention to gender enables us to shed fresh light on our understandings of contemporary socio-political transformations in the Arab region. Yet, by taking gender dynamics and women's issues in the Arab world as a point of departure, we do not intend to single out women from their socio-economic/socio-political contexts. Rather, we aim to deploy feminist analysis as a tool in order to shed light on overlooked aspects of socio-political transformations. This volume explores both continuities and ruptures in gender roles, relations and norms resulting not only from the dramatic uprisings and protests occurring since the end of 2010 but from other moments of upheaval and resistance. We seek to capture the complex constitution of women's subjectivities and agency in relation to structures of power, which cannot be reduced to gender. This volume considers the ways in which women's bodies become objects of control by different actors in order to distinguish the past from the present in processes of political and social change, with particular consequences for different women, but equally it considers how women's bodies become powerful tools of resistance against dictatorship, colonialism and patriarchy. Moreover, we seek to challenge the constructed binary of religion versus secularism that often frames evaluations of socio-political transformations in the Arab world, particularly in relation to the situation of women, whereby secularism is assumed to be a marker of 'progress' and religion a marker of tradition or even 'backwardness'.

Some of the questions that we seek to answer in this volume include:

- What are the epistemological and ontological implications of considering gender and sexualities in the socio-political transformations in the Arab world?
- To what degree do socio-political transformations and other instances of women's resistance activities represent significant ruptures in gender identities, relations and norms?
- How do acts of resistance affect existing perceptions of gender and sexed bodies?

- How do women's various modalities of agency and their gendered experiences disrupt the secular/religious dichotomy?
- What does the case of the Arab world bring to theorizing about gender in revolutions and resistance?

Here, we bring together authors from the Arab world and Europe and from a variety of academic disciplines to rethink the gendered implications of socio-political change and women's resistance activities more broadly, based on previously unpublished and original research. Most of the chapters are based on papers presented at a workshop held at the University of Warwick, UK, in July 2013 and funded by the British Academy and the Department of Politics and International Studies and the Centre for the Study of Women and Gender at the University of Warwick. We are grateful for the contributions of all workshop participants. However, for reasons of space and coherence, we were only able to include a selection of those papers.[4] In order to achieve balance and breadth of coverage in terms of country cases and themes, we have also solicited papers for this volume from other experts in the field. One of the distinguishing features of this volume is the large number of contributing authors from the Arab region, who are not only writing about but also participating in the changing political and social landscapes. Whilst many of the authors in this volume adopt critical views of existing hegemonic Western epistemologies in analyzing the conditions of women in the Arab world, the volume does not seek to reify a binary of Western versus Arab scholarship on women. The chapters here present other positions and arguments, reflecting the diversity of approaches amongst women academics in/from the Arab region.

In this introduction, we introduce the main themes of the volume and discuss some of the key concepts that have been utilized and that we believe, in light of the original empirical material presented in most of the chapters throughout the volume, should be re-thought. We begin by discussing some of the existing arguments regarding gender and socio-political transformations. Next, we discuss three main themes presented in the volume (and which form the basis for organizing the different chapters): the malleability of gender and sexuality in revolutions and resistance; the body and resistance; and gender and the construction of the secular/Islamic binary.

Gender and Socio-Political Transformation

As noted above, at the time of writing, there is only a handful of academic literature examining the Arab Spring from a gender perspective (for example, Al-Ali 2012 and 2014; Elsadda 2011; Hafez 2014; Khalil 2014; Olimat 2014; Salime 2012; Singerman 2013; Skalli 2014). Like those studies, this volume builds on existing work on gender and transformations in the Arab world. In particular, we build on a rich field of work demonstrating women's participation in political struggles and social movements in the colonial and postcolonial periods, including Ellen L. Fleischmann (2000), Margot Badran (1995), Frances Hasso (2005), Julie Peteet (1991), Nadje Al-Ali (2000) and Laurie Brand (1998), amongst others. These authors have highlighted how moments of upheaval and transition create both opportunities and threats for women seeking to participate in public life and raise demands for rights. In some cases women have been able to leverage nationalism and religion to legitimize their presence in the public sphere and frame their demands (Fleischmann 2000; Badran 1995; Hasso 2005; Peteet 1991). However, in other cases nationalism and religion have been used by other actors to delegitimize women's movements and women's rights and to exclude them from political processes (Al-Ali 2000; Brand 1998). In this volume, we certainly find evidence of all of the above in relation to the case studies presented.

We also build on the work of those authors who have examined the ways in which gender is central to political and economic change. The mobilization of women into education and the workforce has been an important instrument for modernizing regimes as well as being held up as a marker of modernity (Al-Ali 2007; Moghadam 2003; Bier 2011; Abu-Lughod 1998). The regulation and control of women's bodies have been central to colonial governance and post-colonial state building (Al-Ali 2007; Bier 2011; Lazreg 1994; Thompson 2000; Charrad 2001). Finally, nationalist and anti-colonial movements have held up women, their behaviour and appearance as symbolic markers of the nation and bestowed upon them responsibility for reproducing the collective and protecting it from foreign influences (Lazreg 1994; Baron 2005; Elsadda 2012). Many of the chapters in this volume highlight continuities with regard to the control and regulation of women's bodies and their use as markers of the nation, as well as contestations over gender norms as part of socio-political transformations and transitions.

Our volume builds on these studies and moves the theoretical debate forward by problematizing the conceptualization of gendered agency, gender identities, gender interests and gender norms in relation to political and social transformations in the Arab world. Overall, the volume emphasizes the different modalities of women's agency in shaping socio-political transformations. Here, it is necessary to expand the notion of the political beyond formal institutions and processes, such as elections, parliaments and constitutions. Although women have been participating in these institutions, their numbers remain small, thereby providing evidence for those who argue that the Arab Spring has been 'bad for women' (Coleman 2011; Langohr 2011; amongst others). Significantly, women have been present in large numbers in street protests and demonstrations as well as initiating new activities in public and virtual spaces. As several of the authors in this volume illustrate, this participation should also be considered political in that it challenges the constructions of gender that underpin claims for and the exercise of political authority.

The Malleability of Gender and Sexuality in Revolutions and Resistance

The first theme highlighted by this volume is the degree to which gendered and sexed norms and identities are malleable in general and particularly in periods of socio-political upheaval. Scholars of gender in the Arab world have highlighted the socially constructed nature of gender norms and identities in specific historical periods, either focusing on state policies and discourses of political and religious elites or on the everyday, context-specific negotiation of gender (for example, within intimate relationships, households, court rooms or government offices) (Abu-Lughod 2000; Bibars 2001; Bier 2011; Hasso 2010; Hoodfar 1997; Joseph 1999; MacLeod 1993; Tucker 2000; amongst others). Whilst many of the chapters in this volume also discuss top-down efforts to regulate normative gender as part of strategies of domination, nevertheless the focus is on the different forms of agency of ordinary women (and often men, too) in constructing new gendered identities and gender norms. Several chapters in this volume illustrate how gender identities and subjectivities emerge in moments of revolution and resistance and also how, in such times, women and men challenge, subvert and resignify existing gender norms, often in creative ways. Moreover, they illustrate how the forging of alternative gender norms is integral to resisting authoritarianism and colonialism, thereby obliging us to rethink 'the political' in revolutions and other transitions. For the most part, observers and commentators have assumed that women's agency in the public sphere, particularly as part of the protests witnessed since the end of 2010, has been an expression of a priori feminist desires for women's rights. Yet, some of the chapters here question the idea that women's identities and subjectivities are fixed according to their gender but rather that these are emergent within the context of political upheaval and conflict. In particular, Shereen Abouelnaga's and Lena Meari's chapters on Egypt and Palestine (respectively) illustrate that the sexual violence to which women are subjected enables them to destabilize and subvert hegemonic norms through their own intentional or unintentional acts and in the process produce new constructs of gendered and sexed identities and subjectivities.

Just as we should avoid assuming a priori gender identities, we must also be careful not to homogenize women's interests in sociopolitical transformations or even to assume that demands for women's rights are expressions of universal feminist desires. Since the 1970s and the introduction of the UN Convention on the Elimination of All Forms of Discrimination against Women (CEDAW), women's interests have increasingly been framed in relation to universal rights. Chapters by Aitemad Muhanna and Sahar Alnaas and Nicola Pratt highlight that there are women in Arab countries using CEDAW to make their rights demands as part of political transitions. Yet, building on Lila Abu-Lughod (2013), Aitemad Muhanna highlights the need for feminists in Tunisia to recognize the significance of religion in shaping the desires and interests of Tunisian women and to localize and contextualize women's rights, rather than simply advocate for women's rights based on a universal rights framework that overlooks the impositions and power structures that the universal entails (Chapter 8, this volume). In discussing 'women's interests' and 'women's rights', we should not fall into a trap of constructing a secular versus Islamic binary (as discussed in a later section) by positing CEDAW against religious understandings of women's rights and interests as the only frameworks through which women can formulate their demands.

In response to critics of her famous typology of women's 'practical' versus 'strategic' gender interests in Nicaraguan women's organizing, Maxine Molyneux has clarified, 'Claims about women's objective interests need to be framed within specific historical contexts since processes of interest formation and articulation are clearly subject to cultural, historical and political variation and cannot be known in advance' (1998: 233). Similarly, the notion of 'women's rights' should be deconstructed not only to reflect the particular contexts of different women but also to recognize that the notion itself is constituted in relation to a specific historical context and is not immune to ideological and political contestations. In other words, 'women's rights' is an 'empty signifier' (Laclau 1996), often strategically deployed by a range of actors, sometimes for purposes that are not related to the needs and interests of specific women. As the chapters on Egypt, Tunisia and Libya illustrate, 'women's rights' have been championed by the spectrum of political forces (including, liberal, leftist, Islamist and military), often seeking to instrumentalize these issues to mobilize women in their support. The need to reconsider what constitutes 'women's interests' and 'women's rights' is politically significant in times of rapid change, when greater numbers of women, particularly women previously marginalized under former regimes, are mobilized.

The chapters by Hala Sami and Sahar Alnaas and Nicola Pratt illustrate how women in Egypt and Libya are drawing on their national heritages and identities to make their claims part of the unfolding socio-political process and legitimize their presence in the public sphere. Meanwhile, in the chapters by Abouelnaga and Meari, women's demands are linked to their specific political contexts of post-Mubarak revolutionary Egypt and anti-colonial struggle in Palestine respectively. These are concrete examples of women contextualizing and localizing their demands, reasserting their belonging to their cities, countries, religions and heritages, and affirming national aspirations rather than characterizing these as being obstacles to their rights. These acts subvert the framework of universal rights and provide an alternative modality of agency to that presented by the 'NGO-ized' women's movement (Jad 2004) that has dominated the field of women's claim-making in the post-Cold War period.

Women's participation in socio-political transformations obliges us to rethink the construction not only of gender identities and interests but also of agency, beyond what has generally been studied in academic literature on women's activism in the Arab world. Saba Mahmood (2005) has critiqued studies of Arab/Muslim women for assuming that women's agency is motivated by an emancipatory agenda and is necessarily resistant of gender hierarchies, even when women's activism is conducted towards other ends (such as embodying piety). Mahmood's ethnography of an Egyptian women's piety movement demonstrates that women's agency may be conducted for the purpose of cultivating norms that underpin gender hierarchies, such as female modesty, rather than resisting such norms. We agree with Mahmood that there is a need to further complicate women's agency with regard to the resistance/subordination binary. However, we also seek to move beyond a secular/religious binary in understanding women's agency (as discussed further in a later section) and to rethink the agency of those women who seek to disrupt hegemonic gender norms.

There has been a general tendency to conceptualize women's agency as an instrument for particular goals (whether national liberation, women's emancipation or family survival). Within such an approach, women's agency is recognizable as an instrument towards achieving a particular end (for example, participating in an association or political movement whose objective is national liberation/women's emancipation, attending rallies denouncing colonialism and occupation, or cultivating patron–client relations to gain access to resources). However, several of the volume's chapters demonstrate that the impact of women's agency in the public sphere cannot be reduced to an *instrument* used for a public or political goal. Rather, chapters by Sami and Alnaas and Pratt illustrate the significance of women's *embodied* agency, of *being* in the public sphere, in disrupting and resisting hegemonic norms. In Sami's chapter, women protesters hold up posters of celebrated women from Egyptian popular culture, and 'can even be seen wearing the posters of such public figures, which suggests their identification with their precursors and emphasizes women's refusal to be interpellated as mere physical vulnerable entities easily accessible for violation' (see Sami, Chapter 3, this volume). In the chapter by Alnaas and Pratt, Libyan women ride bicycles in the streets of Tripoli as a means of forging a new relationship with their city and wear traditional Libyan clothing in public squares associated with the revolution, thereby claiming their place in the public sphere. In other words, socio-political transformation not only consists of changes to institutions and women's participation within those. In addition, women's self-formation, including their bodily performances, is also a subject of socio-political transformation.

Just as women's (and men's) agency cannot be reduced to instruments of change, similarly agency should not be predicated upon *doing*. Western social science has defined agency as the autonomy to 'act' in opposition to 'inaction'. Such an understanding of agency is directly challenged by the concept of *sumud*, which has played an important role in Palestinian resistance (Peteet 1991). Within the

Palestinian struggle, *sumud*, or 'steadfastness', indicates a person's ability to remain in place in the face of indignities, injustices and humiliation at the hands of the colonial power, which seeks to displace and deny the right to exist of the colonized. In other words, steadfastness is not about *doing* but, rather, doing by *not* doing. In her chapter, Meari illustrates the power of *sumud* in the interrogation encounter between Palestinian women strugglers and Israeli security officers. Here, the practice of *sumud* not only enables Palestinian prisoners to withstand sexualized humiliation and torture, but also operates to resignify the meaning of the sexed body within both colonial discourse about the 'other' and Palestinian national discourse.

A reconceptualization of agency enables us to see the significance of women's (and men's) resistance in terms of disrupting hegemonic gender norms through their *alternative* 'stylized gender acts' (Butler 1999: 178–179) (chapters by Shereen Abuelnaga, Lena Meari, Hala Sami, Alnaas and Pratt and El Said, in particular). However, it is also necessary to be attentive to the complex ways in which gender is constituted. As post-colonial theorist Anne McClintock notes, gender 'come[s] into existence in and through relation to [race, class, and sexuality, and, we could add, "nation" as well as coloniality]— if in contradictory and conflictual ways' (McClintock 1995: 5). Several chapters illustrate how hegemonic gender norms are constructed through particular norms of female sexual propriety (as also discussed further in the next section on the body and resistance). Simultaneously, particular notions of female sexual propriety are also constitutive of the boundaries of the nation, between 'us' and 'them'. The interplay between gender, sexuality and nation can render women activists who challenge gender and sexual norms vulnerable to accusations of 'Westernized' (that is, non-authentic) behaviour, even by those who seek to challenge the socio-political status quo, as the chapters by Maha El Said and Abeer Al-Najjar and Anoud Abusalim on Aliaa Elmahdy and Amina Sboui demonstrate. In contrast, other chapters illustrate the ways in which women activists subvert norms of sexual propriety whilst resignifying, rather than repudiating, the nation and, in so doing, reformulate gender norms. Both Abouelnaga's and

Meari's chapters focus on women's refusal to remain silent about the sexual violence committed against them (whether in Egyptian street protests or Israeli colonial prisons) and their smashing of 'the myth of the female body as a symbol of personal and collective national honour and as a site of docility' (Abouelnaga, Chapter 1, this volume). In Egypt, women activists have subverted 'all fixed and monolithic perceptions of the female body as sacred or shameful' by 'shift[ing] the major forms of violence and abuse practised on the female body to the political terrain' of the Egyptian Revolution (Abouelnaga, Chapter 1, this volume). Meanwhile, Meari's study of Palestinian women strugglers in Israeli colonial prisons highlights the way in which they resist sexualized torture through *sumud*, a Palestinian strategy of 'steadfastness' in the face of Zionist oppression and dispossession. In the process, Palestinian women prisoners open up 'the possibility to destabilize the significations of the sexed body, subvert women's daily life routines and social customs that establish women's bodies and sexualities in a fixed manner, and challenge the fixed associations between the female body and the meanings of women's dignity and honour within Palestinian society and the colonial perception of it' (Meari, Chapter 2, this volume).

Alternative gender acts involve both *subversion* of and *compliance* with hegemonic gender-ed and sex-ed norms, thereby dismantling the subordination/resistance binary common to feminist scholarship and critiqued by Mahmood (2005). For example, in Sami's chapter, Egyptian women protesters hold up photographs of Egyptian female celebrities, such as Um Kulthum and Faten Hamama, whose images are strongly associated with normative Egyptian femininity. The validation of these particular female celebrities both conforms to hegemonic gender norms, whilst reinscribing them as subverting the conservative gender discourses of the Muslim Brotherhood through their insertion in political protests. Similarly, in the chapter by Alnaas and Pratt, women's dressing in the traditional Libyan *farashiya* conforms to norms of female modesty in public yet simultaneously the celebration of *farashiya* day reinscribes the *farashiya* as challenging dominant Islamist gender discourses through its insertion into public spaces associated with the 2011 Libyan revolution. The transposing of aesthetic signifiers of (national) patriarchy into revolutionary and political spaces constitutes a creative form of agency that is particularly noticeable in the post-2010 period. In embedding themselves within their local/national context, women activists break down the binary, assumed by dominant strands of second wave feminism (see Cockburn 2007: 192–202), that posits nationalism and national culture in opposition to feminism or women's rights. Rather, these women activists engage in resignifying those elements of nationalist discourse that reduce women to mere symbols of the collective to actively reimagine the nation as a space of equal citizenship.

The Body and Resistance

Bodies and, particularly, women's bodies are key sites of control and contestation in socio-political transformations. Perhaps more so than ever, women's bodies have become 'battlefields' in revolutionary and counter-revolutionary processes since the end of 2010. As women have entered public spaces in ever greater numbers, they have faced a range of measures aiming to control and exclude them, including proposed dress codes, death threats, violence and sexual assaults. Yet, Shereen Abouelnaga argues, in regard to the experience of Egyptian women activists, 'the more the female body was abused, the stronger and more solid the activism that was practised', making the body the 'main protagonist' of the revolution.

In this regard, the Supreme Council of the Armed Forces (SCAF) in Egypt has garnered considerable attention with their use of sexualized violence against women being central to counter-revolutionary processes. Abouelnaga's chapter discusses the case of Samira Ibrahim, a woman activist in her twenties who was arrested and subjected to a 'virginity test' by SCAF in March 2011. Revolutionaries supported Ibrahim in her legal battle against the military doctor who performed the test, recognizing that the use of sexual violence against female activists is aimed at breaking the revolutionary will. In response, SCAF stated that the so-called virginity tests 'were conducted out of self-defence'

(Borkan 2011). According to an interview with a military representative, 'The girls who were detained were not like your daughter or
mine. These were girls who had camped out in tents with male protesters' (Amin 2011); in other words, these were 'loose' girls who
had no respect for authority. The general's statement outlines the definition of the acceptable (Egyptian) woman as one who is confined to
the private realm and complies with normative femininity, as opposed
to 'these girls' who demonstrate boldness and courage and break the
segregation norms observed by 'respectable girls'.

As noted in the previous section, notions of sexual propriety
are key elements in the constructing of gender norms as well as in
marking the boundaries of 'the nation'. The concept of the 'loose
woman' implies defiance of a (gendered) normative order. Within
this paradigm, loose women are potentially a national threat and,
consequently, the control of women's sexuality is necessary to maintain public order. In Egypt, not only were women activists subjected
to violence, they were also accused of being 'sexually frustrated'
and that 'if they had a husband' (that is, a man to control them and
channel their sexual desires in a legitimate way) they would not be
'jeopardizing the whole nation'.[5] The description of revolutionary
women as 'loose' and 'blasphemous' was also used by the authorities
in Yemen to discredit the anti-government protesters (as discussed
by Al-Najjar and Abusalim in Chapter 5).

The use by counter-revolutionary forces of the image of 'loose
women' to discredit mass protests and calls for political change triggered a defensive response amongst many of those struggling in the
name of revolution. In several cases, women and men were segre-
gated during demonstrations. In Bahrain, women were at the front of
demonstrations, whilst their male counterparts protected them from
behind. In Yemen, women were at the back and protected by men at
the front. The Islamist Islah Party (the most important political party
opposing the government in Yemen) went to the extent of building a
wooden fence in Change Square to separate men from women in an
attempt to deflect accusations against them of blasphemy (Sohlman
2012). Perhaps most paradoxically, as highlighted by Al-Najjar and

Abusalim, were the efforts of the April 6 Youth Movement in Egypt to distance themselves from the 'loose' behaviour of Aliaa Elmahdy, who posted a nude picture of herself on the internet in November 2011.

However, it is not only counter-revolutionary forces that have attempted to control women's bodies and sexuality but also post-revolutionary forces. The chapter by Alnaas and Pratt illustrates how Libyan women's bodies have been appropriated and instrumentalized to mark the break from Muammar Gaddafi's Jamahariya and the establishment of an Islamized post-Gaddafi Libyan state, and how newly emerged political forces seek to control women's bodies and sexuality as part of a struggle over authority and power in the 'New Libya'. This magnified focus on women's sexuality leads to a public discourse that focuses on the appearance and behaviour of women; making issues related to women's bodies a matter of state control. In particular, political Islamists, who have dominated the post-2011 political scene, have put the control of women bodies at the forefront of their agendas in line with their notions of 'gendered piety' and 'moralistic politics' (Amar and Vijay 2013). In a critique of Islamist conceptions of citizenship, Fatima Mernissi argues, 'The citizens of the domestic universe are primarily sexual beings; they are defined by their genitals and not their faith' (1985: 139). Political Islamists, including the Muslim Brotherhood and the Salafists, have justified bodily violations and violence, such as female genital mutilation (FGM) and the early marriage of girls, with reference to religion and tradition, enforcing notions of gender hierarchy and patriarchal practices with recourse to conservative interpretations of Islam. Alnaas and Pratt describe efforts by Islamist actors to encourage women to wear 'Islamic' dress and their campaign against CEDAW (and its assumptions of women's bodily autonomy) in order to consolidate their authority by claiming sovereignty over women's bodies and their sexuality in the name of religion. Even in parliament, the presence of female MPs is represented as a threat to the proper functioning of the institution. Alnaas and Pratt recount (Chapter 6) a parliamentary session in which Mohamed Al-Kilani, a Salafist member of parliament 'stated that women and men should never mix in public' and that women's attire and application of make-up creates 'a distractive environment for male members of parliament'. Despite Islamist political agendas to enforce particular notions of sexual propriety and women's bodily conduct, it is important to emphasize that gender and sexuality norms are multidimensional and cannot be reduced to the binary of religion and secularism (as further discussed in the next section).

It is also important to stress that women have been objects and victims of control not only by various political actors. The socio-political transformations since the end of 2010 offer multiple examples of revolutionary corporeal practices that disturb and unsettle power relations as they break the long-standing boundaries that discipline and regulate women's bodies. As several of the chapters in this volume demonstrate, women have rebelled not only against dictatorship but, in so doing, have rebelled against the socially informed body, have shunned the 'docile' female body and used their bodies as weapons of resistance. Employing strategies of resistance that appropriate the oppressive powers of domination, women have been able to 'reconstitute the body in terms that lie outside the hegemonic forms of bodily comportment' (Hafez 2014: 177). Moreover, they have dismantled an essentialized perspective of women in Arab/Muslim countries as submissive and victimized.

A central dimension of women's rebellious behaviour relates to the control of their own bodies and sexuality. The case of Samira Ibrahim is not only an example of the sexualized violence visited upon women's bodies, but also an inspiring example of women breaking the silence over sexual violence and resisting the patriarchal control of their bodies. Al-Najjar and Abusalim argue that Aliaa Elmahdy and Amina Sboui converted the female body from a 'tool of repression' to 'an assertion of power' as they used their bodies to break social norms surrounding the female body. The statement 'my body belongs to me' written on Amina's bare torso is loaded with power as it strips the body of its burden of shame and honour. Maha El Said (Chapter 4) also discusses the case of Elmahdy, noting that 'when Elmahdy poses stark naked she not only reverses the gaze, but also reverses the power relation. She is no longer the passive object of male sexual pleasure;

instead, she challenges this power relation as she defies the performativity norm that reiterates power'. Yet, it is important to note that nudity in itself does not necessarily represent an emancipatory act and may even contribute to constituting sexualized power relations. The issue at stake here is the context of the act and the nature of the shift it produces.

Al-Najjar and Abusalim expose the media responses to Aliaa and Amina, demonstrating the prejudices against women and their bodies. The unthinkable moves by Aliaa and Amina, of posting their naked photographs in order to claim control of their bodies, was so shocking and perplexing that the media reverted to the trope of the psychologically troubled woman, echoing ancient claims of female hysteria, in order to understand the women's actions. In other words, if women break the norm and resist discipline they become unintelligible and disruptive of order. The authors argue that a 'lack of recognition of the socio-political message intended by the women's nudity hindered any serious debate about the message itself'. This is problematic in light of the ways in which women's bodies came to be used and abused in the Arab Spring. Abouelnaga highlights the media narrative in response to a woman who was stripped to her blue bra by military police in Egypt during a demonstration and whose photo went viral on the internet. Whilst Egyptian revolutionaries celebrated the woman's resistance, calling her Sitt el-Banat ('Lady of all Ladies') as a mark of respect, nevertheless Egyptian media asked 'What made her go there?', thereby questioning women's presence in protests as well as reflecting the degree to which control over women's bodies through violence is regarded as a normalized practice.

Another revolutionary use of the body discussed by Maha El Said in her chapter, is the use of belly dancing for political protest. El Said illustrates how Sama El-Masry 'decodes and deconstructs the stereotypes of belly dancing' by using it as a form of protest against the Muslim Brotherhood's efforts to control women's bodies. El Said describes how El-Masry was capable of drawing on folklore to reconfigure belly dancing, employing a 'coercive structure that summons a creative form of resistance'. Similarly, in Libya, as discussed in the previous section, women have resisted political Islam and its attempts to impose Wahhabi style Islamic dress by wearing Libyan national dress, the *farashiya*. In this way, women assert control over their bodies, as well as claiming a national identity that is unique to them.

The bodies in this volume, whether covered up or naked, are rebellious bodies as they 'strip the body of its readings' as an object of sexual desire, causing a 'de-familiarization whose aim is not necessarily that of seeing the female body differently, but of exposing the habitual meanings/values attached to femininity as cultural constructions' (Doane 1981: 24–5). These bodies defy control in creative ways that subvert power by performing and maintaining their bodily integrity and by adopting what Marwan Kraidy calls the 'performative-contentious model of the public sphere', in which 'the gendered human body is at once a medium of expression and a discursive battlefield' (Kraidy 2012: 73).

Gender and the Construction of the Secular/Islamic Binary

We have seen that women's issues in the Arab world in general and in the period of socio-political upheavals in particular are decontextually constructed by the Western and national liberal mind and understood within a paradigm of secular-modern-progressive/Islamic-premodern-traditional binary opposition (see Tadros 2010). Historically, women's rights and women's issues have been intrinsically linked to notions of modernity and national progress in political discourse (Abu-Lughod 1998). In effect, from the early twentieth century, women's rights became a marker of modernity, particularly in secular-orientated modernizing regimes in Tunisia, Egypt and Libya (under Gaddafi). As Omaima Abou-Bakr and Aitemad Muhanna argue in this volume, the intertwining of women's rights with discourses of national modernization has made it difficult for women's movements to maintain their independence from regimes. In addition, it has created a set of binaries, in which the secular (Asad 2003) is heralded as modern and democratic, and as the guarantor of women's rights, whilst political

Islam, or even religion in general, is vilified as 'backward', 'barbaric' and necessarily in opposition to women's rights. Within this vein, the veil has become a master signifier for women's oppression or liberation. Consequently, women's groups or women's rights activists become vulnerable to co-option by secular-orientated dictatorships which suppress political Islam and political Islamists in the name of defending national modernization and women's rights, as has happened in Tunisia and Egypt. Moreover, this logic has justified on the one hand colonial interventions under the pretext of 'liberating' Muslim women from their patriarchal oppressive culture and, on the other hand, an uncritical adoption of the constructions of women and gender in Islam. This has left Muslim women trapped between the colonial-secular discourses versus the local-Islamic discourse.

The secular/Islamist binary as constructed in Western thought does not necessarily apply to the perceptions of large segments of the Arab world. Arab-Muslim subjectivity is not characterized as purely secular or Islamic. There exists another mode of subjectivity that contains both secular and Islamic aspects. Analyzing the relationship between politics and religion in the Arab world, Abd al-Ilah Balqaziz (2013) notes a 'commendable' association between politics and religion existing within the Arab national liberation struggles against colonialism. However, there is another form of association between politics and religion, which has led to internal conflicts and power struggles. This 'uncommendable' form of investing religion in politics is reflected not only within violent groups but also in moderate political-religious groups, and has led to a state of political and cultural polarization and mutual exclusion. In other words, in the context of an anti-colonial national liberation, the struggle occurs between the whole people and the colonizer and religion constitutes a unifying factor. However, in other cases, religion plays a role in instigating conflicts within the same nation for the sake of authority and sovereignty (Balqaziz 2013: 9–11).

Despite Balqaziz's uncritical treatment of nationalism as a unifying force, his words testify to the complicated relationship between (secular) nationalism and Islam. This analysis challenges the construction of 'pure' secular versus religious signs as determinants of Arab sub-jectivities and politics. Balqaziz's argument exemplifies the way in which Arab nationalist intellectuals have analysed the articulation of religion and politics and the different assessment of this relation-ship in anti-colonial versus post-colonial contexts. In this regard, it is interesting to discuss the example of events occurring in the summer of 2013 in Egypt. Following the ousting of former president Moham-med Morsi of the Muslim Brotherhood, the two competing camps (for and against Morsi) were divided spatially between Rabia Al-Adawiya and Tahrir squares, not according to secular versus Islamic conceptions but rather according to different perceptions of Islam and its relationship to national identity as well as differences in the understanding of democracy and its relationship to the politics of the Muslim Brotherhood.

Several scholarly works on Muslim women have engaged more critically with secular-liberal conceptions and Western liberal-feminist viewpoints regarding representations of Muslim women, their rights and agency (for example, Leila Ahmed 1993; Saba Mahmood 2005; Lila Abu-Lughod 2013). Saba Mahmood considers the challenges that women's involvement in Islamist movements poses to feminists in particular, and secular-liberal politics in general. She analyses the moral agency and politics that undergird the practices of the women's mosque movement in Egypt and juxtaposes it with the liberal assump-tions about human nature and its desire for freedom and autonomy and liberal conceptions of agency as acts that challenge social norms. Mahmood's critical analysis informs us of the limits and problematic nature of liberal assumptions, yet it leaves no space for the imagination for an alternative position for challenging secular-liberal assumptions other than the Islamic pious position. Can we speak of the secular and the religious from a different basis, which does not reproduce the non-contextualized secular/Islamic binary and its relation to women's issues? Is there an alternative framing for women's activism, beyond what pretends to be universal values for gender justice (such as CEDAW), on the one hand, and the purely Islamic self-cultivation through piety practices that Saba Mahmood describes, on the other?

Is there a way for a local women's movement to be immersed in the local and for issues to emerge out of the local economic, social, political and cultural modes of life, without reifying the local or the 'authentic'? Could such a movement be motivated by justice and confront all types of oppressions?

Several chapters in this volume call us to go beyond the secular/ Islamic binary in thinking about women's issues and their life experiences. We briefly discussed above women's use and resignification of national heritage and identity in making demands a part of political transition processes. Another way to challenge this binary is by illustrating how women's issues and women's independent movements and organizations have been co-opted and controlled by both secular and Islamist regimes, as the chapters on Egypt (Abou-Bakr), Libya (Alnaas and Pratt) and Tunisia (Muhanna) illustrate. In particular, Abou-Bakr criticizes the strand of elitist-secular state feminism and its association with corrupt regimes that prevailed during the last decades in Egypt and has been reproduced since the ousting of Mohammed Morsi.

Women activists themselves are rethinking this binary through their actual practices. Self-identified secular and Islamic women activists in post-revolutionary Tunisia share common goals and similar activities and actually engage and learn from the experiences of one other (Aitemad Muhanna's chapter). Muhanna traces the construction of an Islamic/secular feminist binary in Tunisian society, arguing that this binary is artificially constructed and does not reflect the gender politics practised by the two groups of activists. Despite differences in discourse (a legal and human rights discursive framework versus an humanitarian and development one) and the convictions of secular-feminist leaders that the Islamist project forms a threat to women's equal rights, there exist common objectives, such as women's access to education, employment, political participation and the struggle against violence against women. There are many shared goals pertaining to women's socio-economic conditions in Tunisia, particularly with regard to poor, marginalized rural women, and there is an overlap in the actual activities of these organizations. The self-identified Islamic and secular women's groups and organizations do not fit into either side of a binary; rather, there are differences among the groups that identify as Islamic or secular. It is more accurate to place women's organizations along a spectrum and to identify the diversity of gender and gender politics amongst them. The trend of 'pragmatic' democratic feminism, for instance, attempts to reconcile feminism with religion and local traditions, instead of constructing a binary of universal women's rights versus local Islamic positions. Muhanna argues that women's activism should emerge from contextualized forms of life and relevant power structures. Thus, for example, instead of working according to a binary logic, feminists and women activists should be critical of a capitalist market economy and the impoverishment it causes, whether it is advocated and led by a secular or an Islamist ruling party.

Another perspective from which to rethink the secular/Islamic binary is offered by Omaima Abou-Bakr's chapter (Chapter 7). Abou-Bakr considers the project of Islamic feminism as an intermediate space between fundamentalist secular rejection of religious referencing altogether and religious conservatism. It criticizes theological patriarchy, contests religious justifications of gender hierarchy and develops gender justice and equality values within Islam's worldview. Nevertheless, Abou-Bakr argues that, if Islamic feminists want to develop as a conscientious social and activist movement, they need to take an ethical political stand against corrupt political regimes, whether ruled by political religious or secular parties/actors. Such a stand has become more pressing in light of political events in Egypt since the ousting of Morsi in 2013. We can read this form of politics as a struggle against all forms of oppression, including economic, political and social injustices, and the basis for a mode of feminism that transcends self-identified secular/Islamic feminisms. Such a feminist project would evoke the demands of the people in 2010/2011 for 'bread, freedom, dignity and social justice'.

Structure of the Book

The chapters that follow are grouped into three parts, reflecting the themes discussed above: The Malleability of Gender and Sexuality in Revolutions and Resistance; The Body and Resistance; and Gender and the Construction of the Secular/Islamic Binary. Each of these parts contains chapters that provide substantive insights with regard to the respective theme whilst also recognizing some overlap in the concerns and subject matter of different chapters across the three sections. Following this introduction, Part I begins with Shereen Abouelnaga's 'Reconstructing Gender in Post-Revolution Egypt', which explores the process of generating novel constructs of gender through a fierce tactical and discursive confrontation with hegemonic gender norms. The insistence of women (and men) to counter the hegemonic discourse by occupying the public sphere has turned hegemonic norms into sites of contestation and challenge. Paradoxically, while the dominant discourse offers a normative form of feminine subjectivity – claimed to be the only politically correct one – its organization and practices, mainly gendered violence, imply the possibility of reversal. The reverse discourse, or resistance discourse, has enabled women to subvert the concept of victimization and transform it into a concept of agency in order to augment their political resistance and to integrate the personal (body) with the political (revolutionary trajectory). Far from being self-indicting, the testimonies of women subjected to violence and harassment prove that gender norms are being fabricated by force in those incidents and that silence is coerced.

Chapter 2, Lena Meari's 'Resignifying "Sexual" Colonial Power Techniques: The Experiences of Palestinian Women Political Prisoners', explores the construction and reconstruction of sexuality and the sexed body within the dynamics of colonial domination and resistance in Palestine. Specifically, the chapter analyses the ways in which shabak (Israel Security Agency) interrogators deploy sexuality and gender conceptions in their interrogation techniques in order to subjugate Palestinian strugglers and the ways in which Palestinian women strugglers resisted and re-signified these techniques through the enactment of the practice of sumud (steadfastness in the interrogation). The chapter illustrates how the praxis of sumud by Palestinian female (and male) strugglers opens up the possibility to destabilize the significations of the sexed body, subvert women's daily life routines and social customs that establish women's bodies and sexualities in a fixed manner and challenge the fixed associations between the female body and the meanings of women's dignity and honour within Palestinian society and the colonial perception of it. Rather than reading the Palestinian women's interrogation experiences from the viewpoint of colonial power, the chapter follows Fanon's approach by approximating the interrogation experiences from the viewpoint of resistance.

The final chapter of this section is Hala Sami's 'A Strategic Use of Culture: Egyptian Women's Subversion and Resignification of Gender Norms', which examines the emergence of a paradigm of women's resistance in post-Mubarak Egypt, particularly under the presidency of Mohammed Morsi, that resorts to intertextuality to challenge women's subjugation. This paradigm is explored through three cases: Baheya Ya Masr (a political activist movement), Doaa Eladl (a woman cartoonist) and Women On Walls (a graffiti movement). Intertextuality as an approach allows these women to draw on Egyptian culture's reservoir of diverse, prominent female figures to provide alternative representations of women, to secure their space in the public arena and to challenge patriarchal discourses that attempt to marginalize them. 'Culture' as a set of shared social meanings as well as various artistic manifestations operates as a weapon of resistance, confronting and affronting a regime that sought to exclude women from civil society and relegate them to the domestic space.

Part II begins with Maha El Said's 'She Resists: Body Politics between Radical and Subaltern', which focuses on two women who made controversial use of their bodies as modes of resistance: Aliaa Magda Elmahdy, known as 'the naked blogger', and Sama El-Masry, a belly dancer. Both attempted to challenge the power dynamics of social control over women's bodies and minds. Despite the fact that both became 'embodied subjects' in the struggle for democracy and freedom at a time of redefining gender roles and the remaking of the nation, the effectiveness of their agency greatly differed. Exploring their tactics of defying the cultural representation of the female body, the chapter considers Elmahdy's resistance as rooted in a radical feminism that is alien to popular appeal, while El-Masry, embedded within popular culture, is rendered as the subaltern agent that challenges power from within grassroots culture.

Chapter 5, 'Framing the Female Body: Beyond Morality and Pathology?' by Abeer Al-Najjar and Anoud Abusalim, also discusses the case of Aliaa Elmahdy as well as that of another woman who posted naked images of herself, the Tunisian Amina Sboui. The chapter examines the media responses to these women's actions in order to identify the emergence of new frames for interpreting women's agency after the Arab Spring. The authors find that, despite generating a lot of local media attention, the Arab media failed to understand the women's actions within the revolutionary context and, therefore, were unable to understand the message behind their actions. Instead, the media resorted to framings of the women's actions as pathological.

The next chapter by Sahar Mediha Alnaas and Nicola Pratt, 'Women's Bodies in Post-Revolution Libya: Control and Resistance' explores how women's bodies have been instrumentalized in post-Gaddafi Libya as symbols of a new, Islamized Libya with implications for women's presence in the public sphere and their bodily and sexual rights. In response, Libyan women have engaged in a number of initiatives and bodily performances in the public sphere in order to legitimize their public presence and secure their involvement in post-Gaddafi transition processes. The chapter argues that there is a need to go beyond studies of women's participation in formal institutions when considering gender and socio-political transformations. Rather, the case of Libya demonstrates the importance of women's agency within the broader public sphere in terms of resisting the hegemonic gender norms that marginalize women within formal transitional processes.

Part III begins with Omaima Abou-Bakr's 'Islamic Feminism and the Equivocation of Political Engagement: "Fair is foul, and foul is fair"', which discusses the precarious relationship (involving both resistance and accommodation) between feminists and the nation state in the modern Egyptian context. This, in turn, provides a backdrop for understanding the rise of Islamic feminism as an intellectual trend. Following this, the chapter explores the moral ambiguities associated with Islamic feminism's political stands in relation to the recent rise and fall of Islamist rule in Egypt. Abou-Bakr argues that the post-Mubarak period necessitates reflection not just on the role of Islamic feminist ideas in society, but also on the question of the relationship between Islamic feminism and different political currents emerging and transforming in this period. The chapter identifies the need to go beyond the framework of the secular/Islamic binary to formulate an ethical and political Islamic feminist position.

The final chapter of this part of the volume is by Aitemad Muhanna and entitled 'Islamic and Secular Women's Activism and Discourses in Post-Uprising Tunisia', in which she maps out the discourses of secular and Islamic women activists and the dynamics between them in post-uprising Tunisia. The research demonstrates that the secular/ Islamic binary in Tunisian society is artificially constructed and does not reflect the actual gender politics adopted by the two self-identified groups. The chapter finds that secular women activists are not a homogenous group, but can be divided into 'radical' and 'pragmatic' secular women activists. Whilst 'radical' secular activists dichotomize the relationship between feminism and Islam, pragmatic secular activists are interested in creating a synthesis between the two discourses for the local Tunisian context. Meanwhile, whilst Islamic women prioritize the moral and social reconstruction of society from below, rather than enshrining 'women's rights' in the constitution, nevertheless, the experience of being in political power has led Islamic women activists to learn from secular feminist discourses. Moderate Islamic women as well as secular women activists seek to preserve the existing Personal Status Code (often considered to be key to protecting women's rights). In addition, the chapter finds much overlap in the goals and methods of self-identifying secular and Islamic women's groups, suggesting the need to go beyond the secular/Islamic binary in understanding women's activism.

Finally, we conclude the volume with a joint chapter that not only brings together the findings of the chapters presented in this volume but also reflects upon some of the questions posed in this introduction. In our conclusion, we suggest alternative ways of theorizing gender in socio-political transformations in the Arab world in particular, but also more generally.

Notes

1. SCAF opened the Rafah crossing in May 2011 to all women, minors and any man under eighteen and over forty, to pass freely without a visa six days a week from 9am until 4pm. However, men between the ages of eighteen and forty were not allowed to cross without a visa for onward travel. See 'Rafah Crossing Open but Restrictions Remain' (*Electronic Intifada* 2011).
2. For example, Dabashi 2012; Gelvin 2012; Haas and Lesch 2013; Noueihed and Warren 2013; Lynch 2013; Henry and Jang 2013; Dawisha 2013; Kamrava 2013; Laremont 2013; Horst, Jünemann and Rothe 2013; Korany and El-Mahdi 2013; Howard and Hussain 2013; Achcar 2013; and Amar and Vijay 2013, to mention just a few of the scholarly books published on the subject.
3. Historicism, according to Chakrabarty (2000: 6), is 'the idea that to understand anything it has to be seen as both a unity and in its historical development'.
4. Abstracts for all the papers can be read at: www2.warwick.ac.uk/fac/soc/sociology/rsw/research_centres/gender/research/birzeit/workshop_3/abstracts
5. Tawfik Okasha in his daily *Al-Masry Al-Youm* programme brought this up several times, discussing Nawara Negm and Asmaa Mahfouz. See *Al-Masry Al-Youm* 2011 and 2012.

References

Abu-Lughod, L. (2000) *Veiled Sentiments: Honor and Poetry in a Bedouin Society*, University of California Press, Berkeley.
Abu-Lughod, L. (2013) *Do Muslim Women Need Saving?*, Harvard University Press, Cambridge, MA, and London.
Abu-Lughod, L., ed. (1998) *Remaking Women: Feminism and Modernity in the Middle East*, Princeton University Press, Princeton.
Achcar, G. (2013) *The People Want: A Radical Exploration of the Arab Uprising*, University of California Press, Berkeley.
Ahmed, L. (1993) *Women and Gender in Islam: Historical Roots of a Modern Debate*, Yale University Press, New Haven, CT.
Al-Ali, N. S. (2000) *Secularism, Gender and the State in the Middle East: The Egyptian Women's Movement*, Cambridge University Press, Cambridge.
Al-Ali, N. S. (2007) *Iraqi Women: Untold Stories from 1948 to the Present*, Zed Books, London.
Al-Ali, N. S. (2012) 'Gendering the Arab Spring', *Middle East Journal of Culture and Communication*, 5 (1), pp. 26–31.
Al-Ali, N. S. (2014) 'Reflections on (Counter-) Revolutionary Processes in Egypt', *Feminist Review*, 106, pp. 122–28.
Amar, P., and P. Vijay, eds (2013) *Dispatches from the Arab Spring: Understanding the New Middle East*, University of Minnesota Press, Minnesota.

Amin, S. (2011) 'Egyptian General Admits "Virginity Checks" Conducted on Protesters', CNN.com, 31 May. Available at: http://edition.cnn.com/2011/WORLD/meast/05/30/egypt.virginity.tests/index.html (accessed on 4 September 2014).

Amnesty International (2014) 'Egypt: Human Rights in Crisis: Systemic Violations and Impunity: Expanded Amnesty International Submission to the Universal Periodic Review', October–November, 1 July. Available at: www.amnesty.org/en/library/asset/mde12/034/2014/en/63d8f6f3-2cad-4553-bded-563bcf593170/mde120342014en.pdf (accessed on 11 August 2014).

Asad, T. (2003) *Formations of the Secular: Christianity, Islam, Modernity*, Stanford University Press, Stanford.

Badran, M. (1995) *Feminists, Islam, and Nation*, Princeton University Press, Princeton.

Balqaziz, A. (2013) *State and Religion in the Arab World*, Center for Arab Unity Studies, Beirut.

Baron, B. (2005) *Egypt as a Woman: Nationalism, Gender, and Politics*, University of California Press, Berkeley.

Bibars, I. (2001) *Victims and Heroines: Women, Welfare and the Egyptian State*, Zed Books, London.

Bier, L. (2011) *Revolutionary Womanhood: Feminisms, Modernity, and the State in Nasser's Egypt*, Stanford University Press, Stanford.

Borkan, B. (2011) 'Military Intelligence Head Says Virginity Tests Conducted out of Self-Defense', *Daily News Egypt*, 26 June. Available at: www.dailynewsegypt.com/2011/06/26/head-of-military-intelligence-confirms-virginity-tests-conducted-out-of-self-defense/ (accessed on 30 January 2014).

Brand, L. A. (1998) *Women, the State, and Political Liberalization: Middle Eastern and North African Experiences*, Columbia University Press, New York.

Butler, J. (1997) *The Psychic Life of Power: Theories in Subjection*, Stanford University Press, Stanford.

Butler, J. (1999) *Gender Trouble: Feminism and the Subversion of Identity*, Routledge, New York and London.

Chakrabarty, D. (2000) *Provincializing Europe: Postcolonial Thought and Historical Difference*, Princeton University Press, Princeton and Oxford.

Charrad, M. M. (2001) *States and Women's Rights: The Making of Postcolonial Tunisia, Algeria, and Morocco*, University of California Press, Berkeley.

Cockburn, C. (2007) *From Where We Stand: War, Women's Activism and Feminist Analysis*, Zed Books, London.

Coleman, I. (2011) 'Is the Arab Spring Bad for Women?' *Foreign Policy*, 20 December. Available at: www.foreignpolicy.com/articles/2011/12/20/arab_spring_women (accessed on 13 August 2014).

Dabashi, H. (2012) *The Arab Spring and the End of Postcolonialism*, Zed Books, London.

Dawisha, A. (2013) *The Second Arab Awakening: Revolution, Democracy, and the Islamist Challenge from Tunis to Damascus*, W. W. Norton, New York.

Doane, M. A. (1981) 'Woman's Stake: Filming the Female Body', *The New Talkies*, 17 (Summer), pp. 22–36.

Electronic Intifada (2011) 'Rafah Crossing Open but Restrictions Remain', 2 June. Available at: http://electronicintifada.net/content/rafah-crossing-open-restrictions-remain/10037 (accessed on 28 December 2014).

Elsadda, H. (2011) 'Women's Rights Activism in Post-Jan 25 Egypt: Combating the Shadow of the First Lady Syndrome', *Middle East Law and Governance*, 3, pp. 84–93.

Elsadda, H. (2012) *Gender, Nation, and the Arabic Novel: Egypt 1892–2008*, Syracuse University Press and Edinburgh University Press, Syracuse, NY, and Edinburgh.

Fleischmann, E. L. (2000) *The Nation and Its 'New' Women: The Palestinian Women's Movement, 1920–1948*, University of California Press, Berkeley.

Gelvin, J. (2012) *The Arab Uprisings: What Everyone Needs to Know*, Oxford University Press, Oxford.

Haas, M. L., and D. W. Lesch, eds (2013) *The Arab Spring: Change and Resistance in the Middle East*, Westview Press, Boulder.

Hafez, S. (2014) 'The Revolution Shall Not Pass through Women's Bodies: Egypt, Uprising and Gender Politics', *The Journal of North African Studies*, 19 (2), pp. 172–85.

Hasso, F. S. (2005) *Resistance, Repression, and Gender Politics in Occupied Palestine and Jordan*, Syracuse University Press, Syracuse.

Hasso, F. S. (2010) *Consuming Desires: Family Crisis and the State in the Middle East*, Stanford University Press, Stanford.

Henry, C., and J. H. Jang, eds (2013) *The Arab Spring: Will It Lead to Democratic Transitions?*, Palgrave Macmillan, New York and London.

Hoodfar, H. (1997) *Between Marriage and the Market: Intimate Politics and Survival in Cairo*, University of California Press, Berkeley.

Horst, J., A. Jünemann and D. Rothe (2013) *Euro-Mediterranean Relations after the Arab Spring*, Ashgate, Aldershot.

Howard, P. N., and M. M. Hussain (2013) *Democracy's Fourth Wave? Digital Media and the Arab Spring*, Oxford University Press, Oxford.

Jad, I. (2004) 'The NGO-isation of Arab Women's Movements', *IDS Bulletin*, 35 (4), pp. 34–42.

Joseph, S. (1999) *Intimate Selving in Arab Families: Gender, Self and Identity*, Syracuse University Press, New York.

Kamrava, M. (2013) *Beyond the Arab Spring: The Evolving Ruling Bargain in the Middle East*, Hurst and Co., London.

Khalil, A. (2014) 'Tunisia's Women: Partners in Revolution', *The Journal of North African Studies*, 19 (2), pp. 186–99.

Korany, B., and R. El-Mahdi, eds (2013) *Arab Spring in Egypt: Revolution and Beyond*, American University in Cairo Press, Cairo.

Kraidy, M. M. (2012) 'The Revolutionary Body Politic: Preliminary Thoughts on a Neglected Medium in the Arab Uprisings', *Middle East Journal of Culture and Communication*, 5, pp. 66–74.

Laclau, E. (1996) 'Why Do Empty Signifiers Matter to Politics?', in E. Laclau, *Emancipation(s)*, Verso, London, pp. 36–46.

Langohr, V. (2011) 'How Egypt's Revolution has Dialed back Women's Rights', *Foreign Affairs*, 22 December. Available at: www.foreignaffairs.com/articles/136986/vickie-langohr/how-egypts-revolution-has-dialed-back-womens-rights (accessed on 13 August 2014).

Laremont, R., ed. (2013) Revolution, Revolt and Reform in North Africa: The Arab Spring and Beyond, Routledge, London.

Lazreg, M. (1994) The Eloquence of Silence: Algerian Women in Question, Routledge, New York and London.

Lynch, M. (2013) The Arab Uprising: The Unfinished Revolutions of the New Middle East, Public Affairs, New York.

MacLeod, A. (1993) Accommodating Protest: Working Women, the New Veiling and Change in Cairo, Columbia University Press, New York.

Mahmood, S. (2005) Politics of Piety: The Islamic Revival and the Feminist Subject, Princeton University Press, Princeton.

Al-Masry Al-Youm (2011) Al Faraeen Channel, 19 December. Available on YouTube at: https://www.youtube.com/watch?v=m7c50QYL6yI

Al-Masry Al-Youm (2012) Al Faraeen Channel, 5 May. Available on YouTube at: https://www.youtube.com/watch?v=d74oLPczyYA

McClintock, A. (1995) Imperial Leather: Race, Gender, and Sexuality in the Colonial Contest, Routledge, New York and London.

Mernissi, F. (1985) Beyond the Veil: Male-Female Dynamics in Muslim Society, Saqi Books, London.

Moghadam, V. (2003) Modernizing Women: Gender and Social Change in the Middle East, Lynne Rienner, Boulder.

Molyneux, M. (1998) 'Analyzing Women's Movements', Development and Change, 29 (2), pp. 219–45.

Noueihed, L., and A. Warren (2013) The Battle for the Arab Spring: Revolution, Counter-Revolution and the Making of a New Era, Yale University Press, New Haven.

Olimat, M. S., ed. (2014) Arab Spring and Arab Women: Challenges and Opportunities, Routledge, London and New York.

Peteet, J. (1991) Gender in Crisis: Women and the Palestinian Resistance Movement, Columbia University Press, New York.

Salime, Z. (2012) 'A New Feminism? Gender Dynamics in Morocco's February 20th Movement', Journal of International Women's Studies, 5 (5), pp. 101–14.

Singerman, D. (2013) 'Youth, Gender, and Dignity in the Egyptian Uprising', Journal of Middle East Women's Studies, 9 (3), pp. 1–27.

Skalli, L. H. (2014) 'Young Women and Social Media against Sexual Harassment in North Africa', The Journal of North African Studies, 19 (2), pp. 244–58.

Sohlman, E. (2012) 'Yemen's Many Factions Wait Impatiently for a Resolution', New York Times, 23 May. Available at: www.nytimes.com/2012/05/24/world/middleeast/24iht-m24-yemen-change.html?pagewanted=all (accessed on 28 December 2014).

Tadros, M., ed. (2010) ''Religion, Rights and Gender at the Crossroads', IDS Bulletin, 42:1.

Thompson, E. (2000) Colonial Citizens: Republican Rights, Paternal Privilege, and Gender in French Syria and Lebanon, Columbia University Press, New York.

Tucker, J. E. (2000) In the House of the Law: Gender and Islamic Law in Ottoman Syria and Palestine, University of California Press, Berkeley.

PART I

The Malleability of Gender and Sexuality in Revolutions and Resistance

ONE

Reconstructing Gender in Post-Revolution Egypt

Shereen Abouelnaga

Introduction

The prefix 'post' might suggest that the revolution is over, in the sense of either having been crushed or having fulfilled its aims. I use 'post' in neither sense because I fully adopt the slogan 'the revolution continues'. The prefix means what happened after the famous 'Eighteen Days'. Egyptians also generally use the word 'revolution' to refer to the same period (25 January–11 February 2011). The title of this chapter is highly misleading in another sense. It suggests that 'reconstructing gender' has been a corollary of the revolution. Perhaps the revolution has been one of the epistemic incentives but not the only one. It seems that the huge numbers of women who took to the streets during those Eighteen Days in 2011 led the media, analysts, writers and observers to conclude that such a conspicuous presence meant that gender was being revolutionized. It is impossible not to notice the plethora of studies, articles and conferences that took the Egyptian and Tunisian Revolutions to be markers of the liberation of women.[1] Surely, this is an oversimplification that does not take into consideration the mish-mash of socio-cultural complexities along with power relations.

To conflate the public sphere with the streets and to assume that women were previously physically incarcerated is quite a mistaken hypothesis that keeps generating more simplistic views about the dynamics and polemics of the context. It was a revolution against the corruption and barbarity of a regime – with a special focus on the physical torture that had become systematically perpetrated by the security services – in which almost every citizen was willing to play a role regardless of gender, religion or class. Gender roles and women's rights were not listed on the agenda of protesters, in spite of a few feeble unheard voices;[2] and, in retrospect, that was the mistake.

This chapter argues that the initial formulation, or rather unfolding, of new constructs of gender appeared as a result of the incessant violations of women's rights, where the body stood as the main protagonist. That is to say, gender became a priority when the utopia of the Eighteen Days turned into a dystopia.

Back to the 1990s

In order to understand and explore the malleability of gender in the current period, it is necessary to go back to the 1990s. This decade derives its importance from the plethora of activities related to women's rights. For example, in 1994 the UN held the International Conference on Population and Development in Cairo. The conference received considerable media attention due to disputes over the question of reproductive rights. Muslim and Christian authorities were equally staunch critics. That was followed by the 1995 Beijing Conference, which was a catalyst for the formation of several task forces in Egypt to promote women's rights. At the same time, there was a remarkable surge in activism with the establishment of many NGOs that were actively engaged in defending women's rights. Put differently, it is essential to understand, or rather to remember, how the Mubarak regime perceived gender and how it kept it as a decorative not a functional tool. Literally speaking, all international conventions were signed and even ratified only to pose a stance of modernity (Mernissi 2002).[3] Whilst the state sought to keep a certain 'image' intact regarding women's rights, it feared that women's rights and other civil society organizations could mobilize against the regime and, hence, attempted to suppress their efforts. This authoritarian attitude gained even more power and momentum as the state presented its own version of 'women's rights' as covered by and consistent with the teachings of Islam. This attitude continued until 2011 without the slightest change. What changed indeed was the vision of the ruled.

Not surprisingly, violations of women and their rights have been just a continuation of the techniques of the ex-regime, where the female body, the most sensitive issue in Islam, was the major player in identity politics. Prior to the 2011 Revolution, state feminism monopolized the official enunciation of the demands of women through a form of co-option that failed to engage with the plurality of women's voices. In an interview, Hoda Elsadda, Egyptian feminist activist and academic, explains that:

> Under Mubarak's rule, and as he sought to present himself as the
> sole guardian of the commitment of Egypt to modern values in
> the battle against the rising power of Islamists in the Arab region,
> the role of the ex-First Lady as the foremost champion of women's
> rights was fore-grounded and celebrated. What actually happened
> was that the work and struggles of women's rights activists was
> appropriated and manipulated by state representatives. (Elsadda
> 2013a)

The distorted relation between women and the 'governmental' discourse meant that women had to find alternatives to a suffocating agenda. The challenge was to avoid any confrontation with the state discourse that turned out to be catering to an international image. As for women activists, they had to abide by the law of non-governmental organizations. According to Law 32 issued in 1964 and the modifications to it that took place in 1999 and 2002, no organization was allowed to engage with politics. NGOs were forced either to do charity work or to replace the state in providing the most fundamental basic services, including the issuing of voter IDs for women as a priority, for example. When the issue of violence against women was raised by the

New Woman Research Centre in 1995, the regime's denial of its existence was really shameful. Meanwhile, the masses of women had to
manoeuvre the economic and cultural difficulties of daily life without
clashing with the government.

Propagated heavily was the image of women as markers of the cultural identity of the nation. The state-run media, politicians, political
parties and even intellectuals adopted this discourse that is reminiscent of, for example, Ahmed Fuad Nijm's famous poem 'Masr yamma
ya Baheya'.[4] That is to say, the cultural – Egypt as a woman – intertwined with the political to facilitate the elimination of individuality
and diversity and to prioritize nationalism in its more orthodox form.
The ex-regime's nationalism did not highlight national independence
in front of foreign economic and political powers. It was a discursive
form of nationalism that relied upon, among other things, women's
bodies. Moreover, these discursive practices justified, or even legitimized, coercing women into accepting a uniform political path and a
monolithic practice and conduct, where all socio-political and cultural
differences were dismissed. Political suppression along with a monolithic discourse about women and their rights augmented frustration
and pessimism and left no room for negotiation. Therefore, women
had to find their own way in the politics of daily life: transportation,
work, writing, clothing, self-image, self-esteem, self-defence, getting
married and struggling.

One cannot deny that sexual abuse and domestic violence were
among the concerns of a rising feminist agenda; yet, the image created
by the state, which celebrated Egypt as the 'safest place', obstructed
any efforts to mobilize around such critical issues and almost prohibited women from revealing such atrocities. The state ignored such
violations for the sake of a touristic image. The furore provoked by a
CNN film that showed the circumcision of a young Egyptian girl cannot be forgotten.[5] In addition to being labelled a national scandal, the
reactions to the film proved that women were 'subsumed symbolically
into the national body politic as its boundary and metaphoric limit'
(McClintock 1997: 90).

It was in the same decade when the idea of women's honor was translated as the synonym of the nation's honor. To pillar a whole nation on a gendered subject was another translation of the assumption that women are the markers of cultural identity. The crisis of the material gendered body fully erupted in 1993 when a young girl- known as Ataba[6] girl- was sexually harassed on a public bus. The public opinion was shocked; yet, that did not protect the girl from taking all the blame.[7] And ever since that time, indictment has been the regular reaction to any sexual molesting. Concomitantly, domestic violence became an issue that the state either denied or accepted ambivalently, on the basis that it is an 'individual and aberrant' case. In other words, the national body politic depended upon controlling and disciplining women's bodies, especially in the private sphere where all violations are not only considered to be private, but also legitimate according to a specific interpretation of Islam and a strong tendency of patriarchal patronization.

In many instances, women suffered from collective sexual harassment. However, it was never employed as a means of political discipline and punishment of those taking to the streets until 2005. In May of that year, and during a protest organized by the Kefaya movement for political reform, journalist Nawal Ali was sexually assaulted on the stairs of the Journalists' Syndicate. This incident demonstrated the audacity and brutality of the regime and Ali courageously recounted the details of her scandalous assault by pro-Mubarak thugs. Meanwhile, the media conducted an unprecedented and fierce smear campaign against her. In spite of the solidarity with Ali, the fierce public vilification earned her a divorce and the complaint she filed disappeared from the court archives. That incident, so fierce and ugly, declared the female body to be a site of contest. Apparently, the incident resided in the collective unconscious and in May 2013 the memory of Ali was commemorated in several papers and on many social media sites. The commemoration signifies a shift in the way women's bodies have come to be perceived, as a result of the rising challenge to the previously undisputed orthodox constructions of gender. However, shamefully, those who condemned Ali earlier were amongst those who hailed her as a champion now that they had realized that they had become targets of sexual violence.

From the above discussion, it is clear that the dominant paradigm governing women's agency and subjectivity before 2011 was generated by a set of modern patriarchal values, set implicitly by society and consolidated crudely by the state, that reduced female identity to the corporeal body by which abuse, mutilation, isolation and harassment were justified culturally. That is to say, since women's bodies stand for national honour, then these bodies must be 'protected' through discipline and punishment.

The 1990s witnessed another controversy over the term 'writing the body', which popped up in the literary and critical arena as a result of women's writings.[8] The writings of this generation focused on female subjectivity through narrating the personal and the particular, rather than the national and societal. They were concerned with the position of the self in the world. Yet, the literary milieu was not willing to integrate women's writings that introduced different epistemological approaches into the canon. Women writers who came of age in the era of the 1990s were, therefore, sidelined at best and attacked on the ground that they dropped the 'national cause' for the sake of trivial bourgeois details, that is, the body. The dismissal of these writings from the literary and critical discourse sprang from the refusal to deal with the misnomer 'writing the body', which is not to be taken as an echo of the French school of l'écriture féminine. That term meant simply that those women writers talked about the violations and aspirations of their bodies. It was then that visual and textual practices – theatre, painting, films and writing – managed to carve discursive spaces in which women were represented and addressed as subjects, possessed of both specificity and a history. These creative forms provided a safe exit from the strait jacket of the pseudo-feminist discourse advanced by the state, a discourse that was bent on marginalizing any different claims and demands.[9] The absence of any outright confrontation

with that institutional discourse meant that Egyptian women chose to
reject the act of enunciation in favour of 'silence as a will not to say or
a will to unsay and as a language of its own' (Minh-ha 1997: 416). It
is very likely that such tactical silence was translated by all observers
and analysts as exclusion from the public sphere. The silence that was
translated as passivity was in fact a cruel form of indifference, hence
retaliation, where women divorced the regime from their daily life
and resorted to their own strategies to cope without the least attempt
at confrontation.

Space of Appearance Lost

The long-deferred public confrontation between women and a solid
patriarchal paradigm – with all the reservations on the word 'patriarchy'[10] – was triggered by the post-revolution socio-cultural clash,
where women's bodies turned into a battlefield. The sense of struggle
and the weight of oppression formed a point of departure from which
women decided to restore the utopian experience of Tahrir Square,
which had come to stand for the 'space of appearance' as defined by
Hannah Arendt. This space is a creation of action and, thus, is highly
fragile. It 'comes into being wherever men [and women] are together
in the manner of speech and action, and therefore predates and pre-
cedes all formal constitution of the public realm' (Arendt 1958: 178).
Its peculiarity, as Arendt says, is

> unlike the spaces which are the work of our hands, it does not
> survive the actuality of the movement which brought it into being,
> but disappears not only with the dispersal of men – as in the case of
> great catastrophes when the body politic of a people is destroyed –
> but with the disappearance or arrest of the activities themselves.
> Wherever people gather together, it is potentially there, but only
> potentially, not necessarily and not forever. (1958: 199)

Naturally, with the arrest of socio-political activities that were smoothly
practised in Tahrir Square by men and women on an equal footing,

Egyptian women protesters in particular not only wanted to secure
this space of appearance but were also working on recreating it in the
liminal spaces of the personal and political. As I see it, the departure
of the people from Tahrir Square on 11 February – myself included –
signified a political naivety that aborted all the discursive practices of
the utopian Eighteen Days. That a 'New Egypt' was waiting to embrace
the 'New Woman' that emerged from the Square turned out to be a
mirage. The dispersal of the masses led to the arrest of activities and
the aspiration to revolutionize socio-cultural practices was challenged
by the lack of power, which is not the same as strength, force and
violence (Arendt 1972: 143–55). Women did not have to wait long
for the big disappointment: they were not welcomed in the streets as
protesters anymore. On the one hand, the power needed to actualize
women's agency was absent and, in the best-case scenario, fragile. The
neo-conservative voices were much louder and fiercely determined
to keep women's agency mediated through the male designation. On
the other hand, we are reminded by Foucault that resistance is never
in a position of exteriority to power relations;[11] that is, we have to
examine the networks of practices, institutions and technologies that
sustain positions of dominance and subordination. In other words,
we should be concerned not only with how the body is perceived and
given meaning, but with the manner in which what is most material
in it is invested and solidified. At the crossroads of culture and politics,
women lost the 'space of appearance', and the body was turned into
a site of contesting ideologies. This is where the confrontation started
and the process became irreversible. Never before has such a confrontation taken place outright; ambivalence was the rule. What augmented the inevitability of this confrontation was the fact that women
'tasted' the power to endow their lives with meaning, discursively
and physically, during the Eighteen Days. That is why resistance to the
process of denying them this agency became irreversible.

In March 2011, a huge women's march celebrating International
Women's Day turned ugly and the participants were heckled and
harassed.[12] The next day, a few hundred men and women took to
Tahrir Square again and were arrested. While men and women were

tortured and jailed in the Egyptian Museum and later in a military prison, women had to bear a bigger share of humiliation. In full view of several officers, they were forced to go through a series of 'virginity tests'. That was a defining and turning moment. Body disciplining as a means of socio-political control started to be a systematic practice against women protesters. Whereas physical abuse and torture of men was interpreted as political, all forms of abuse practised on women's bodies were taken by society – supporters and opponents of the women protesters – to be cultural. Foucault explains that the purpose of using and perceiving the body as a means of discipline and punishment is that

> it define[s] how one may have a hold over others' bodies, not only so that they may do what one wishes, but so that they may operate as one wishes, with the techniques, the speed and the efficiency that one determines. Thus, discipline produces subjected and practiced bodies, 'docile bodies'. (1979: 138)

However, Foucault treats the experiences of the human body as if there is no difference between men and women. One should ask how the disciplinary practices engender the bodies of women. Since this analysis aims at explaining how the engendered violence was transformed by women into a means of resistance and a route to agency, we should try to capture the point of irreversibility to fathom how the transformation of meaning started to take place, slowly but surely. Conditions that were constraining and enslaving became liberating and transforming. Put differently, what was disciplined as a docile body turned into a body that revolted. However, the reactions to and interactions with the gendered disciplinary practices were not monolithic. The vicissitudes of reception form the process of transformation.

Although possessing the female body and coercing it into certain degrading activities related to sexuality is not new in history,[13] what happened in March 2011 is still deemed shocking. Several women who were forced to go through the shameful experience of 'virginity tests' chose to resort to silence. Only one, Samira Ibrahim, decided

to file a lawsuit against the Supreme Council of the Armed Forces
(SCAF).[14] The courage this girl exhibited was shockingly subversive
of a docile society that had learnt not to break silence over the question of sexual harassment and rape – both acts entailing an offensive
questioning of the woman's 'honour'. We cannot forget the vilification of Nawal Ali and the utter silence in the media over the victory
of Noha Rushdi.[15] Throughout a long tedious process, Ibrahim came
out both victorious and defeated. Yet, her decision to break the silence
surely positions her as the precursor of the transformation process.
On the occasion of the second anniversary of the Revolution, *Jadaliyya*
launched a series of articles, amongst which Sherine Seikaly wrote
an article entitled 'The Meaning of Revolution: On Samira Ibrahim',
where she concluded that Ibrahim

> did not claim the category of the Virgin as a sacred space of refuge.
> She did not fight her brutalization in the tired terms of honor and
> righteousness. She fought it on political grounds. She confronted
> the precipice at which her flesh and its openings had become the
> terrain of public scrutiny, and defying descent she decided to walk
> over it. (Seikaly 2013)

Whereas Ibrahim ought to be credited for taking the fight to 'political
grounds', the general who was interviewed on CNN took the fight to
a different terrain, that of the 'private' sphere. He said that the arrested
women 'were not like your daughter or mine. These were girls who
had camped out in tents with male protesters', only to express the
views of a wide sector of society. When an interview with Ibrahim
was uploaded to YouTube, the comments posted underneath it differed little from the general's, and were maybe even worse.

In the face of what Sharon Marcus calls 'a gendered grammar of
violence' (1992: 392), Ibrahim and her supporters subverted the
dominant discourse. The 'grammar of violence' exerted over the
female body

> assigns women a disadvantageous position in the rape script
> because it identifies us as objects of violence and because it offers

the insidious inducement of a subject position which assigns
us an active role vis-à-vis fear – a role which is all the more
insidious for its apparent agency. Whereas masculine fear triggers
the notorious 'fight or flight' response, feminine fear inspires
the familiar sensations of 'freezing' – voluntary immobility and
silence. (Marcus 1992: 394)

That Ibrahim did not stick to the rules of the script triggered a hugely
hostile social reaction. By smashing the myth of the female body as
a symbol of personal and collective national honour and as a site of
docility, Ibrahim and her generation were able to shift the major
forms of violence and abuse practised on the female body to the
political terrain. It is worth remembering that this is not the only
atrocity that targeted female protesters. Every time a female protester
was arrested, she had to be harassed by the police physically or ver-
bally. In spite of all that, the supposed victim turned into a warrior.
The result is a new discourse, still in the making, that has puzzled the
old patriarch and has forced a rethinking of all forms of femininity
and masculinity equally.

Space of Appearance Restored

As expected, there was an extreme socio-cultural resistance to the
endorsement of such a discursive shift, which led to another conflict
over the concept of identity. The vilification of Samira Ibrahim sprang
from a fixed discourse of gender identity that echoed and comple-
mented the image created previously by the state. Discursively, wom-
en's subjectivity was viewed from within an orthodox paradigm of
values and roles, very similar to if not identical with the bourgeois
nineteenth-century Victorian paradigm. On the other hand, Ibrahim's
generation was developing a new discourse of identity that was a corollary of the concept of the revolution itself and within a context characterized by extreme political fluidity, not to mention polarization. Put
differently, this incident with all its repercussions was employed by
protesters to revolutionize a hegemonic cultural discourse that plays
on the position of the subject.[16] The staunch networks of resistance

and solidarity formed around this crisis, and other similar ones, declared the female body as a site of not only conflicting interpretations but ideological (re)inscriptions. The banner Samira Ibrahim was carrying before the verdict of her case was announced said defiantly 'you cannot break me'. At first glance, one might assume that the statement was directed at the military junta, whereas in fact Ibrahim was addressing a whole culture. In Arabic, the metaphorical use of 'break' implies defeat psychologically. Ibrahim astutely summarizes the whole crisis: the virginity tests were meant to break/defeat/finish/banish those women. Yet, Ibrahim has politicized the private and employed her body as an alphabet of resistance in opposition to the 'gendered grammar of violence'.

The girl stripped to her blue bra towards the end of 2012 problematized the female body even more.[17] The huge efforts to vilify that woman through a toxic mix of culture and religion inspired the process of irreversibility with more strength and stamina. One cannot interpret this event without knowing its complexity. The shocking image of a stripped woman triggered a national furore and widespread international condemnation. On the national level, the controversy – banal and offensive – reduced the whole issue to the presence of the female body in prohibited territory, something already perceived as illegitimate. 'Why did she ever go there?' was a rhetorical question that resonated heavily throughout the controversy.[18] It was a question that re-enacted the beliefs of the ex-regime where the 'victim' is not to be defended since she tarnished the gendered national image, because her photo spread virally across international media. It is worth mentioning here that the controversy over this horrendous violation marked one of the main points of gender polarization in postrevolution Egypt. The fierce controversy was pillared on whether to reveal or to conceal, a question that almost came close to Hamlet's dilemma: 'To be, or no to be'. Yet, the question, posed in relation to the female body, was not a soliloquy. It was a socio-political question of blackmail, in response to which women chose 'to take arms against a sea of troubles'.[19]

The incident of the stripped girl introduced into the agonizing political scene a new factor, that of the dialectic between absence and presence.
While several images became symbolic, this particular one was 'a flesh-
and-blood human being who becomes virtual and goes viral, returning
within a few days to haunt the real space of Tahrir Square as the banner of
the Egyptian women's movement', as W. J. T. Mitchell noted (2012: 16).
Actually it returned to occupy several places in different forms, graffiti
being one of them. It is a form of solidarity, reflected highly in chants, that
is bent on smashing the paradigm of shame and guilt. With this incident,
it became apparent that the conflict was over the categorization of the
assaults: the regressive traditional camp wanted to lock and locate these
abuses in the personal and private, while the revolutionary camp pushed
the issue forward to the political and public, insisting that the personal is
political and cultural. Feminists have always adopted this equation. However,
the merging of the political and personal at this point marked the beginning of a new discourse in post-revolution Egypt.

From this moment onwards, there was a horrific rise in incidents
of sexual harassment targeted at female protesters, which were 'performative', in the words of Judith Butler, 'in the sense that the essence
or identity that they otherwise purport to express are *fabrications* manu-
factured and sustained through corporeal signs and other discursive
means' (1999: 173). One cannot ignore the other specific forms of
abuse of women to understand how gender was being enacted. Two
years after the virginity tests, in March 2013, while drawing graffiti
in front of the headquarters of the Muslim Brotherhood (MB) activists
were attacked, and I cannot avoid adding 'as usual'. The whole situation spun out of control and Mervat Mousa,[20] a journalist, was fiercely
slapped. That action re-enacted a common form of domestic violence
against women, based on sex inequalities consolidated by a socio-
cultural discourse. Slapping a woman is an act that is reminiscent of all
the violations committed in the private sphere.

All forms of violence against women protesters were extremely
challenging culturally, politically and psychologically and represented a crossroads for the strategies of feminist activists. The position

taken towards such highly visible and systematically recurrent acts of harassment and abuse could have reproduced the image of a 'victim'. However, instead, women engaged in a direct confrontation with the power that assaults the body physically and discursively. The disruption caused by the trauma of violence made direct confrontation a necessity.

If we agree that the success of power 'is proportional to its ability to hide its own mechanisms' (Foucault 1990: 86), we can conclude that the sexual abuse of female protesters completely failed to sustain itself as a means of control. With the disguise of power withering, the wider socio-cultural context was open to the negotiation of new constructs of gender, implicitly and slowly, but surely. Chris Weedon explains how a marginal discourse can carve a space in the mainstream:

> The degree to which marginal discourses can increase their social power is governed by the wider context of social interests and power within which challenges to the dominant are made. It may well take extreme and brave actions on the part of the agents of challenge to achieve even small shifts in the balance of power. (1987: 108)

When the oppressive and reckless measures of power brought the masses to the verge of explosion, the wider social context started to acknowledge the fact that the female body had become a site of ideological contest. What used to be a marginalized discourse under the rule of the ex-regime managed to affect some 'small shifts' so as to turn the body from a site of victimization into a site of resistance. Hence, 'the gender paradox' in the words of Nicola Pratt (2013). That is to say, most analysts and observers assumed that women's agency and visibility in the public sphere should lead to remarkable improvements in women's rights. Yet, the exact opposite was happening. The path to democracy – 'a democratic paradox' (Kandiyoti 2012) in itself – meant excessive violations of women's rights due to the fact that the women's rights agenda never achieved legitimacy at the popular level. It was always imposed from the top by an authoritarian regime and, consequently, the violations were perceived as part of 'democracy'. That is to say, they were perceived as part of demolishing all that had to do with the ousted president.

From Victim to Warrior

One should ask how activists managed to make such 'small shifts'. In order for the new reverse discourse to have a socio-political effect, women activists started by circulating it through different forms. Thus, the public transversality of all forms of protests against disciplinary practices was a point of strength. In his article 'The Subject and Power', Foucault explains that transversal protests 'are not exactly for or against the "individual" but rather they are struggles against the "government of individualization"' (1982: 781). Therefore, in their marches, demonstrations, artistic initiatives and all forms of coalition, even if only temporary, women shattered the discursive, social and cultural barriers erected by the former regimes. Collectives such as Baheya Ya Masr,[21] Fouada Watch,[22] and OpAntiSH,[23] amongst others, were the rapid and spontaneous outcome of outrage over the phenomenon of sexual abuse and rape. Some of these initiatives even decided to dismantle the master's house with his own tools by threatening to castrate any harasser,[24] an impulsive reaction that never gained momentum. The rallies, brochures, posters and graffiti lobbied the hitherto fragmented women's movement. These forms of protest, expressed aesthetically as well, supported a new discourse of subjectivity. They reflected – in form and content – a new mapping of territories and the dialectic play between margin and centre. The more the female body was abused, the stronger and more solid the activism that was practised. That this activist discourse basically stems from different positionalities – locked for a long time in the margins of a monolithic entity – endows it with power. In other words, activism against sexual harassment derived its power from lobbying across ideologies and strategies and turning multiplicity into a point of strength.

Since resorting to silence was what power expected from the assaulted women, activists countered that by encouraging the women to testify to what happened to them, after which the testimonies were published and circulated widely on the internet.[25] Over time, documenting the experience of harassment became part of documenting the revolution; the politics of the body became part and parcel of the body politic, if not the cause in many instances. The testimonies, some of which were truly frightening, circulated virally on social media, gaining wide readership and leading to a snowballing of resistance. These testimonies, from my point of view, are one of the strongest techniques of resistance, in that women broke the absolutely sanctioned silence on questions of the 'gendered grammar of violence' by changing their epistemic vision. The vision that was governing this testimonial literature showed an acute awareness of the risks lurking in such a project. Basically, the essential drawback of documenting experience is that it 'precludes analysis of the workings of this system and of its historicity; instead it reproduces its terms' (Scott 1992: 25). That is why the testimonies were not posted and circulated in isolation from the necessary analysis. In all the statements, articles and interviews activists exposed the workings of power where the testimonies are used as primary sources.

First, they historicized the use of sexual harassment as a weapon against women in all political protests. Second, the details of the testimonies focused on the discourse of the harasser where he (more often, they) used sexist terms. Third, the testimonies of the harassed revealed awareness that the female body was being used as a weapon to produce shame and incite fear. That the testimonies were far from being self-indicting and that the testifiers were not deterred from going back to the struggle (solidarity and campaigning cannot be overlooked) are huge achievements, especially when compared with the consequences of the same events in 2005. Only when sexual abuse stopped being perceived as an honour-tarnishing act did the personal – or, rather, what was perceived to be so – turn into the political. Moreover, testimonial literature gave women their voice, without which agency cannot be fulfilled. Having restored their voice, women are capable now of weaving their own discourse about the body. Similar to the dialectic of absence and presence of the body, that between 'voice' and 'silence' motivated women to relocate their 'space of appearance'.

The massive outpouring of creativity related to the revolution –
millions of photographs, banners, slogans, T-shirts, stickers, graffiti,
songs and video clips – contributed a great deal to putting the body on
the agenda of revolutionary concerns. While these creative initiatives
imply a high awareness of the effective role of art, they also enhance
the possibility of transversality. The term 'transversality' was originally coined by Guattari in the field of psychological therapy. In his
activist work he focused more on how modes of transversality might
produce different forms of collective subjectivity that shatter the barriers between the individual and the group.[26] The idea was further
elaborated by Foucault in his article 'The Subject and Power', where
he suggested that these forms of connection shatter the alienation
that power has worked so hard to insinuate (Foucault 1982: 780).
Recently, Gerald Raunig (2007) used the term to describe new ter-
rains of open co-operation between activists, in artistic, social and
political practices. Such new alliances, if only temporary, set to deter-
ritorialize the disciplines and fields they work across. Transversality
is not a form or an institution that one joins, but rather it is continuously constituted through events that require and trigger certain acts
of alliance where art and the revolution connect.[27] For instance, in a
graffiti that portrays three women, veiled, face-covered and unveiled,
the caption says 'do not categorize me'. By circulating these images
on social and alternative media, a collective imagination emerged and
generated transversal solidarity not only across classes and genders but
also across borders.

Similar to the imaginary community, the collective imagination
fuelled action and established a link between the virtual and the physical, the local and global (Appadurai 1996: 5–7). 'The Uprising of
Women in the Arab World', a virtual campaign, is the outcome of
such a transgression of borders and circulation of images. It started
in 2011 on the internet and then took to the streets with the rise of
sexual abuse in Egypt.[28] Global protests against the 'sexual terrorism'
practised on Egyptian female protesters took place in February 2013
in front of several Egyptian embassies. In synchronization with these
protests, women took to the streets of Cairo in a huge march in which

they brandished symbolic weapons, such as knives and rolling pins. It is noteworthy that bringing the instruments of the private space – the kitchen, in this case – to the public space is reminiscent of the women pouring hot water from utensils on British soldiers in Port Said in 1956 during the Tripartite Aggression. Apparently, women have always known how to empower and be empowered by the private space. Yet, in 2013, such an act was a direct declaration of the end of victimization and the restoration of agency.

In Conclusion?

One cannot say that these strategies simply generated new constructs of gender. Such a statement would be glaringly inaccurate. However, since transformation is a process not an operation, there are certain material and discursive signs that ascertain the activation of the process. The most striking sign is how the victim has turned into a warrior who is 'calling into question the model of construction whereby the social unilaterally acts on the natural and invests it . . . with . . . meaning' (Butler 1993: 4). All fixed and monolithic perceptions of the female body as sacred or shameful are being (re)visioned and subverted. In addition, it is an oversimplification to say that this revision has stemmed only from the feeling of anger and humiliation. As much as anger is important for any revolt, it was the persistence of women to revolutionize gender by setting a new paradigm that does not limit gender to the benefit of hegemonic power relations. Although these atrocities were co-opted by the Morsi government, essentially the Muslim Brotherhood, to consolidate political polarization,[29] women have taken them to be the route to subjectivity and agency. Put differently, all forms of 'gendered' violence have helped the process of reversal from victim to warrior and the message was clear: 'stop using crimes of violence against women in your political bargaining; you are part of the reason why this continues to happen' (Kirollos 2013). Emptying the space of appearance never aborted the aspirations towards revolutionizing gender and subverting the masculine gaze. If repression started from the highest point – that is, deforming a painting published in the most official paper – it was met by the most radical form of resistance: performing ballet on the streets.[30]

The empty space is populated by voices and discourses that refuse to give in; they are defiant voices that do not seek any ambivalence. When Hoda Elsadda wrote, 'I deplore the continued exploitation of women's bodies as political battlefields', she was representing the stance of the revolutionary protesting camp (2013b).[31] Collective struggle, individual testimonies, revolutionary aesthetics and incessant discursive and physical violations helped to formulate a discourse that reads the empty space against the grain. It is transformed into a sign of possibility and a democracy not yet realized. This empty space is being filled gradually with new intersections of gender, politics and resistance in preparation for a new 'space of appearance'. Apparently, gender was in dire need of the wild spirit of autumn's West Wind, so that we might find an answer to Shelley's question: 'If Winter comes, can Spring be far behind?' (Shelley, 'Ode to the West Wind').

Notes

1. There is a huge literature about the role of women in both the Egyptian and Tunisian Revolutions; one cannot even start to document it. However, there are some common features that one cannot help but notice: the romanticization of the revolutions, the glorification of the idea and the obsessive references to women's presence.

2. During the famous Eighteen Days of 2011, banners, slogans and chants never expressed any particular demands related to women or their rights. The discourse of protest focused on 'national' demands.

3. In her book *Islam and Democracy* (2002), Fatima Mernissi argues that 'Islamic' governments rush to sign international conventions just to prove that they have joined the wagon of modernity. In reality, these conventions remain as ink on paper.

4. This is one of the most famous poems in Egyptian colloquial poetry. It was written by the late Ahmed Fuad Nijm and sung by Sheikh Imam. In this poem, Egypt is personified as a woman named Baheya. It has been an inspiration up to the present day, to the extent that a feminist collective established in 2012 called itself 'Baheya Ya Masr'. That is to say, the name Baheya has become a feminized symbol for Egypt.

5. A CNN reporter had travelled to Upper Egypt and filmed a young girl being cut. CNN aired the story a day before the opening in Cairo of the ICPD

(International Conference on Population and Development) in 1994 (Amin 2012).

6. Ataba is a well-known, busy district in the heart of Cairo. The girl's name is not remembered and the incident became known as 'Ataba girl'.

7. This incident happened during Ramadan (the fasting month) and caused a huge furore in Egyptian society. A few marginalized voices expressed their solidarity with the girl, whereas the majority, backed by the media, blamed the girl for her clothes. That was the dominant discourse then, where women were held at fault. The offenders were later acquitted and the case was closed.

8. Around 1995, only a few women were able to earn the title of being 'a writer'. These were May Telmissany, Sahar El Mougy, Miral Al-Tahawy, Afaf Al Sayed, Noura Amin and Bahiga Hussein.

9. NGOs have always been active, especially in the 1990s, in lobbying for a feminist agenda. Yet the restrictions imposed by the state were extremely hindering.

10. I am in full agreement with the opinion of Deniz Kandiyoti, in her article 'Fear and Fury' (2013), that patriarchy is an abstract term that does not provide space for responsibility or accountability. In addition, patriarchy is not a coherent project that stands on its own without the support of power relations.

11. Foucault explains that, 'where there is power, there is resistance, and yet, or rather consequently, this resistance is never in a position of exteriority in relation to power' (1990: 95).

12. If you google 'International Women's Day in Egypt 2011' you will get hundreds of entries that narrate and, of course, condemn what happened on that day. I am citing this entry because the writer was one of the protesters who participated in the march. See Jumanah Younis, 'Egypt's Revolution Means Nothing if its Women are not Free' (2011).

13. In *A Dying Colonialism*, Frantz Fanon draws upon his experience as a psychiatrist and emphasizes the violent fantasies of the military doctrine: 'thus the rape of the Algerian woman in the dream of a European is always preceded by the rending of the veil' (1994: 45). Similarly, in Egypt, harassment that might amount to rape is originally a fantasy that oscillates between fascination and anger with the aim of subjugation.

14. See Rana Allam, 'Samira Ibrahim and the Plaque of Courage' (2013).

15. In 2008, the first known case of a ruling against a harasser occurred when Noha Rushdi filed a lawsuit (see BBC News 2008). In Rushdi's case, the government never hesitated to cast itself as a 'modern' defender of women's rights because the case was not political per se. On the other hand, while the harassment of Nawal Ali in 2005 in a political protest by the thugs of Mubarak caused a large-scale uproar, nothing happened. The government would not acknowledge that harassment took place on political grounds. Ali was severely vilified and attacked, to the extent that her husband divorced her (*Egypt Independent* 2013).

16. Ibrahim's position deserves a closer look. She is a young single woman in her twenties. She is Upper Egyptian (that is, from the south of the country, which is generally considered to be more conservative), an activist, veiled, and her family has Islamic leanings. Thus, Ibrahim is oppressed by her gender and upbringing, privileged by her veil and thus more blameworthy by religious rules; privileged by her revolutionary spirit and thus used as a living proof of the immorality of the rising generation. This concept of contradictory subject positions was shown clearly in the reception of Ibrahim's public testimony of the brutality she experienced.

17. In November 2012, a woman was stripped to her blue bra and jeans by the police. In solidarity with her, the revolutionaries called her *Sitt el-Banat* ('Lady of all Ladies') as a mark of honour. Her photograph was front page in all local and several international papers and magazines, as proof of the brutality of the regime of SCAF. It is noteworthy here to mention that the infamous question 'why did she ever go there?' started with this incident in an attempt to condemn the girl. For more details, see Soraya Morayef, 'Women in Egypt through the Narrative of Graffiti' (2013).

18. 'Why did she ever go there?' is a banal and meaningless question that members of the counter-revolution would immediately pose whenever a woman was attacked. So, instead of condemning violations, this question implies that the woman is already at fault.

19. In his famous soliloquy, Hamlet asks:

> To be, or not to be: that is the question:
> Whether 'tis nobler in the mind to suffer
> The slings and arrows of outrageous fortune,
> Or to take arms against a sea of troubles,
> And by opposing end them?
>
> (Shakespeare, *Hamlet*, 3: 1)

20. For details of the Mervat Mousa story, see Shounaz Mekky, 'Slapped Egyptian Activist to File Case Against Brotherhood Member' (2013).

21. See Dina Wahba, 'Baheya: New Movement, New Alliances? Revolutionizing the Women's Movement' (2012).

22. See www.facebook.com/FouadaWatch.

23. See @OpAntiSH (Twitter) and www.facebook.com/opantish.

24. Not Afraid is an organization that was established after the horrific rise in the sexual abuse of protesters.

25. All testimonies are available on the website of the NGO Nazra for Feminist Studies: http://nazra.org/terms/sexual-harassment.

26. There is a whole part entitled 'Transversality' in Guattari's book *Molecular Revolution: Psychiatry and Politics* (1984).

27. See Gerald Raunig, *Art and Revolution: Transversal Activism in the Long Twentieth Century* (2007).
28. See http://uprisingofwomeninthearabworld.org.
29. Faced with massive demonstrations in Egypt on 30 June, the presidency held a press conference in which the spokesperson spent not fewer than five minutes speaking about sexual harassment in Tahrir Square as proof of the thuggery dominating the opposition.
30. In June 2012, *Al-Ahram*, the Egyptian state newspaper, reprinted 'The Popular Chorus' by Abdel Hadi El-Gazzar, painted in 1948, with the naked woman in it covered. Almost a year later, in May 2013, during discussions by members of the Shura Council over the budget for the Cairo Opera House, an Islamist member suggested that ballet performances should be cancelled because of the 'nudity' that they entail. In protest over this statement, ballet dancers decided to perform Zorba on the streets.
31. This article was published on openDemocracy as a reaction to the statement issued by the Muslim Brotherhood expressing their disagreement with the draft declaration by the UN Commission on the Status of Women to combat violence against women.

References

Allam, R. (2013) 'Samira Ibrahim and the Plaque of Courage', *Daily News Egypt*, 11 March. Available at: www.dailynewsegypt.com/2013/03/11/samira-ibrahim-and-the-plaque-of-courage (accessed 9 April 2014).

Amin, S. (2012) 'The Battle Against Female Genital Mutilation', *Daily News Egypt*, November 15. Available at: www.dailynewsegypt.com/2012/11/15/the-battle-against-female-genital-mutilation/ (accessed on 11 January 2015).

Appadurai, A. (1996) *Modernity at Large: Cultural Dimensions of Globalization*, University of Minnesota Press, Minneapolis.

Arendt, H. (1958) *The Human Condition*, Chicago University Press, Chicago.

Arendt, H. (1972) *Crises of the Republic: Lying in Politics, Civil Disobedience, On Violence, Thoughts on Politics and Revolution*, Harcourt Brace Jovanovich, New York.

BBC News (2008) 'Egyptian Sexual Harasser Jailed', 21 October. Available at: http://news.bbc.co.uk/go/pr/fr/-/2/hi/middle_east/7682951.stm (accessed on 11 January 2015).

Butler, J. (1993) *Bodies that Matter: On the Discursive Limits of 'Sex'* Routledge, New York.

Butler, J. (1999) *Gender Trouble: Feminism and the Subversion of Identity*, Routledge, New York and London.

Egypt Independent (2013) 'This Day in History, 25 May 2005: Mubarak Thugs Sexually Assault Journalist Nawal Ali', 25 May. Available at: www.egyptindependent.com/news/day-history-25-may-2005-mubarak-thugs-sexually-assault-journalist-nawal-ali (accessed on 11 January 2015).

Elsadda, H. (2013a) 'Egypt: The Battle over Hope and Morale. An Interview', *openDemocracy*, 8 August. Available at: www.opendemocracy.net/print/62390 (accessed 9 April 2014).

Elsadda, H. (2013b) 'A War Against Women: The CSW Declaration and the Muslim Brotherhood Riposte', *openDemocracy*, 3 April. Available at: www.opendemocracy.net/5050/hoda-elsadda/war-against-women-csw-declaration-and-muslim-brotherhood-riposte (accessed 9 April 2014).

Fanon, F. (1994) *A Dying Colonialism*, Grove Press, New York.

Foucault, M. (1979) *Discipline and Punish: The Birth of the Prison*, Vintage Books, New York.

Foucault, M. (1982) 'The Subject and Power', *Critical Inquiry*, 8 (4) (Summer), pp. 777–95.

Foucault, M. (1990) *The History of Sexuality: Volume 1: An Introduction*, Random House, New York.

Guattari, F. (1984) *Molecular Revolution: Psychiatry and Politics*, trans. Rosemary Sheed, Penguin, Harmondsworth.

Kandiyoti, D. (2012) 'Disquiet and Despair: The Gender Sub-Texts of the "Arab Spring"', *openDemocracy*, 26 June. Available at: www.opendemocracy.net/print/66458

Kandiyoti, D. (2013) 'Fear and Fury: Women and Post-Revolutionary Violence', *openDemocracy*, 10 January. Available at: www.opendemocracy.net/print/70324 (accessed 9 April 2014).

Kirollos, M. (2013) 'Sexual Harassment in Tahrir: A Message from Mariam Kirollos', *Tahrir Squared*, 1 July. Available at: www.tahrirsquared.com/node/5131

Marcus, S. (1992) 'Fighting Bodies, Fighting Words: A Theory and Politics of Rape Prevention', in J. Butler and J. W. Scott, eds, *Feminists Theorize the Political*, Routledge, London and New York.

McClintock, A. (1997) '"No Longer in a Future Heaven": Gender, Race and Nationalism', in A. McClintock, A. Mufti and E. Shohat, eds, *Dangerous Liaisons: Gender, Nation, and Postcolonial Perspectives*, University of Minnesota Press, Minneapolis.

Mekky, S. (2013) 'Slapped Egyptian Activist to File Case Against Brotherhood Member', *Al Arabiya*, 20 March. Available at: http://english.alarabiya.net/en/2013/03/20/Slapped-Egyptian-activist-to-file-case-against-Brotherhood-member.html (accessed on 11 January 2015).

Mernissi, F. (2002) *Islam and Democracy: Fear of the Modern World*, Basic Books, New York.

Minh-ha, T. T. (1997) 'Not You/ Like You: Postcolonial Women and the Interlocking Questions of Identity and Difference', in A. McClintock, A. Mufti and E. Shohat, eds, *Dangerous Liaisons: Gender, Nation, and Postcolonial Perspectives*, University of Minnesota Press, Minneapolis, pp. 415–19.

Mitchell, W. J. T. (2012) 'Image, Space, Revolution: The Arts of Occupation', *Critical Inquiry*, 39 (1) (Autumn), pp. 8–32.

Morayef, S. (2013) 'Women in Egypt through the Narrative of Graffiti', *EgyptSource*, 5 March. Available at: www.atlanticcouncil.org/blogs/egyptsource/women-in-egypt-through-the-narrative-of-graffiti (accessed on 11 January 2015).

Pratt, N. (2013) 'Egyptian Women: Between Revolution, Counter-Revolution, Orientalism, and "Authenticity"', *Jadaliyya*, 6 May. Available at: www.jadaliyya.com/pages/index/11559/egyptian-women_between-revolution-counter-revoluti (accessed on 11 January 2015).

Raunig, G. (2007) *Art and Revolution: Transversal Activism in the Long Twentieth Century*, Semiotext(e), New York and Los Angeles.

Scott, J. (1992) 'Experience', in J. Butler and J. W. Scott, eds, *Feminists Theorize the Political*, Routledge, London and New York.

Seikaly, S. (2013) 'The Meaning of Revolution: On Samira Ibrahim', *Jadaliyya*, 28 January. Available at: www.jadaliyya.com/pages/index/9814/the-meaning-of-revolution_on-samira-ibrahim# (accessed 9 April 2014).

Wahba, D. (2012) 'Baheya: New Movement, New Alliances? Revolutionizing the Women's Movement', *Aswat Masriya*, 3 October. Available at: http://en.aswatmasriya.com/analysis/view.aspx?id=86123bfd-dc5c-4a8d-8d9e-7dc02578eccf (accessed on 11 January 2015).

Weedon, C. (1987) *Feminist Practice and Poststructuralist Theory*, Blackwell Publishing, Oxford and New York.

Younis, J. (2011) 'Egypt's Revolution Means Nothing if its Women are not Free', *The Guardian*, 9 March.

TWO

Resignifying 'Sexual' Colonial Power Techniques

The Experiences of Palestinian Women Political Prisoners[1]

Lena Meari

Women change at the same time that they change the world. This trial
of strength not only remodels the consciousness that woman has of
herself, and of her former dominators or of the world, at last within
her reach. This struggle at different levels renews the symbols, the
myths, the beliefs, the emotional responsiveness of the people.[2]

Frantz Fanon's text, *A Dying Colonialism*, addresses the Algerian Revolution and the ways in which 'it changes man and renews society'
(Fanon 1965: 181). In an introduction to the text, Adolfo Gilly writes
that Fanon's main preoccupation was not to document the brutality
of the oppressor nor the sufferings of the oppressed, rather 'his main
interest has been to go to the essentials: the spirit of struggle, of opposition, of initiative of the Algerian masses; their infinite, multiform,
interminable resistance' (Gilly 1965: 2). The spirit of struggle encompasses changing one's daily life, one's routines, prejudices and imme-
morial customs that hinder the revolutionary struggle (ibid).

Fanon's preoccupation with the spirit of revolutionary struggle and
its multiform incessant resistance, I believe, does not undermine the
importance of exposing the brutality of the oppressors or the subsequent

suffering of the oppressed; rather, it stresses the revolutionary spirit necessary for the oppressed's struggle for liberation, the only option available to them to overcome the oppressive structures. Considering the fact that epistemological positions intertwine with ontological assumptions and political sensibilities, approaching colonial structures from the viewpoint of resistance carries critical value for the processes of liberatory knowledge production and anti-colonial politics.[3]

In this chapter, I explore the reconstruction of sexuality and the sexed body within the dynamics of colonial domination and anti-colonial resistance in Palestine. Based on testimonies by *munadilat* (women strugglers) who were part of the Palestinian resistance movement, the chapter analyses the ways in which Shabak (Israel Security Agency) interrogators deploy sexuality and gender conceptions in their interrogation techniques in order to subjugate Palestinian strugglers and the ways in which Palestinian women strugglers resisted and re-signified these techniques through the enactment of the practice of *sumud*[4] (steadfastness under interrogation). I illustrate how the praxis of *sumud* by Palestinian female (and male) strugglers opens up the possibility to destabilize the significations of the sexed body, subvert women's daily life routines and social customs that establish women's bodies and sexualities in a fixed manner, and challenge the fixed associations between the female body and the meanings of women's dignity and honour within Palestinian society and the colonial perception of it. Rather than reading the Palestinian women's interrogation experiences from the viewpoint of colonial power, I follow Fanon's approach by approximating the interrogation experiences from the viewpoint of resistance. Particularly, I expose the ways in which Palestinian women political prisoners subvert the sexual colonial power techniques employed in interrogation at the same time as they change themselves, their society's cultural values and perceptions of women's sexuality that hinder revolutionary struggle in the specific case of Zionist settler colonialism in Palestine. Throughout this transforming process, the enactment of *sumud* in interrogation changes the Palestinian revolutionary struggle and the Palestinian revolutionary movements at large by re-constituting the perceptions of the constructed category of woman and her body in new revolutionary ways.

The chapter begins by opening up constricted perceptions of sexuality through highlighting the ways in which it is articulated within other categories and domains. The second section addresses the literature on sexual torture in colonial contexts in order to go beyond those constricted perceptions; it exposes the methodological limitation of approaching sexual torture from the perspective of power. The third section considers the academic literature on Palestinian women prisoners. In spite of the critical contribution of this literature in displaying Palestinian women's interrogation experiences, the focus of this body of literature on Shabak interrogation techniques and the subsequent suffering of women overlooks Palestinian women's resistance practices under interrogation and its potential to subvert colonial domination and its sexual perceptions. In the fourth and main section of the chapter, I present and analyse the interrogation experiences of the Palestinian women with whom I had long, in-depth conversations. I explicate the modes in which Palestinian women political prisoners have confronted sexual torture techniques and the ways in which material practices of *sumud* constitute alternative ontological premises regarding women's bodies and sexuality and a new mode of revolutionary subjectivity within the Palestinian resistance movement.

The Articulations of Sexuality

The regulation of sexuality and gender conceptions had been central to colonial regimes. Nevertheless, sexuality had never been 'a *discrete* regime in its own right' (Stoler 2011: 187) and gender as a constructed category is articulated with other categories (McClintock 1995). Hence, sexual and gender based torture techniques employed by the Israeli Shabak in the interrogation of Palestinians should be framed and analysed within the broader context of Zionist colonial rule in Palestine. As Ann Stoler argues, 'key to the sexual politics of colonial rule was never just enacted sexual violation but the distribution of social and political vulnerabilities that nourished the **potential** for them' (Stoler 2011: 186; emphasis in original). In this sense, sexuality is one domain in the constellation of colonial power techniques

and it converges with the physical and psychological management
of other domains (ibid.; Stoler 2006). Sexual torture techniques are
entangled with other interrogation techniques and broader colonial
techniques and make no sense when perceived in isolation. Thus, we
need to analyse sexual torture as simultaneously sexual and not sexual.
This analysis is central to understanding the workings of the structures
of colonialism and its resistance.

Within interrogation encounters in general, including those
explored in this chapter, the Israeli colonial state has always employed
sexuality as part of the broader complex physical-psycho-social interrogation techniques.[5] This is evident through the practice of strip and
body searching, and verbal insults such as the Shabak interrogators'
obsessive reiteration of the term *sharmuta* (whore) to refer to interrogated Palestinian females or to female family members of Palestinian males. It is also evident in the deprivation of feminine hygiene
products, threats to disseminate photos of naked bodies, to undress
females, to unveil veiled women or to threaten with or enact rape. In
the last decade the Shabak have also relied on concepts and practices
of sexuality when positioning female interrogators to interrogate Palestinian males, particularly Islamist activists.

These interrogation techniques emerge from the dominant Zionist
conceptions of Palestinian sexuality and gender dynamics and aim to
subjugate Palestinians by disintegrating their intimate selves. However, in order to analyse and understand the construction of sexuality
within the interrogation encounter and the ways in which Palestinians
subvert it, we need to go beyond the narrow perceptions and definitions of the sexual. For instance, narrow definitions of sexual torture
have focused on (or even sensationalized) images of the raped interrogated woman (or man) and naked bodies, such as those disseminated
in the photos from Abu Ghraib prison in Iraq. This understanding of
sexual torture does not help in understanding the narrative of Palestinian women such as Aisha with whom I had a long conversation about
her attempted rape during the interrogation. Aisha never referred to
her rape by Shabak interrogators as an individual, private sexual act;

she does not describe the rape act, nor her resistance to it, in sexual terms but in political ones. She states: 'While resisting the interrogators and shouting "No!", I felt I was struggling against all types of oppression the Zionists committed against Palestinians and Arabs'. The narrative of Aisha cannot be contained only in sexual terms or in what is called 'sexual torture'. Further, it cannot be contained in her own sexed body. Her narrative is perhaps the best reflection of the notion that the personal or the sexual is political, and this is intensified in colonial contexts.

Aisha's narrative, then, reconsiders the constricted definition of sexuality. It necessitates rethinking and reformulating the concept of 'sexual torture' and a deep examination of the articulation of sexuality and politics in colonial contexts. We need to re-examine how the logic of 'sexual torture' works as a technique of domination and oppression under colonialism and, more importantly, how it is perceived and resisted by different political actors. Sexuality in Aisha's narrative should be conceived as a subscript for other forces. Aisha perceives her 'sexed body' as Palestine, broadening how we define the body and the sexual. In this sense, sexuality and sexual torture, as Ann Stoler (2010) suggests, go beyond the individual body towards other social-political planes. Yet, Stoler constricts her investigation of sexuality and colonialism to the perspective of power: the strategies of colonial rulers and colonial techniques. Reading sexuality from the perspective of the interrogated Palestinian, such as Aisha's, adds new insight into the order of colonial sexuality and the diverse ways in which it is conceived and confronted by the colonized. Analyzing the workings of colonial structures is important; however, I am interested in reading colonialism and its complex sexual power techniques from the perspective of the colonized. Engaging with the colonized not as the constituent subjects of colonialism, but as revolutionary subjects engaged in and generated through anti-colonial struggles, elucidates the subversive force of the colonized through the resignifications of the sexual and the body, as the experiences of Palestinian women prisoners presented below demonstrate.

Sexual Interrogation Techniques in Colonial Contexts

Israel's colonial state terrorism and the routinization of torture of Palestinian men and women by Shabak interrogators are not exceptional. Considering the decolonization/recolonization war during the 1954–1962 Algerian Revolution, Marnia Lazreg argues that torture was not an epiphenomenon of the war but a central strategy to the army's defence of a colonial empire: 'the systematic use of torture was a logical outcome of revolutionary-war theory and doctrine developed in the 1950s by a group of veterans of colonial wars, especially in Indochina' (Lazreg 2008: 3). As Lazreg illustrates, torture is part and parcel of a subjugation ideology to combat revolutionary struggles. Thus, torture is intimately linked to the nature of the colonial state and its anti-subversive techniques towards resistance movements. This explains why the 'conduct of the Algerian war has been a source of information, if not inspiration, for the U.S. governments' (ibid.: 10), as reflected in the interest of the Pentagon and its use of the film The Battle of Algiers as a training tool during the colonization of Iraq (Lazreg 2008).

Torture aims to subjugate revolutionaries regardless of their gender. French military strategists became aware of the active participation of women within the FLN (Front de Libération Nationale) during the Algerian Revolution, as they 'display[ed] the consciousness and will to actively undo the colonial system, they became enemies to be fought with the same ferocity as men' (Lazreg 2008: 160) and were arrested and subjected to torture; 'when a woman was taken prisoner, the sexual nature of torture was a matter of fact. It was born by her gendered body' (ibid.). However, as the testimonies below of Palestinian women prisoners illustrate, the gendered body and gendered identities are undone through the resistance to the sexual colonial torture. That is, revolutionary anti-colonial acts destabilize the gender of the struggler, transform the struggler as well as the resistance movement and potentially subvert colonialism.

The signification of sexual torture has been widely discussed following the dissemination of photos from Abu Ghraib prison in Iraq in 2004. Most scholars place the photographs within the workings of the sexual aspects of the US project of empire and the tradition of sexual Orientalism and racism. Sherene Razack reflects on the sexualized violence inflicted on Iraqi prisoners by both men and women guards and argues that the project of empire requires the infusion of violent heterosexuality and patriarchy. She considers the racial hierarchies and the role of ritualized violence in enabling white men to achieve a sense of mastery over the racial other (Razack 2005: 341). Mary Ann Tétreault situates the politics of Abu Ghraib in a tradition of Orientalism that fetishizes and feminizes the sexuality of subjugated people as part of a strategy of domination affirming power relations between the occupiers and the occupied (Tétreault 2006: 34–35). Nicholas Mirzoeff notes that in the photographs from Abu Ghraib, 'sodomy was visualized as embodied spectacle, a mass of alterity that confirmed the long standing sense of the "Oriental" as deviant' (Mirzoeff 2006: 21). Jasbir K. Puar situates torture in Abu Ghraib within social discourses and practices related to sexuality, race, gender and nationalism. She argues that the torture of Iraqi prisoners at Abu Ghraib was 'neither exceptional nor singular' as liberals depict it. Puar considers bodily torture as one element in a repertoire of techniques of occupation and subjugation; however, what distinguishes Abu Ghraib's case within the 'torture industry' is its sexual feature (Puar 2005: 13). Puar argues that the administration's response to Abu Ghraib, particularly to the same-sex or homosexual acts demonstrated in the photographs, reinstantiate a liberal regime of multicultural heteronormativity intrinsic to US patriotism (ibid.: 14). She points to the argument of cultural difference raised by many commentators on the Abu Ghraib case, particularly the discourse about sexual repression and the taboo of homosexuality within Islamic cultures: 'the Orient is the site of carefully suppressed animalistic and perverse homo- and hypersexual instincts. This paradox lies at the heart of Orientalist notions of sexuality that are reanimated through the transnational production of the Muslim terrorist as torture object' (ibid.: 19).

Orientalist knowledge production, including the employment of anthropological methodologies, is evident in the working of the Israeli Shabak. Studying, representing and fixing culture and the Palestinian Other's mentality, specifically in relation to bodies and sexualities, are vital in determining Israeli 'effective' torture techniques. In Yakoov Peri's memoir *Habaa Le Horgecha* (*My Profession as a Man of Intelligence* 2001), the head of the Israeli General Security Service from 1988 to 1994, Peri notes that, as part of his training in the Shabak, he lived with an Arab family to learn the language and, more importantly, the 'culture and mentality' of Arabs, as if such fixed notions exist. What Peri does not declare is that this knowledge was also employed in developing torture techniques, as the process of torture requires 'understanding' the culture and mentality of the tortured in relation to her world and body. Evidences on the employment of this knowledge come from the testimonies of Palestinian political prisoners regarding the interrogation techniques deployed by the *Shabak* interrogators.

The above critical reflections on the torture at Abu Ghraib are revealing in pointing to the embeddedness of sexual torture techniques within colonial, racist systems and their role in reproducing imperialist Orientalist homophobic sexual fantasies. Nevertheless, most reflections on torture in Abu Ghraib read sexual torture from the perspective of power. The objects of analysis are the photographs of the Iraqi prisoners not the prisoners themselves. This methodological limitation creates reflections that, despite their critical value, reproduce the centrality of the empire and contribute to the erasure of the colonized subjects. This can be seen most clearly in Susan Sontag's reflection on the Abu Ghraib photographs, in which she argues that the acts of violence are enabled by the American administration's policies and, therefore, 'the photographs are us' (Sontag 2004). That is, the acts of violence deployed in Iraq reflect the image of Americans. In this way, Sontag, like other scholars, marginalizes the agency of the Iraqis in dealing with/confronting the American acts. Rather than reading sexual torture as reflection of the empire and its desires, this chapter examines the perception of torture from the viewpoint of those subjected to it and resisting it.

Writing Palestinian Women Political Prisoners

The methodological limitation regarding the exclusion of Iraqi prisoners from the analysis has been avoided in writings on Palestinian women prisoners, which have been based on ethnographic work with women prisoners themselves.[6] Elham Bayour (2004) and Nahla Abdo (2011) provide examples of this literature and their important analysis emerges out of in-depth interviews and conversations with Palestinian women ex-detainees, revealing crucial aspects of their experiences. Their analysis exposes the biased representations of Palestinian women strugglers by Western feminist writers, the brutality of the sexual torture techniques deployed on Palestinian women and the suffering of Palestinian women strugglers. While their research explicates the workings of Zionist and Western colonial power techniques and their effects on Palestinian women, what is also needed, and can be exposed through an anti-colonial resistance approach, is an analysis of the subversive role undertaken by Palestinian women and their resignification of those techniques employed in their interrogation.

Elham Bayour addresses Palestinian women's experiences of imprisonment as part of their contribution to the national liberation struggle. She argues that the occupation policies towards Palestinian women prisoners constitute 'sexual terrorism' (Bayour 2004: 201). Bayour conducted her research into Palestinian women political prisoners in three refugee camps in Gaza during the years 1998, 1999 and 2000. She interviewed fifty-two former prisoners about their involvement in the national liberation struggle, their detention experiences and their lives after prison. She analyses Palestinian women's conditions within the context of 'Zionist colonization' and 'patriarchal Arab traditions'. Bayour exposes the sexual violence deployed against Palestinian women political prisoners and illustrates the ways in which sexual terrorism is a fundamental part of their experience. She details the sexual interrogation techniques employed by the Shabak, which include 'repeated threats of rape, sexual assaults, beating women's breasts and genitals, fondling, verbal sexual abuse, and bringing the women's father and/or a Palestinian male political prisoner and ordering him to rape her' (Bayour 2004: 206). These practices, Bayour asserts, illustrate 'how the interrelated practices of occupation and sexual violence disrupt Palestinian society' and how 'rape attacks the integrity of the woman as a person as well as her identity as a woman' (ibid.: 207). Palestinian women prisoners continue to 'experience physical and psychological suffering' (ibid.: 209) after their release and also suffer 'from the reaction of their own community, which responded by blaming them' (ibid.: 210). Hence, Bayour concludes, 'in the face of dispossession and loss of land, colonized men and women hold fiercely onto their heritage, at times adhering to cultural dogmas that negatively affect women and children' (Bayour 2004: 211). Bayour's analysis overcomes the limitation of marginalizing the experiences of those subjected to torture and exposes crucial aspects of the interrogation experiences of Palestinian women. Yet, the focus on the brutality of the acts of sexual torture and the resulting psychological suffering reproduces a fixed conception of sexuality and gender dynamics and misses the resignifications of sexuality and gender dynamics that emerge from the Palestinian women's acts of *sumud* during the interrogations.

Nahla Abdo's study (2011), based on interviews with seventeen Palestinian women who were detained between the 1960s and the 1980s, constitutes a critique of the body of de-historicized, de-contextualized and Orientalist literature produced by several Western feminists on Palestinian women's military resistance after 2000. Abdo criticizes the writings of Andrea Dworkin, Barbara Victor and Mia Bloom, among others, for representing the Palestinian *munadilat*'s resistance as emerging from family oppression and for 'focusing on cultural symbols, such as family, patriarchy and religion' (Abdo 2011: 59) and ignoring the settler colonial order. In contrast, the women interviewed by Abdo joined the national liberation struggle voluntarily and 'were not silent victims of Palestinian patriarchy or male dictates' (ibid.: 61). Abdo notes that the explanations proposed by Western feminists as the motivation for Palestinian women's resistance acts are similarly used by the Israeli prison system as colonial torture tools to force women to confess during interrogation (ibid.: 60–61). Interrogation techniques are underpinned by an a priori image of Palestinian women as 'docile', 'subservient', 'obedient', 'religious' and fearful of any relationship or act that concerns their body or sexuality, and employs it as torture techniques against Palestinian women (ibid.: 62). Abdo presents examples of the sexual-psychological means employed by the Shabak interrogators and the ways in which women's bodies and sexuality are used to force confessions, concluding that, 'culture, family and sexuality are used as means of torture and control' (ibid.: 66). While Abdo rightly criticizes the ways in which Western feminists construct Palestinian women strugglers and Palestinian women detainees, and highlights their agency in choosing to participate in the liberation struggle, she still dwells on torture techniques and the employment of culture, family and sexuality as torture techniques. She overlooks the ways in which Palestinian women prisoners destabilize and resignify perceptions of culture, family and sexuality.

In what follows, I focus on the sumud of Palestinian women in the interrogation encounter. Sumud in the interrogation context means not to confess.[7] It offers Palestinian strugglers the possibility to challenge the colonial power structure with the potentiality to destabilize power relations, resignify colonial techniques aiming to humiliate them, transform themselves and the society's values and subvert the ontological bases of the body while constituting their revolutionary subjectivity. Since concepts of the Palestinian woman's body and sexuality are shaped with and through power structures and relations, including colonial power structures, sumud also subverts Zionist colonial power itself.

Sumud: Opening Up Possibilities for Resignification

As a major agent of the Zionist colonial regime, the Shabak draws upon culturally loaded knowledge produced about Palestinians to develop interrogation techniques. Shabak interrogators deploy fixed Orientalist/colonialist perceptions of Palestinian sexuality, such as those related to the concepts of women's dignity and honour.[8] Suha, a Palestinian ex-political prisoner, recounted to me her interrogation experiences, which illustrated the failure of Shabak interrogation techniques based on fixed constructs of cultural values and family upbringing of women. Suha explained to me the formation of the concept and practice of sumud and the possibilities it opens for resignifying gendered conceptions and, therefore, subverting interrogation techniques based on them. Suha had her first experience of arrest and interrogation in 1979. She states:

> At that time, sumud was not prevalent . . . The threat of rape had been one of the most effective methods to make females and males confess.
>
> During the eighty days of my interrogation, I didn't cooperate with the interrogators. However, my sumud at the time did not stem from a heroic position; it stemmed from my mother's personality. My mother was a very stubborn and proud person . . . She encouraged us, her daughters, to be strong and proud . . . My mother planted ethical values in us. That's what mobilized our sumud. In that interrogation, my ethical upbringing didn't allow me to say anything about anyone. I couldn't cause damage to anyone I knew. I refused to write anything in front of the interrogator, even my name . . . It is not that I wasn't afraid during the interrogation. I was horrified when they called me to the interrogation room or when they stripped off my clothes and threatened to rape me, or to bring my mother to the interrogation. But I was able to gather all my power and remember the pride my mother cultivated in us. For me, dignity is key. If you have dignity you can resist. The significance of the dignity that my family instilled in me was intensified during my political activities, specifically during the Eighties with the development of the culture of sumud in the interrogation. The personal dignity intertwined with the political-ethical collective dignity. A whole political culture of collective dignity and support developed. Sumud took root within this culture.

During her first interrogation in 1979, a time when sumud was not yet prevalent as an actualized practice, Suha's sumud was not mobilized by political positions. Instead, her sumud was an extension of her relationship with her mother, who was a model of women confronting oppressive apparatuses. Suha's narrative of her experience in the interrogation explicates how familial relations and nurture within the colonial context contribute to the practice of sumud. Dignity for Suha is not associated with her sexuality; rather it is associated with sumud and not revealing information about others. Suha was terrified of the interrogators and their capabilities, including rape. Yet, she engaged in a process of rearranging her internal fears and strengths. She was able to gather her strengths and reassert the milestones of her mother's nurturing, which involved pride, dignity and, consequently, the practice of *sumud*. Sumud, as Suha points out, involves adopting and highlighting facets that are cultivated through familial and social nurturing, such as dignity and defiance. It also involves undermining and undoing other aspects, such as the fear of being forced to strip, or even raped. Some scholars have analysed the rape of women and men prisoners in the interrogation as targeting their dignity (Lazreg 2008: 158). Yet, the experience of Suha shows that, despite her horror in front of the interrogators' threats, the dignity and pride that her mother instilled in her was the motivation for overcoming her fear and practising her *sumud*. What is understood as Palestinian women's dignity undergoes a process of resignification that accompanies and affects the political culture of struggle.

During Suha's second interrogation experience in 1992, she was subjected to 'deprivation of sleep, persistent annoying music, strong lighting in the cell, putting [her] in a cell full of shit, and not giving [her] [sanitary] pads during [her] menstrual cycle'. Yet, she states:

I faced all this with pride. Once the Red Cross came to visit me and I went and sat on a white chair, and I showed them how they treated me in the interrogation and didn't allow me access to [sanitary] pads. These things didn't make me feel ashamed, as my pride and dignity stem from my struggle not from these things. The extent of the oppression was reinforcing my defiance. The form of oppression they used didn't aim to oppress, but to humiliate you. It is not beating, but preventing you from basic necessities that are intended to lead you to feel humiliated.

As Suha illustrates, the techniques used by interrogators to humiliate her only reinforced her defiance. Instead of perceiving interrogation techniques as dehumanizing her, Suha understood them to be a systematic technique used to subjugate her and discourage her resistance and, therefore, she needed to confront and defeat those techniques. For Suha and other Palestinians, torture is intertwined with the colonial regime that they must challenge through *sumud*. They do not refer to torture as a violation of their human rights under colonialism, nor perceive themselves as being dehumanized by torture. Frantz Fanon approximates this stance when he argues that the revolutionary Algerian woman, 'arrested, tortured, raped, shot down . . . testifies to the violence of the occupier and his inhumanity' (Fanon 1965: 66). Similarly, rather than dehumanizing Suha and other women prisoners, torture testifies to the inhumanity of the occupier.

Sexual interrogation techniques are also employed with Palestinian men, as this segment of Mohammad's narration of his third interrogation experience illustrates:

> I already experienced all the interrogation techniques, but this time they were harsher . . . One technique used was hitting the genitalia and threatening to affect my sexual abilities and, on the other hand, suggestions of bringing beautiful girls to my cell if I confess. Threats and suggestions for relief took other forms as well. They threatened to bring my mother and sisters if I didn't confess or to let me out to finish school if I did. One interrogator told me, 'You have four sisters. We will bring them and do things with them that won't satisfy you'. I told him, 'Bring them if you want'. He got mad and replied, 'You are not a man and have no honour. You Marxists have no morals'. Anyway, this interrogation lasted for forty-seven days and I didn't give up anything.

The interrogators threatened to bring Mohammad's sisters, suggesting that they would sexually abuse them. They resorted to this technique presuming that a Palestinian man would protect his honour, perceived as being dependent upon women's bodies. This presumption is based on fixed Orientalist/colonialist perceptions of 'Arab masculinity', which went awry when Mohammad told the interrogators to go ahead and bring his sisters. The failure of this interrogation technique angered the interrogator, who continued to resort to the fixed perception of masculinity by telling Mohammad that he was not a 'real man' and had no 'honour'. As in the case of Suha, this incident exposes the failure of the interrogators as they assume a fixed perception of morality, honour and masculinity. For Mohammad, his morality and honour resided in protecting other comrades, not in his sisters' sexuality. Mohammad's engagement with political struggle involved transformations in how morality and honour are perceived. It also pointed to the malleability of gender within the Palestinian anticolonial movement.

Palestinian resignification of violent colonial acts does not take place only in interrogation centres. Julie Peteet explored the Israeli policy and practice of beating Palestinian males during the First Intifada, and how Palestinians appropriated the Israeli violence and beatings in a dialectical and agential manner (Peteet 1994: 37). The physical marks of violence on Palestinians' bodies signified not only the violence of the occupier but also the sacrifice and the honour that comes from resisting the occupier (Peteet 1994). Overall, the conception of honour undergoes a transformation in the context of resisting Zionist colonization in Palestine. Acts of resistance become signs of Palestinian honour, reformulating conceptions of femininity and masculinity.

The Potential Failure of Repetitious Sexual Power Techniques

As Palestinians testify, Shabak interrogators resort to repetitious speech and tangible acts of violence. Nevertheless, the practices of *sumud* enacted by Palestinian women strugglers bear the possibility of challenging those techniques and expose their potential failure to attain their intended goals of intimidating and humiliating Palestinian women in order to lead them to confession. Whenever Shabak interrogators interrogate a Palestinian woman they obsessively reiterate the term *sharmuta* (whore) and other derogatory sexual terms in referring to them. The repetition of the terms aims to insult women, to humiliate and fragment them.

Palestinian women can actually be affected by these speech acts. Sana states 'I was brought up in a house in which we never used bad language and the interrogators' reiteration of bad language annoyed me'. Yet, 'after a while the terms lost their effect on me and I started to utter them before the interrogator did'. The failure of the technique of using bad language in attaining its goal can be analysed through the examination of the efficacy/inefficacy of hate speech acts. Judith Butler argues that the utterance itself does not necessarily reconsolidate the power structure of domination, as the speech act can go wrong. Power structures can 'suffer destructuration through being reiterated, repeated, and rearticulated' (Butler 1997: 19). That is, the act of hate speech can fail because it is prone to innovation and subversion. For, if a structure is dependent upon its enunciation for its continuation and if it requires a future repetition to endure, then 'the repetition might disjoin the speech act from its supporting conventions such that its repetition confounds rather than consolidates its injurious efficacy' (ibid.: 20).

The potential failure of a power technique throughout its reiteration does not attain only to speech acts. It applies to tangible acts of violence. Whenever the occupation forces want to arrest a Palestinian, they raid the house with huge numbers of military jeeps and soldiers between midnight and five o'clock in the morning. This ritual of power aims to reinstate the colonial dominance, intimidate Palestinians and soften them for the phase of interrogation. Ilham provides an example of the failure of this repetitious ritual. Ilham was twenty-four years old when she was arrested for the first time in 1987, four months before the outbreak of the First Intifada. Before her arrest, Ilham had witnessed the arrest of Palestinians in her area and the ritual of the arrest performed by the occupation forces. At the moment of her arrest, Ilham remembers that a huge number of occupation forces filled the area around her home. Instead of being threatened by the scene of being pulled by soldiers along the road filled with people, Ilham says that, 'while walking quietly from the home to the military jeeps, the road was full of people and I felt like I was in a wedding'. The ritual of arrest as a performance of power failed to reconsolidate the colonial power structure. Ilham resignified the scene that was intended to threaten her. This suggests the possibility of transformation within the Palestinian community itself, as Ilham's perception of her arrest as a wedding march involves the community's perception of her as a Palestinian bride/heroine.

Suha provides another example of the failure of repetitive acts during interrogation:

> There was a young conservative woman with me in the cell. Before her interrogation I told her they will call you *sharmuta* – whore – on a regular basis and threaten to rape you. If they do this, don't show any signs of distress. Instead, take off your shirt and tell them to do it. She was shocked and told me that I am crazy. In the interrogation session, they threatened to rape her and she did exactly as I told her. This angered them, and they didn't use this technique with her again.

Suha helped the *sumud* of another Palestinian woman by encouraging her to overcome the fear of being stripped and threatened with rape, a routine, repetitive interrogation technique intended to intimidate women and lead them to confession. Resistance of this technique through *sumud* leads the interrogators to stop using it as it loses its efficacy and, in the process, the colonial power balance is altered.

Subverting the Ontological Bases of the Body

Ilham, a Palestinian Islamist activist, tells me that in the interrogation sessions interrogators attempted to make her confess through exploiting what they perceive as cultural and religious sensitivities. In addition to unveiling her, the interrogator would get very close to her to create sexual proximity as intimidation. As a response, Ilham states, 'Within the interrogation, I never felt my body was a female body. I did not perceive my position as being a female. For me, the interrogator was an enemy to confront'. Ilham says that she did not perceive the interrogator as a 'male', but merely as an 'enemy to confront' and that the bodies involved in this encounter were not gendered bodies. The interrogator attempted to sexualize her body, but, for Ilham, there was nothing sexual taking place. Within her framing/conceptualization, her own body was not a sexualized, brutalized, tortured female body but, instead, a site of resistance and a vehicle for remaining strong in the face of the enemy's violence. This conceptualization of Ilham's experience resonates with Aisha's account of her experience of rape in the interrogation:

> During my interrogation, I realized that the body is the house of the roh (spirit). During the interrogation, I did not experience my body as a body in the common sense, as encompassing my sex. The body was the place on which you are being beaten so that the pain moves to the wa'i (consciousness) and spirit. The body is the place they hurt you through . . . The body is the gate through which they get to your consciousness in order to transform it. The real struggle is over the consciousness. If they get to your consciousness and succeed in convincing you that you and your people are weak and can be defeated, and that your people don't deserve your loyalty, all your walls of defence collapse. With your sumud you can defy them and remain strong.

For both Ilham and Aisha, the body has a unique status. It transcends the body's sex and becomes a space through which another battle is waged: the battle against the spirit and consciousness. This perception of the body comes to the forefront as Aisha talks about the interrogators' attempt to rape her during the interrogation:

> The rape initiated by the interrogators was not something related to my sexual body or honour. For me, it was an assault on my being and existence as a Palestinian Arab. This is what gave my body the astonishing energy and power to prevent them from penetrating it. I decided at that moment that I am not going to allow them to penetrate my core. They wanted to penetrate me at my core, yet, at that moment the whole energy of resistance in the world, the whole energy of the cosmos and of history gathered in my body and rejected them. I sensed that their absolute injustice, the highest level of the arrogance of their power and their sense of victory had permitted them to be villainous to this degree. When I saw that they want to get to my core, I sensed that their absolute

injustice should be resisted and defeated. At that moment I felt hope. I didn't perceive my body as my own body; it was the body of all Palestinian Arabs and all those oppressed. And I shouted, 'Nooooooo!'

For Aisha and Ilham, in their interrogations the body was redefined and was given a different ontological meaning. It was not perceived as a sexed female body or an autonomous individual body. Aisha's body absorbed the bodies of all Palestinians, all Arabs and all oppressed peoples, and it radiated the resistance of this collective body. Ilham and Aisha's experiences destabilize the perception of the body as a universal, 'naturalized material given of human substance' (Kirby 1989). By stating that 'the body is the gate through which they get to your consciousness in order to transform it', Aisha does not privilege one side, rather she deconstructs the well-established body–mind binary. Aisha's expression testifies to the disruption of the categorization of phenomena as relating to either the body or the mind.

Transforming the Self and Society's Values

Ghada, who was nineteen years old when arrested and interrogated in 1982, was a student at Damascus University. She was arrested immediately after her visit to her family in Nablus. The interrogation lasted for one month. The massacre of Sabra and Shatila took place while Ghada was in the interrogation and she states 'the guard of the prison came to me to tell me about the massacre. She was laughing while telling me we killed all Palestinians in Lebanon; we will kill you all and no one will remain'. Ghada responded to her 'if you kill Palestinians we will give birth to others and they will continue the struggle against you . . . I will give birth to forty kids and they will become strugglers'. During the interrogation, Ghada was charged with the events and scenes of Palestinian refugees removed from Lebanon to Syria. She describes with tears the scenes of trucks holding Palestinians. This, according to Ghada, gave her strength during the whole interrogation. The resignification of the interrogation techniques are reflected in

Ghada's words as she says 'while in interrogation and the long periods I was kept in a dark cell and my head covered with a filthy bag, I was proud that the filthy bag that covers my head was put on Palestinian *feda'iyin* who sacrificed for Palestine'. The oppression that Palestinians endured and Ghada witnessed had transformed her in such a way that she became an integral part of the collective Palestinianess constituted through resistance and *'amal fida'iyi*.

Rape threats and the interrogator's hold on her body parts were the most prominent interrogation techniques employed on Ghada. Ghada says that the interrogator kept telling her '"I will rape you and let everyone talk about you" . . . they kept employing the cultural sensitivity of Palestinians to try to stress me'. Against the intended goal of the interrogator to elicit fear in Ghada by employing Orientalist/colonialist fixed perceptions of Palestinian society, Ghada told me that she was thinking that even if she was raped and got pregnant she would give birth to a *fida'i* who would kill his colonizer father.

Ghada describes how she was working to undo her fears of the interrogator and how she considered death as a viable option. 'I was thinking that I am not better than the Palestinians who do not find food to eat or who were killed, and this gave me strength to confront the harsh experience of the interrogation'. During the whole interrogation, 'I was surprised to discover my own strengths not only in the interrogation but also in the prison itself . . . I met lots of women strugglers who had long experiences and they had an effect on me. We shared our experiences and this gave me more strength to resist'. The experiences of being interrogated and imprisoned transformed Ghada and strengthened her. An effect that she says has stayed with her long after these experiences.

The arrest and interrogation of Ghada was a shock for her family. Ghada comes from a family that is not involved in political activities and no member of the family had ever been arrested. Ghada was active when she was at school in Nablus and she remembers the killing of Lina Al-Nabulsi, who was at her school, and how her martyrdom affected her and instigated her involvement in struggle. She was arrested several times at the age of fourteen and was always taken with her father. The colonial authorities used to tell her father 'educate your daughter, she is involved in activities that endanger the security'.

The interrogators employed the issue of the family and kept telling Ghada that she needed to confess and to cooperate with them and think about the situation of her parents. On the transformation of her family, Ghada says:

> For my family, social perceptions were important. I was the eldest in my family and they were happy that I went to study in Damascus. My arrest was a shock to the family and others started to say, 'look what happened because you sent her to study abroad'. In court, my father was sad and very worried for me. This affected me but I was convinced that I had done the right thing and that he needed to understand that. Some family members told my father that he should be proud of me and that Ghada opened up the way in the family for political engagement . . . as for my mother, she was very affected; she was always crying in court and during the visits to me in prison. At the end I told her if you want to continue crying don't visit me and she stopped crying. The issue is not easy but when you feel that there is a cause that is bigger than the family and bigger than the parents, then you feel strong and that you need to bear all things. During my prison time my parents met and got to know the families of other prisoners and this supported them and raised their spirits. At the beginning it was a disaster for my family to know I was involved in the struggle but afterwards they became proud of me.

After her release, Ghada says that she had a greater motivation to continue the struggle. 'They think that the arrest, interrogation, torture and prison would stop the struggler but all this motivated me to continue. The experience strengthened and hardened me and gave me the conviction that I am strong, especially the experience of hunger strike that we had in prison in 1983'. According to Ghada, this experience not only strengthened her to confront the interrogators but also to confront the society and to be more confident in herself. In her two other arrests and interrogations in 1989 and 1992 during the First Intifada, she confronted her interrogators, who were unable to obtain any information from her. During the interrogation in 1992, Ghada told the interrogators 'you can continue hitting me for the next ten years but you will not get anything from me'. When the interrogators noticed Ghada's strong conviction they did not threaten to bring in her parents but focused on other techniques to break her, such as threatening to spread rumours about her or causing her pain. Ghada says, 'the amazing thing is that when you feel yourself strong you don't feel pain. While getting hit harshly I did not feel pain'. Ghada's words testify to how culturally based interrogation techniques lose their effect.

Ghada describes the transformations that she underwent and the constitution of a revolutionary subjectivity: 'I felt I am a struggler and need to be a model for others'. The struggler, according to Ghada, 'has conviction in her cause, has strong connections with her comrades and community and is ready to sacrifice for them'. Ghada's words outline features of Palestinian revolutionary subjectivity constituted through resisting Zionist colonization. It is a subversive subjectivity enmeshed within the Palestinian cause and community.

Subverting Western Feminist Constructions of Palestinian Women

Women of colour and women from the colonized world have criticized the concept of 'women's sisterhood' by highlighting the different modes of life that they live, which form their feminism in a different way from that of Western liberal feminists. The notion of 'women's sisterhood' continues to be employed by different parties, including the Shabak, to weaken Palestinian women's anti-colonial struggle. Nadia provides an example of the deployment of 'women's sisterhood' in her interrogation, telling me that, 'once an interrogator initiated a conversation to convince me that women are oppressed in Palestinian society and that I should be allied with Israeli women against Palestinian patriarchal oppression'. The employment of this technique – aiming to weaken the connective relationality of the Palestinian woman to her community, and specifically the males within the community, and at the same time to strengthen her positive relationality towards women within the colonizing society – is revealing. It demonstrates the attempts to generate a form of normalization through alliance between specific sectors of the colonized and the colonialists, impeding the ability of the colonized to confront and destabilize colonial power relations. The interrogator highlights power relations on the basis of gender while erasing colonial power relations and their articulation with other power structures. In other words, the discourse of 'women's sisterhood' is used to justify colonization. Reflecting on that, Nadia tells me that, in spite of her awareness of the gendered power relations within her own community, she does not separate the struggle for social and gender justice from the struggle against colonialism.

Tahreer provides another example of a technique widely used by the Shabak in the interrogation of Palestinian women. In addition to the interrogators' attempts to get information from her regarding her activities and the people she is associated with, one of the main goals of Shabak interrogators was to get a statement from her testifying that she was exploited. 'One of the interrogators', says Tahreer, 'spent a long time trying to convince me to say that I was manipulated by the organization and the male leadership. He said, "I will get you out of prison if you say that you were deceived to get involved in these activities"'. What the interrogator was trying to get from Tahreer is also one of the arguments of several Western feminists in their writings about women in general, and Palestinian women in particular, concerning their involvement in the national liberation struggles of their people. They portray Palestinian women's participation in the national liberation struggle as the co-optation of women within patriarchal structures at the expense of their feminist aspirations. Most Western feminist writing on Palestinian women focuses on culture and religion as the main aspects of women's condition, ignoring the colonial aspect.[9] A main strand of Western feminism had failed to understand the multiple meanings of feminism and the meaning of feminism for colonized women and women of colour – especially how, for colonized women, feminism has developed within broader liberation movements. As my research has shown, for Palestinian women like Tahreer who have been interrogated, resisting sexism and colonization have always gone hand in hand. Colonialism, exemplified here by Israeli interrogation practices, is already gendered and sexualized, so it makes no sense to reach out to Palestinian women for solidarity around sexism especially when this form of solidarity does not capture or account for the forms of sexism Palestinian women actually face, particularly the sexism enacted by the Zionist colonization.

Conclusion

Approaching the interrogation as a micro site for the Zionist settler colonial regime in Palestine is revealing of the dialectic of oppression–resistance in relation to the colonial condition in Palestine. The gender analysis of the dynamics of the interrogation, offered in this chapter, illustrates that the analysis of sexual techniques employed in the interrogation and the gender constructs and practices of the interrogation and its resistance by Palestinians provides a nuanced understanding of the dialectic of oppression/resistance in colonized Palestine. Israeli Shabak interrogators deploy every means to combat resistance, to subjugate Palestinian strugglers and to extract confessions from them, based on a priori perceptions of Palestinian sexuality and gender norms and identities. Approaching the interrogation from the perspective of Palestinian women (and men) reveals how sumud as a revolutionary praxis opens up possibilities for resignifying interrogation techniques and for transforming the self and perceptions of sexuality. Sumud changes the meanings of the oppressive interrogation techniques and transforms the interrogation into a practice of resistance to both colonialism and the fixed perceptions of Palestinian sexuality and sexed bodies. Further, it exposes gender malleability and shifts in gender norms, and the meanings of femininity and masculinity within the Palestinian resistance movement. As Frantz Fanon suggested in relation to the Algerian Revolution, throughout revolutionary processes and resistance practices, cultural values are destabilized and new community and revolutionary subjectivities are produced. The testimonies of Palestinian women provided in the chapter illustrate how new Palestinian revolutionary subjectivities were in the making through the practices of *sumud* and how these practices transformed the sexual perceptions of Palestinian women, men and the community of strugglers.

Notes

1. The idea for this chapter is based on my ethnographic research carried out between 2008 and 2010 for my PhD dissertation, titled 'Sumud: A Philosophy of Confronting Interrogation'. For this chapter, I conducted more research and in-depth interviews with Palestinian women political prisoners during 2014. The English translations of quotations are mine unless otherwise indicated. I would like to thank Nadine Naber for her valuable comments on different drafts of the text, and Suad Joseph for her supervision of the original research project.
2. This paragraph is a gendered paraphrasing of Frantz Fanon's following words: 'The thesis that men change at the same time as they change the world has never been so manifest as it is now in Algeria. This trial of strength not only remodels the consciousness that man has of himself, and of his former dominators of the world, at last within his reach. This struggle at different levels renews the symbols, the myths, the beliefs, the emotional responsiveness of the people' (Fanon 1965: 30).
3. Mark Lewis Taylor's article 'Decolonizing Mass Incarceration: "Flesh Will Wear Out Chains"' (2014) provides an example of the form of knowledge produced by approaching mass incarceration from the perspective of resistance. Taylor analyses the decolonizing practices that serve as liberating spectre to what he calls 'the colonial carceral' (Taylor 2014: 123).
4. For a genealogy of the praxis of *sumud* in interrogation and how the interrogation encounter and broader colonial relations are conceptualized through *sumud*, see Meari 2014.
5. For documentation of the Shabak interrogation techniques in general and the routinization of torture see, for instance, Al-Haq 1993; B'Tselem 1998; B'Tselem and HaMoked 2007. For human rights organizations' accounts of Shabak sexual- and gender-based interrogation techniques, see, for instance, The Public Committee Against Torture in Israel 2013; Addameer n.d. For detailed accounts of sexual violence, sexual assaults and threats of rape deployed towards Palestinian women political prisoners as narrated by them see Elham Bayour 2004 and Nahla Abdo 2011.
6. There is another form of analysis of Palestinian women prisoners, which uses quantitative methods and focuses on the long-term psychological and physical consequences of torture for Palestinian women; see, for instance, Zaqut et al. (2010). For a critical reading of the construction of suffering and the trauma

discourses surrounding Palestinian political prisoners see Meari, 'Reconsidering Trauma: Towards a Palestinian Community Psychology' (2015), in which I examine the working of the discourses of trauma and the ways in which it excludes the politics and practices of *sumud* by individualizing and de-politicizing the 'victim' of torture.

7. For an analysis of the concept and practice of *sumud* in interrogation, the mode of subjectivity and the form of politics it produces, see Meari (2014).

8. For an account of how the concept of honour and 'honour crime' has become 'the most iconic of the cultural-legal categories created to describe the deplorable state of women's rights in the Muslim world', see Lila Abu-Lughod (2013: 113).

9. See Amira Silmi's (2009) text on the Western academic discourses and the Western feminist representations of Palestinian women who participate in the national liberation struggle.

References

Abdo, N. (2011) 'Palestinian Women Political Prisoners and the Israeli State', in A. Baker and A. Matar, eds, *Threat: Palestinian Political Prisoners in Israel*, Pluto Press, London.

Abu-Lughod, L. (2013) *Do Muslim Women Need Saving?*, Harvard University Press, Cambridge, MA, and London.

Addameer (n.d.) *Palestinian Women Political Prisoners: Systematic Forms of Political and Gender-Based State Violence*, Addameer, Ramallah.

Bayour, E. (2004) 'Occupied Territories, Resisting Women: Palestinian Women Political Prisoners', in J. Sudbury, ed., *Global Lockdown: Race, Gender, and the Prison-Industrial Complex*, Routledge, New York and London.

B'Tselem (1998) *Routine Torture: Interrogation Methods of the General Security Service*, 19 May, B'Tselem, Jerusalem.

B'Tselem and HaMoked (2007) *Absolute Prohibition: The Torture and Ill-Treatment of Palestinian Detainees*, May, B'Tselem and HaMoked, Jerusalem.

Butler, J. (1997) *Excitable Speech: A Politics of the Performative*, Routledge, New York and London.

Fanon, F. (1965) *A Dying Colonialism*, Grove Press, New York.

Gilly, A. (1965) 'Introduction', in F. Fanon, *A Dying Colonialism*, Grove Press, New York, pp. 1–21.

Al-Haq (1993) *Palestinian Victims of Torture Speak Out: Thirteen Accounts of Torture During Interrogation in Israeli Prisons*, Al-Haq, Ramallah.

Kirby, V. (1989) 'Corporeographies', *Inscriptions: Journal for the Critique of Colonial Discourse*, 5.

Lazreg, M. (2008) *Torture and the Twilight of Empire: From Algiers to Baghdad*, Princeton University Press, Princeton.

McClintock, A. (1995) *Imperial Leather: Race, Gender, and Sexuality in the Colonial Contest*, Routledge, New York and London.

Meari, L. (2014) 'Sumud: A Palestinian Philosophy of Confrontation in Colonial Prisons', *South Atlantic Quarterly*, 113 (3), pp. 547–78.

Meari, L. (2015) 'Reconsidering Trauma: Towards a Palestinian Community Psychology', *Journal of Community Psychology*, 43 (1), pp. 76–86.

Mirzoeff, N. (2006) 'Invisible Empire: Visual Culture, Embodied Spectacle and Abu Ghraib', *Radical History Review*, 95, pp. 21–44.

Peri, Y. (2001) *My Profession as a Man of Intelligence: 29 Years of Working in the Shabak*, trans. Bader A'qili, Dar Aljaleel, Amman. (Arabic).

Peteet, J. (1994) 'Male Gender and Rituals of Resistance in the Palestinian Intifada: A Cultural Politics of Violence', *American Ethnologist*, 21 (1), pp. 31–49.

Puar, J. (2005) 'On Torture: Abu Ghraib', *Radical History Review*, 93, pp. 13–38.

Razack, S. (2005) 'How is White Supremacy Embodied? Sexualized Racial Violence at Abu Ghraib', *Canadian Journal of Women and the Law*, 17 (2), pp. 341–63.

Silmi, A. (2009) *On Women and Resistance: The Colonial Narrative*, Muwatin: The Palestinian Institute for the Study of Democracy, Ramallah. (Arabic).

Sontag, S. (2004) 'Regarding the Torture of Others', *The New York Times Magazine*, 23 May. Available at: http://www.nytimes.com/2004/05/23/magazine/regarding-the-torture-of-others.html (accessed 7 July 2014).

Stoler, A. (2006) *Haunted by Empire: Geographies of the Intimate in North American History*, Duke University Press, Durham, NC.

Stoler, A. (2010) *Carnal Knowledge and Imperial Power: Race and the Intimate in Colonial Rule*, University of California Press, Berkeley.

Stoler, A. (2011) 'Beyond Sex: Bodily Exposures of the Colonial and Postcolonial Present', in A. Berger and E. Varikas, eds, *Genre et Postcolonialismes: Dialogues Transcontinentaux*, Éditions des archives contemporaines, Paris.

Taylor, M. L. (2014) 'Decolonizing Mass Incarceration: "Flesh Will Wear Out Chains"', *Journal for Cultural and Religious Theory*, 13 (1), pp. 121–142.

Tétreault, M. A. (2006) 'The Sexual Politics of Abu Ghraib: Hegemony, Spectacle, and the Global War on Terror', *NWSA*, 18 (3), pp. 33–50.

The Public Committee Against Torture in Israel (2013) *From the Testimony of a Palestinian Woman Prisoner*, PCATI, Jerusalem.

Zaqut, S., Abu Daqa, M., and Sarraj, E. (2010) 'The Psychological and Physical Long Term Effects of Torture on Released Palestinian Prisoners in Gaza Strip', The Palestinian Developmental Women 'Studies Association', Gaza (Arabic). Available at: www.pdwsa.ps/ar/?page=newsdetails&id=124 (accessed on 15 September 2014).

THREE

A Strategic Use of Culture

Egyptian Women's Subversion and Resignification
of Gender Norms

Hala G. Sami

Introduction

Since 2011, in the context of post-revolutionary Egypt, there has been a tendency, even an urge, to reassess Egyptian national identity and socio-cultural values, particularly those pertaining to women's position and role in society. As Nira Yuval-Davis argues, women are historically viewed as the symbolic markers of the nation and its culture (Yuval-Davis 1997: 45). When the nation's cultural identity is in question, women have always been implicated.

National cultural identity often attributes to women characteristics such as 'self-sacrifice, benevolence, devotion, religiosity, and so on' (Chatterjee 1993: 131), as well as connecting women to the land. Such representations of women are compromizing, as they usually constrain women's roles (Loomba 2005: 180), while various other potentials are denied to them.

Political Islamist groups, which became particularly powerful after the January 2011 Revolution, have led debates over women's role within the public and private spheres and sought to marginalize and discredit women's presence in public life. However, it is worth noting that the compromizing approach to handling women's social status and role is not exclusive to right-wing fundamentalists, but is an over-all political standpoint that continues to emerge in transitional phases of the nation's history. As Hoda Elsadda notes: 'secular and Islam-ist discourses on gender are similar, in other words . . . liberal posi-tions on the woman question are not more supportive of women's empowerment and are fraught with contradictions and ambivalences' (Elsadda 2012: xxv).

In her article 'The Technology of Gender', Teresa de Lauretis points out that the 'construction of gender . . . is both a socio-cultural con-struct and a semiotic apparatus, a system of representation which assigns meaning . . . to individuals within the society' (de Laure-tis 1998: 717). In order to counteract any hegemonic discourse, de Lauretis suggests it is necessary 'to create new spaces of discourse, to rewrite cultural narratives, and to define the term of another perspec-tive – a view from elsewhere' (ibid.: 719).

Following the 25 January Revolution, several initiatives emerged to create new spaces of discourse and rewrite cultural narratives in order to challenge women's marginalization within the public sphere. This chapter will explore three of these initiatives, which, I argue, are innovative in their intertextual use of Egyptian culture[1] and history to subvert the conservative discourse about women that emerged in the wake of the revolution, to resignify women's representation in Egyptian civil society and to highlight the subaltern voice. Indeed, at a time of vigorous opposition and rebellion, popular culture manifests itself as an appropriate medium for political upheaval and transition in Egyptian history. In the face of a comparatively monolithic interpella-tion of society, popular culture as 'the voice of dissent' (El Hamamsy and Soliman 2013: 9) proposes itself as an avant-garde socio-cultural manifestation: it 'has become a prime site for contestations of value embedded deep within fields such as television and film criticism, popular music and "modern" art' (Edensor 2002: 16).

The present chapter, thus, proposes to illustrate the strategic decon-struction of gender norms through popular culture by three particu-lar politically active manifestations. The first section will engage with

the reappropriation of national iconic figures by Baheya Ya Masr, a
political activist movement that emerged in 2012. The second section examines the caricatures of Doaa Eladl, a woman satirical cartoonist, whose daily subversive production is a genuinely pronounced
update on Egyptian current affairs. The third and final section examines the graffiti movement, Women On Walls, whose wall designs aim
at resisting women's marginalization within the public sphere. The
chapter, thus, engages with the dynamics of emerging paradigms that
attempt to resist a truly conservative mentality, one that is inclined to
relegate women to the periphery of civil society, in which they would
occupy their traditional role of hearth and home, while limiting the
public sphere to men. In the dichotomous private-versus-public formula, the private sphere is believed to be associated with 'the emotional, sexual, and domestic' (Spivak 1987: 103). The public sphere,
on the other hand, encompasses 'the political, social, professional,
economic, intellectual arenas' (ibid.), which are socially and culturally acclaimed and deemed to be 'more important', 'more rational'
and 'more masculine, than the private' (ibid.). In her seminal essay,
'Is Female to Male as Nature is to Culture?', Sherry B. Ortner echoes
this social phenomenon in which 'the domestic is always subsumed
by the public' (Ortner 1974: 79). The attempt to exclude women
from the public arena, which encompasses 'places for social encounter
and exchange, places for political action and participation in political life and plays an important role as places for economic activities'
(Grundström 2005: 1), becomes an issue to contend with. It calls for
an examination of the representation of women within an emerging
ideological context that has the tendency to overlook their pivotal role
in social development.

Baheya Ya Masr: Women's Political Activism

Baheya Ya Masr[2] is a popular movement that was founded in 2012.
On its Facebook page, it states that the movement's objective is to
mobilize people on a large scale and lobby for the rights for both
women and men. The name of the movement is culturally significant,

as, primarily, it evokes the character of Baheya, who is one of two figures depicted by the Egyptian sculptor Mahmoud Mokhtar in his famous statue, *Nahdat Misr*, or 'Egypt's Awakening' (the other figure being the Sphinx). Mokhtar designed and accomplished the statue a year after the 1919 Egyptian uprising against British occupation. 'Baheya' is a typical Egyptian peasant woman's name that is meant to symbolize Egypt. In her book *Egypt as a Woman*, Beth Baron elaborates on the symbolic significance of Baheya, as a peasant woman: at that time (1919–1920), the nationalist movement considered the peasant to be 'culturally authentic' and, therefore, seen as, 'the soul of Egypt' (Baron 2005: 68).[3] In the sculpture, Baheya lifts her veil and gazes towards the horizon, simultaneously symbolizing Egypt's 'authentic national identity' and its future as an independent and modern state. Such representations of women as standing in for the nation have been problematized by post-colonial feminists. As Anne McClintock argues:

> Women are represented as the atavistic and authentic body of national tradition . . . embodying nationalism's conservative principle of continuity. Men, by contrast, represent the progressive agent of national modernity . . . embodying nationalism's progressive, or revolutionary principle of discontinuity. (1993: 66)

The logo of Baheya Ya Masr resignifies the character of Baheya by attributing to her the words, in both Arabic and English, *horriyati wa kar-amati wa haqi*, 'my freedom, dignity and rights'. In other words, Baheya is not only a nationalist symbol but becomes an agent in achieving citizens' rights. This agency is also underscored by the association of 'Baheya' with the late revolutionary poet Ahmed Fuad Nijm and musician Sheikh Imam. '*Masr yamma ya Baheya*' was one of several political songs performed by the duo.[4] This and other songs would be sung by workers and students in strikes and protests in the late 1960s and 1970s, and were often heard in 2011 during the eighteen-day occupation of Tahrir Square. Moreover, like many of the people who took to the streets against the Mubarak regime in 2011, Baheya is painted with the three colours of the Egyptian flag. Baheya Ya Masr, therefore, resolves the 'temporal anomaly within nationalism – veering between nostalgia for the past and the impatient, progressive sloughing of the past' not 'by figuring the contradiction as a "natural" division of *gender*' (McClintock 1993: 66), but through the reappropriation and resignification of Baheya as an active Egyptian (female) citizen, thereby resisting conservative discourses seeking to marginalize women in public life.

The movement's political activism is varied and ranges from organizing demonstrations to holding discussions and showing feature and documentary films, particularly pertinent to women's issues. For instance, on 8 March 2012, on the occasion of International Women's Day, it led a march to parliament to request fair representation of women in the constitution that was being drafted during that period. On 6 February 2013, it mobilized people to march to Tahrir Square to protest against the premeditated and organized sexual harassment of women participating in demonstrations.

During the movement's marches and demonstrations, many women and men were seen raising posters of prominent Egyptian female public figures, such as Nefertiti (the ancient Egyptian queen), Faten Hamama (the famous actress), Umm Kulthum (the renowned singer), Safiya Zaghlul (early twentieth-century political activist, supporting women's rights, and wife of national leader Saad Zaghlul) and many other women from both ancient and modern Egyptian history. The appropriation of these figures in protests operates to highlight the long history of powerful, influential and venerable women, creating continuity between Egypt's past and the present day demands of Baheya Ya Masr. Moreover, the celebration of an ancient Egyptian queen, a singer, an actress and a political woman challenges Islamist discourse, which repudiates Egypt's pre-Islamic history, believes that singing and acting are irreligious and seeks to marginalize women's political roles.

Women's social status, especially their roles within the public and private arenas, became one of the frequent issues debated by a conservative current of thought, particularly led by fundamentalist religious groups. They came to the surface and became the highlight of the political scene immediately after the January 2011 Revolution.

They began to openly air their conservative views after their sweeping victory in the parliamentary elections of November 2011–January 2012 and their ideological vantage point was further corroborated by the Muslim Brotherhood's hold on power from June 2012 to June 2013. For instance, they suggested that women should be totally banned from appearing in films, that is, they should not play roles as actresses. If it is necessary for women to appear in the public sphere, paradoxically, their invisibility is underlined. During the parliamentary elections of November 2011, such a view was endorsed by a radically conservative political party, which, to circumvent the law requiring a female nominee amongst the list of candidates, omitted the picture of its female candidate standing in one of the constituencies. The candidate's picture was replaced by a rose.

In response to such gender subordination, as 'the ideological construction of gender keeps the male dominant' (Spivak 2005: 28), literary theorist G. C. Spivak proposes the 'subaltern' woman's strategic use of culture, by means of which 'all feminist activity' would be engaged in a 'deconstruction of the opposition between the private and the public' (Spivak 1987: 103), whereby the two terms of the binary opposition are not merely reversed, but a 'deconstruction as reversal-displacement' (ibid.) takes place. She relates such a notion of displacement to the dichotomous position of margin and periphery: 'The only way I can hope to suggest how the center itself is marginal is by not remaining outside in the margin and pointing my accusing finger at the center. I might do it rather by implicating myself in that center' (ibid.: 107). Spivak, therefore, invites the subaltern to subvert her marginalization by taking over the centre.

As such, some of the protesters of Baheya Ya Masr can even be seen wearing the posters of such public figures, which suggests their identification with their precursors and emphasizes women's refusal to be interpellated as mere physical vulnerable entities easily accessible for violation. In the lower corner of these posters, the word el-sitt ('the woman' in colloquial Arabic) is written in a large font. This use of the term el-sitt operates on multiple levels. First, it highlights and serves as a reminder that women have been ancient rulers, political activists, singers and actors, and have fulfilled many other roles. Second, all these figures are placed on an equal footing, as citizens who have actively contributed to Egyptian public life. Third, *el-sitt* is also the title by which the late great Egyptian diva Umm Kulthum (1898–1975) is famous (she was known as 'El-Sitt Umm Kulthum' or simply 'El-Sitt'). In Egyptian society, and with reference to Umm Kulthum in particular, the title has always been understood as one of reverence, carrying the bourgeois connotation of 'a lady', a woman who boasts a respectable social position. One can venture to add that Umm Kulthum was invested with a socio-cultural aura of respectability, reflected by the social title assigned to her name despite the fact that she was a singer, a vocation frowned upon by the bourgeoisie at that time. However, her unusual talent, the careful cultivation of her image of respectability, her nationalist political role and her association with the late president Gamal Abdel Nasser meant that Umm Kulthum was celebrated as a national icon. Fourth, by appropriating *el-sitt*, both the Egyptian diva and the title of 'lady', Baheya Ya Masr reinscribes street protests and political activity as socially respectable roles for all women, thereby subverting the conventional connotations of the term and resisting conservative Islamist discourses. The fact that the demonstrators are in the streets and literally wrapping the posters around their bodies signifies their deliberate adoption of this particular image of woman's identity. In other words, after subverting the conventional identity of *el-sitt*, they deliberately choose to perform this newly resignified identity.

The resistance of Baheya Ya Masr is varied, creative and unrelenting, as revealed in the way it addressed a very significant and fundamental political move that took place on 22 November 2012, about four months after ex-president Mohammed Morsi had taken office. By means of a constitutional declaration, he gave himself additional executive privileges at the expense of democracy for the Egyptian people.[5] The day immediately following the declaration, there began continual demonstrations in Tahrir Square, as well as a series of protest marches in various parts of the country, in opposition to the declaration. In response, on 1 December 2012, a large number of Morsi's supporters rallied at Nahdat Misr Square in a show of strength. The Islamists' choice of place to assert their overwhelming presence is accounted for by the fact that the then-ruling Muslim Brotherhood's political programme was called Al-Nahda (The Awakening), thus echoing the name of the statue. This in turn provoked Baheya Ya Masr to call for a protest in the square on 19 December 2012 at the foot of the Nahdat Misr statue to object to the proposed constitution drafted by a constituent assembly dominated by Islamists.

Nahdat Misr Square witnessed a dialogue between two opposing parties, a dispute, as it were, and a cultural tussle between the theocratic regime and the demonstrators led by Baheya Ya Masr, who insisted on preserving their human rights and space. With reference to the significance of occupying space, Charles Tripp notes that public spaces become contesting sites, 'a shifting frontier' between the supporters of the authoritarian voice and those who resist them (Tripp 2013: 74). Despite their small number, in contrast to the overwhelming crowd of Islamists gathered about two weeks earlier, the women's occupation of this particular space is very telling. Moreover, it becomes a metaphorical struggle over the identity of the nation itself and, in turn, 'a site for the competing imaginings of different ideological and political interests' (Loomba 2005: 173).

The choice of Baheya Ya Masr to rally at the Nahdat Misr sculpture reinscribes the 'culturally authentic' Baheya as part of a protest movement for rights and a symbol of the protesters' empowerment. In the process, the pristine and passive Egyptian peasant woman is divested of her rural 'culturally authentic' attribute and is brought to bear upon an urban setting. She departs from the rural periphery to occupy the urban centre as she is resignified as an Egyptian activist citizen standing her ground and becomes the iconic figure of political activism.

It is also worthy of note to shed light on another substantial example of gender resignification, which unravelled during the protests against women's constitutional marginalization in early 2012. Some of the demonstrators are seen holding a poster of Shadia, a famous Egyptian singer and actress, who played the role of an empowered Upper Egyptian peasant woman called Fouada in a famous feature film

based on the novel *Shay' min al-khawf* (*A Taste of Fear*).[6] The film presents
a courageous peasant woman, who, despite her vulnerability and poverty, manifests a defiantly resistant stance against Atreess, a powerful
and tyrannical patriarchal figure, who imposes high taxes and determines the peasants' share of water to irrigate their patches of land. At
one point, Fouada is depicted as valiantly opening the water lock for
the peasants, who were suffering from water scarcity, as well as rejecting the ruthless Atreess's marriage proposal.

The novel was published in the 1960s at a time when the Egyptian
people suffered from much oppression and coercion. It had political
implications and was even deemed as a political manifesto in defiance
of Nasser's regime. It is written in the guise of a folktale of resistance,
thus highlighting the voice of the marginalized and downtrodden factions of society.

One of the posters by Baheya Ya Masr gives voice to Fouada, who
states two propositions: *Ana illi gayya aftah hawees al-horreyya* (I've come to
open the gateway to freedom) and *'ew'a tehammish door el-mar'a* (Beware
of marginalizing women's role). As such, Baheya Ya Masr brings
material from a story that is very well known to the Egyptian collective
consciousness into the present context. It allows the popular movement to adopt the stance of an empowered woman, hitherto doubly
marginalized as a woman and a peasant, in an attempt to mobilize
against women's marginalization in the constitution. Once again,
Fouada, who is a variant of Baheya, is viewed in a different light. She
is not a helpless subordinate peasant woman, but is represented standing in solidarity with the mobilizing women activists. She becomes
the source of the protesters' empowerment, as her valiant resistant
stance in the face of tyranny overlaps and is transposed to women's
current marginalization.

The innovativeness of Baheya Ya Masr has been its strategic use of
female figures (both fictional and historical) significant to Egyptian
nationalist discourse and Egyptian national culture. The movement
has appropriated these metaphors of the nation, thereby clearly locat-
ing itself within the nation, yet has resignified them beyond hegemonic nationalist discourse. Moreover, the movement has also imbued

these national icons with the legitimacy of the 25 January Revolution. In this way, it has legitimized Egyptian women's active citizenship role, subverted the conservative gender discourse that seeks to exclude Egyptian women from public life and reimagined the nation.

Doaa Eladl: Subversive Caricature

Another political activist and resistant figure is the Egyptian woman cartoonist, Doaa Eladl,[7] who publishes her cartoons in Al-Masry Al-Youm, the most widely circulated independent Egyptian daily newspaper. She started practising as a cartoonist before the 2011 Revolution and carved for herself a niche in a traditionally male-dominated profession. Not only do her cartoons evoke political resistance, but they question rigid and fossilized socio-cultural precepts.

In an unstable post-revolutionary Egypt, her cartoons react to the current political issues, many of which were directed against the emerging autocratic discourse in 2012 and 2013. During this time, some right-wing extremists began to endorse abuses of women's rights, claiming to be abiding by Islamic scriptures. As a response to such detrimental practices and beliefs, Eladl uses her cartoons to condemn the trafficking of women, the early marriage of girls, as well as the widespread custom of female genital mutilation.[8]

For instance, during a march on 6 February 2013 to mobilize against the sexual harassment of women during demonstrations, some women had brandished knives in their hands as a threatening act against their physical violation. The demonstrators' menacing measure was addressed at state security thugs, who hoped to discourage women from mobilizing and demonstrating in the streets and, eventually, banish them from the public scene altogether.

Parallel to this activist stance, Eladl borrowed a photograph of the late great Egyptian diva Umm Kulthum and inserted it into her cartoon, with knife in hand, and assigned to her a line from one of her love songs in which she sings *innama lil-sabr hudoud* (but my patience has a limit). Here, the words of the song no longer reflect the emotional outburst of a woman in love. Instead, the words are transposed to the public arena, in which the great singer becomes an active participant, resisting the attempt to limit her existence to the domestic space.

The correlation between the contemporary Egyptian woman and her female precursor sheds light on an obvious identification between prominent women who form and belong to the very core of the collective Egyptian culture, on the one hand, and those who live the socio-cultural challenges of the present, on the other. The cartoon achieves its subversive message by means of parody, highlighting the discrepancy between the diva's dressy attire worn during one of her public shows and the menacing tool held in her hand. The cartoonist depicts her threatening stance as a public warning from all demonstrating women to their would-be sexual harassers. The singer becomes their mouthpiece.

As a reaction to the constricting cultural representations that are usually available for women, Eladl makes use of pastiche and parody to address the daily challenges met by the Egyptian people. In one of her cartoons, she draws upon Naguib Mahfouz's famous female character Amina in his renowned novel Bein el-Qasrein (Palace Walk), published in 1956. In the Egyptian collective consciousness, Amina is the epitome of a woman's helplessness and subservience. She also symbolizes domesticity imposed on her by her rigid and oppressive husband. The cartoonist depicts the famous female actor who played the role of Amina on television as the futile cabinet of ministers appointed by Morsi, a cabinet that claimed to be 'the empowered cabinet' (hukumat al-salahiyyat), while proving to be totally inadequate.

In the cartoon by Eladl, the character of Amina's husband, or 'Si El-Sayed', is a metaphor for the autocratic President Morsi. El-Sayed is an Arabic word, which is a male name but also means 'the master', whilst Si is a form of address in Egyptian Arabic. In a confrontation with the president, the government/Amina appears to be totally submissive towards 'Si El-Sayed'/Morsi, who is reluctant to grant the cabinet of ministers power and authority to take decisions. He tells Amina: 'Are you asking for full prerogatives? . . . You must've been hit on the head, Amina!' To this, Eladl assigns to Amina (the new government) a sentence well known from the televised version of Mahfouz's novel. In the famous scene, Amina is required to account for a foot injury, which she incurs during her husband's absence. She finds herself helpless in the face of her autocratic husband's anger for disobeying him and temporarily leaving the house. She openly discloses to him the cause of her mishap as she subserviently replies: '*el-sawaress khabatetni ya Si El-Sayed*' ('The cavalrymen hit me, Si El-Sayed'). In the cartoon, Amina/the government reiterates the famous sentence of a passive humiliated woman, totally relinquishing her basic rights.

By representing the relationship between Amina and Si El-Sayed as a metaphor for the relationship between the government and the presidency, Eladl exaggerates recognizable gender norms in order to criticize the passiveness of the government (which is hyper-feminized) and the despotism of Morsi (who is hyper-masculinized). Moreover, the cartoonist generates what Judith Butler describes as 'strategies of subversive repetition'. Butler notes that 'there is a subversive laughter in the pastiche-effect of parodic practices in which the original, the authentic, and the real are themselves constituted as effects' (1999: 186). The repetition of the female actor's well-known statement has a subversively humorous effect, which results from the discrepancy between the two different contexts of the same dialogue. The whole instance illustrates Butler's notion of parody in relation to gender identity, whereby a person's gender is based on what s/he performs or utters. The fluidity of the whole concept of gender identity leads it to be constantly subject to subversion and resignification:

> The parodic repetition of gender exposes as well the illusion of gender identity as an intractable depth and inner substance. As the effects of a subtle and politically enforced performativity, gender is an 'act,' as it were, that is open to splitting, self-parody, self-criticism, and those hyperbolic exhibitions of 'the natural' that, in their very exaggeration, reveal its fundamentally phantasmatic status. (Butler 1999: 187)

The well-known scene, which represents the epitome of women's domestic oppression, is entirely transposed onto the political level.

The 'pastiche-effect' of combining the television series with the present political condition allows Eladl to subvert both the voice of authority as well as the dominant discourse which compromises women's socio-cultural representation. She pits the two interlocutors against each other (one of them is assigned the role of a helpless woman), thus totally subverting authority. Moreover, this pastiche equally dismantles the public–private dichotomy. In other words, by means of repetition, parodic imitation is achieved, which, in turn, dismantles gender identity (Butler 1999: 188). In addition, bringing a televised scene to bear upon the current political context reveals the use of popular culture as a strategy of resistance.

Political Women on Walls

Sitt el-Heita, or Women On Walls (WOW),[9] is another resistant manifestation which initially consisted of a graffiti campaign that was launched in early April 2013. It encompasses a group of thirty graffiti artists, both women and men,[10] who seek to highlight various issues related to women, even to shock people so as to provoke them to reflect upon gender-sensitive matters. The campaign initially consisted of two phases.[11] The first phase held a series of workshops for artists revolving around gender issues. The second phase included travelling to four major Egyptian cities to create street art: Mansoura (12–14 April), Alexandria (17–21 April), Cairo (20–28 April) and Luxor (1–5 May). Street art, in general, is considered to be an example of 'subculture', or 'a popular form' of art, and allows for subtle 'political participation' (Douglas 2005: 7). It is, above all, 'an act of transgression' (ibid.: 8). Women On Walls use graffiti with the aim of 'increasing women's visibility and positively affecting the collective consciousness of each community' (ElNabawi 2013), thereby reappropriating physical public space for women.

The meaning of the movement's name in Arabic, Sitt el-Heita, literally translates as 'the woman/lady of the wall', which contrasts with the traditional clichéd label sitt el-beit ('the lady of the house' or 'housewife'), hence underscoring women's appropriation and control

of their own space, particularly public space, as well as highlighting women's representation in such public space. One of the graffiti
women artists, for instance, draws women as strong and empowered
cats who wear halos over their heads. In Mansoura, one of the mural
designs portrays women sticking their tongues out as an act of defiance against society. Another graffiti entitled 'Super Fawzeya' depicts a
heavily burdened woman, wearing Superman's flowing cape together
with a badge of her name's initial on her chest. She is carrying one
child, holding another by the hand, while her head accommodates
a big pile of boxes and grocery shopping. In the lower foreground,
there is a globe, which underscores the universality of such a resilient,
multitasking super woman.

In Alexandria, a very significant graffiti[12] depicts once again an
actress who became principally known for playing the role of Amina,
this time in the 1964 feature film of Mahfouz's novel (see Figure
3.1). On the wall, and contrary to the character in the novel and film,
Amina is portrayed, in accordance with the project's objective, as
mastering the whole scene and occupying centre stage. She hosts a
group of prominent Egyptian women, the late singer Umm Kulthum,
the late Egyptian nuclear scientist Samira Moussa, the contemporary
political activist and head of the Egyptian Farmers' Union Shahenda
Maqlad, the revolutionary activist who challenged the military over
'virginity testing' Samira Ibrahim,[13] the ancient Egyptian Queen
Nefertiti and the ancient Greek-Alexandrian philosopher Hypatia,
among many others. The normally subservient character of Amina is
resignified as powerful through her association with these prominent
women from Egyptian public life. They are depicted in overwhelming sizes and are juxtaposed to and contrasted with the two sole male
figures in the graffiti, who appear to be totally belittled and defeated.
The conventionally hidden woman is very visibly captured, as she
becomes the mistress of the wall, while the hitherto dominantly visible male figures are, in this context, rendered almost suppressed and
invisible. In short, the status of the women and the men are reversed,
thereby subverting conservative discourses that attempt to exclude
women from the public sphere.

Figure 3.1 WOW movement artist, Lamis Suleiman from Alexandria, depicts
Amina looming large in this graffiti, which is a celebration of
empowered womanhood (© WOW).

However, in the present example, and unlike the cartoon by Doaa
Eladl mentioned above, Amina materializes as an empowered woman
who breaks her silence and strikes back at her master, telling him 'Bik-
fayak zift ya Si El-Sayed' ('Enough shit, Mr Sayed/my lord/my master')[14]
while she appears to lean on and empower herself with the company
of fellow women. The words that she utters are paradoxical as the
graffiti designer keeps the usual phrase Si El-Sayed that Amina utters
in the renowned film, yet it is preceded by an insulting interjection,
which also subverts her usual image of a subjugated woman. The discrepancy between the two halves of the statement parody and subvert
the famous statement of subservience Si El-Sayed, which harks back to
Butler's view vis-à-vis reiteration. The constant reiteration loses its significance and becomes a source of laughter. In this context, Amina

stands on the same par as the prominent female figures and is no longer merely a domesticated woman.

Moreover, in the graffiti, the public and the domestic spheres become one, thereby deconstructing the opposition between public and private. In this way, Amina gains a voice and is displaced from periphery to centre (Spivak 1987: 107). Simultaneously, the patriarchal voice is suppressed, which is equally reflected by the spatial dimension, as the two sole male figures in the graffiti are reduced to a dwarf-like size in contrast to the number and size of their female counterparts. Whereas Amina is conventionally and collectively viewed as a marginalized figure, she reclaims the spatial centre by means of a popular marginalized form of art. The socio-cultural domestic norm of *sitt el-beit* (the lady of the house), traditionally epitomized by the submissive docile Amina, is reinscribed into an empowering representation of the public *sitt el-heita* (the lady/woman of the wall).

Conclusion

The revolution of 2011 served as a catalyst to bring to the fore resistance to the marginalization of women. The political activist movement Baheya Ya Masr, the cartoonist, Doaa Eladl and the graffiti designers of Women On Walls are all politically resistant and activist manifestations who subvert the subjugating and discriminative discourse that advocates women's invisibility and relegation to the domestic realm. Instead, respectively, they march and demonstrate in the streets, secure a niche in a profession traditionally restricted to men and unravel women's present concerns on public walls. Popular culture constitutes a medium through which women activists/artists have been able to appropriate famous stereotyped female representations from the Egyptian cultural context and to resignify them in order to empower and legitimize women's contemporary resistance activities.

The women activists challenge the relegation to the domestic sphere by refusing the notion of a woman as merely *sitt el-beit* (the lady of the house). Instead, they appropriate the term *el-sitt* (the woman/

lady) to signify an active citizen and to validate women's presence in
the public sphere as by no means detracting from a woman's respectability. The process of resignification is further developed as the name
is transformed into *sitt el-heita* (the woman/lady of the wall), where
the shift from the private to the public, that is, from the home to
the wall, is an obvious transformation from an invisible to a visible
condition and where the private–public dichotomy, which debili-
tates women's potential, is altogether displaced and eliminated. As a
matter of fact, women's appropriation of, and presence in, the public space appears to be ubiquitous, as *el-sitt* seizes space previously
usurped by *el-sayed* (the man). This echoes Spivak's call to displace the
private–public dichotomy (Spivak 1987: 103) and, in so doing, as
de Lauretis proposes, the activists attain 'new spaces of discourse'
(1998: 719).

The three resistant paradigms go beyond the compromizing
dichotomy by abolishing the binary divide, as female representations
take over the central/public space. The resistant subaltern implicates
herself in the centre, as proposed by Spivak (1987: 107). El-sitt validates her presence, her role in and her right to the public sphere. In
fact, she deconstructs the conventional principle that 'the domestic is
always subsumed by the public' (Ortner 1974: 79).

In a similar attempt to resignify gender norms, authority is depicted
in a parodic light. In a dichotomous subordinating formula, the female
gender becomes the tool by which oppressive authority is subverted.
Butler's notions of gender performativity (1999: 173) (the role of the
subordinated character is assigned to the dominant voice) and repetitive signifying (ibid.: 185) (a famous sentence of total acquiescence
is attributed to the dominant voice) create the parodic effect (ibid.:
177), which causes the subversion of the dominant subordinating
discourse.

The activists remind us that women throughout Egyptian history
and culture have been part and parcel of the public realm. The resistant
paradigms, which are the subject of the present chapter, deconstruct
and transcend the confines of the problematic private–public dialectic
to offer women alternative parameters of signification and existence.

This is achieved through the appropriation of national cultural female figures and their resignification beyond their metaphorical role to become active citizens whose very existence in the public domain is fully substantiated, simply because of their strong national belonging.

Notes

1. The present chapter does not claim to delve into the nuances of what constitutes 'culture', a term and concept deemed very challenging to define. See Raymond Williams, 'Culture Is Ordinary' (2002) and Terry Eagleton, The Idea of Culture (2000). In the present context, 'culture' is used to refer to the arts in general.

2. For further information regarding Baheya Ya Masr, see www.facebook.com/BaheyaYaMasr/photos_stream.

3. Unlike urban people, the peasants, untainted by cosmopolitan life and closely connected to the land, are deemed an appropriate 'embodiment of the nation' (Baron 2005: 68–69).

4. There is also a well-known Egyptian folktale and myth entitled 'Yasseen wa Baheya' (Yasseen and Baheya), which portrays Yasseen, though an outcast, as a mythical hero. Baheya, the Egyptian peasant woman from Upper Egypt, is, above all, collectively perceived as a metonym for Egypt, as well as Yasseen's beloved, who supports him in his adventures to defy authority for the benefit of the poor.

5. Article II stated that any future declarations, laws or decisions decreed by the president would be final, cannot be challenged or cancelled, and will not be subject to court appeal. Article III decreed that the president has the authority to appoint the new attorney general (rather than selecting one from several candidates nominated by the judiciary). Article V indicated that no judicial institution would be allowed to dissolve the Shura Council (the upper house of parliament) or the Constituent Assembly. Both the Shura Council and the Constituent Assembly were, at this time, dominated by conservative and religious fundamentalist political currents.

6. The film was produced in 1969 and is based on a novel carrying the same title by Egyptian novelist Tharwat Abaza.

7. For further information regarding Doaa Eladl, see www.facebook.com/doaeladl/photos_stream.

8. It is significant to point out that such malpractices already existed during Mubarak's regime. However, in the wake of the 2011 Revolution, and in the face of an attempt to vigorously condemn such detrimental practices, right-wing extremists appeared to support them.

9. For further information regarding Women On Walls, refer to the website http://womenonwalls.org.

10. The 2011 Revolution has revealed a new generation of young people, including men, who take part in women's empowerment.
11. WOW has launched a new phase, WOW 2: Going Into the Streets Again, which started on 31 January 2014. For more information, refer to their website.
12. The graffiti was designed by one of the members of the Alexandria team, Lamis Suleiman.
13. Samira Ibrahim is the woman who chose to break her silence and recount the traumatic ordeal of undergoing a virginity test, together with other young women, at the hands of the Supreme Council of the Armed Forces (SCAF) in March 2011.
14. The graffiti designer's original translation of the title is 'Enough Shit'.

References

Baron, B. (2005) *Egypt as a Woman: Nationalism, Gender, and Politics*, University of California Press, Berkeley.

Butler, J. (1999) *Gender Trouble: Feminism and the Subversion of Identity*, Routledge, New York and London.

Chatterjee, P. (1993) *The Nation and Its Fragments: Colonial and Postcolonial Histories*, Princeton University Press, Princeton, NJ.

Douglas, G. (2005) 'The Art of Spatial Resistance: The Global Urban Network of Street Art', Unpublished MSc. thesis, London School of Economics.

Eagleton, T. (2000) *The Idea of Culture*, Blackwell Publishing, Malden, MA.

Edensor, T. (2002) *National Identity, Popular Culture and Everyday Life*, Berg, Oxford and New York.

El Hamamsy, W., and M. Soliman, eds (2013) *Popular Culture in the Middle East and North Africa: A Postcolonial Outlook*, Routledge, New York and London.

ElNabawi, M. (2013) 'Women on Walls Campaign Empowers Women Via Street Art', *Egypt Independent*, 9th April. Available at: www.egyptindependent.com (accessed 3 June 2014).

Elsadda, H. (2012) *Gender, Nation, and the Arabic Novel: Egypt, 1892–2008*, Syracuse University Press and Edinburgh University Press, Syracuse, NY, and Edinburgh.

Grundström, K. (2005) *Gender and Use of Public Space*, Housing Development and Management – HDM, Lund University, Sweden. Available at: www.n-aerus.net/web/sat/workshops/2005/papers/11.pdf (accessed on 21 July 2014).

de Lauretis, T. (1998) 'The Technology of Gender', in J. Rivkin and M. Ryan, eds, *Literary Theory: An Anthology*, Blackwell Publishers Inc., Malden, MA, pp. 713–21.

Loomba, A. (2005) *Colonialism/Postcolonialism*, Routledge, London and New York.

McClintock, A. (1993) 'Family Feuds: Gender, Nationalism and the Family', *Feminist Review*, 44 (Summer), pp. 61–80.

Ortner, S. B. (1974) 'Is Female to Male as Nature Is to Culture?', in M. Z. Rosaldo
    and L. Lamphere, eds, *Woman, Culture, and Society*, Stanford University Press,
    Stanford, pp. 67–87.

Spivak, G. C. (1987) *In Other Worlds: Essays in Cultural Politics*, Methuen, New York
    and London.

Spivak, G. C. (2005) 'Can the Subaltern Speak?', in B. Ashcroft, G. Griffiths and
    H. Tiffin, eds, *The Post-Colonial Studies Reader*, Routledge, London and New York,
    pp. 28–37.

Tripp, C. (2013) *The Power and the People: Paths of Resistance in the Middle East*, Cambridge
    University Press, Cambridge.

Williams, R. (2002) 'Culture Is Ordinary', in B. Highmore, ed., *The Everyday Life
    Reader*, Routledge, London and New York, pp. 91–100.

Yuval-Davis, N. (1997) *Gender and Nation*, Sage Publications, London.

PART II

The Body and Resistance

FOUR

She Resists

Body Politics between Radical and Subaltern

Maha El Said

If we don't find our body's language, it will have too few gestures to accompany our strategy.

(Luce Irigaray, *This Sex Which is Not One*, 1985)

Introduction

The remarkable contribution of women in the Egyptian Revolution of 25 January 2011 inspired a lot of research in an attempt to re-examine and redefine the state of women in Egypt. Although 25 January seemed to have a feminist face, with prominent women activists at the forefront, as the events progressed women were relegated to the sidelines and, even more seriously, were aggressively violated. Typical to most revolutions, the public participation of women was accepted, even encouraged, yet it was to remain within the confinement of what was perceived as 'culturally acceptable feminine conduct' (Kandiyoti 1996: 9). Accordingly, different ideas about nationalism and feminism were being contested, putting the national agenda and gender interests at the forefront of the debate. The earlier acceptance of women as

equal partners in the revolution, even the attribution of the first spark
of the revolution to Asmaa Mahfouz,[1] was revoked and their mere
presence on the streets was questioned. The two misogynistic systems
that came to power after the revolution, namely the Supreme Council
of the Armed Forces (SCAF) and the Muslim Brotherhood (MB), both
systems based on an androcentric value system that cherishes hierarchy and obedience and is blind to women, made sure to formulate
a post-revolution Egypt that cherishes masculinity and sustains the
patriarchy.[2] Therefore, it was no surprise that both systems favoured
the suppression of women's political participation and practised different forms of atrocities against women that led to a more forceful
resistance by women. As Shereen Hafez notes, 'Women's bodies, once
mobilised (and mobilising) to take to the streets to support the revolution became, after the end of Mubarak's regime, the source of conten-
tion and debate' (2014: 173).

In their struggle to hold on to their public space and political
place, the women of Egypt formed coalitions and political groups to
confront the various forms of violence that were being practised to
inhibit their participation. Independent from these different collective
efforts, two Egyptian women chose to resist differently: Aliaa Magda
Elmahdy, known as 'the nude blogger', and Sama El-Masry, a belly
dancer. In spite of the difference of their strategies, both attempted at
breaking the power dynamics of social control over women's bodies
and minds. Instead of the streets of Cairo, the internet with its public/
private bearings became their site of resistance, where each found her
'body language' through a different strategy of defying the 'fixed sites
of corporeal permeability and impermeability' (Butler 1990: 135).

Aliaa Magda Elmahdy is an Egyptian blogger in her twenties, who
posed nude and publicized her nude picture on the internet on 23
October 2011. Her picture went viral on the internet and became the
main topic for TV talk shows, blowing the incident out of proportion
and inviting different interpretations of this 'shocking' act. On the
other hand, Sama El-Masry, a previously unknown belly dancer who
became famous only after a scandal involving her marriage to a Salafist
parliamentarian, performed a series of satirical belly dancing skits on

YouTube where she criticized the MB outright with a special focus on their attempts at controlling women and women's bodies in the name of Islam.

Although both women used their bodies as 'a site for opposition to established power relations and ideological hegemonies' (Burkit 1999: 6), the reactions to each of these women's bodily being and bodily performance were extremely different. Elmahdy stirred up a frenzy of criticism and was rejected by both the conservative Islamists and the liberal revolutionaries. El-Masry, on the other hand, while offending Islamists, was applauded by the liberals and her seductive moves were perceived as resistance.

Engaging with post-colonial and feminist theories, this chapter aims to explore the reasons behind this incongruent reaction towards the two women. Despite the fact that both became 'embodied subjects' in the struggle for democracy and freedom at a time of redefining gender roles and the remaking of the nation, the effectiveness of their agency seems to have been poles apart.[3] Exploring their tactics of defying the cultural regulation of the female body and the modes of control of female sexuality that are very much influenced by Islamization in a patriarchal system shows Elmahdy rooted in radical feminism and alien from popular appeal, while El-Masry was entrenched in popular culture, making her the subaltern agent that challenges power from within grassroots culture. This comparison of agency reflects the need to ground resistance and agency in a cultural context that embraces public consent in order to secure its effectiveness.

Body as Resistance

Perhaps Foucault's 'docile bodies' and 'unequal gaze', in spite of many feminists' disapproval, should be a starting point to conceptualize both 'body' and resistance. According to Foucault, the body is 'the anchoring point for a manifestation of power' (1975: 55). Yet feminists such as Nancy Fraser and Nancy Hartsock, amongst others, argue that Foucault's work 'fails to provide the normative resources required to criticize structures of domination and to guide programs for social change' (Armstrong 2003). To my mind, understanding 'docility' and the power relations at play is an eye-opener that charts the way towards resistance and enables us to identify embodied resistance. This understanding is in itself an urge to regain control of the body and alter the scrutinizing gaze that enforces discipline, creating an informed refusal of fixed, stable or naturalized identities. Without understanding the 'power' behind the formation of the 'docile body' it would be impossible to transform it into what Ian Burkit calls the 'productive body': a body that is capable of defying power relations, hence, transforming them (1999: 3).

Regardless of positions on Foucault or others, I can safely say that the body has been used – and still is used – as the battleground for power. Who controls what? Whose gaze defines whom? Which body parts can be revealed? What body language is appropriate? Endless questions arise from this power conflict.

The case of the body, especially the female body, is an issue that is highly complex in an Islamic culture. As Jeremy Carrette rightly states, 'culture is born out of religious traditions' (1999: 33), and the traditions (whether Muslim or Christian) that govern women's sexuality and bodily acts in Egypt are based on a conservative patriarchal culture justified by religious dogma, creating social norms and practices that assume the power of tradition. As Charmaine Pereira and Jibrin Ibrahim note 'women's bodies constitute key sites mediating the experience of religion by the ways in which they configure gender and sexuality' (2010: 922). Talking of sexuality and power, Foucault states:

> I believe that Christianity found the means to establish a type of power that controlled individuals by their sexuality, conceived as something of which one had to be suspicious, as something which always introduced possibilities of temptation and fall in the individual. (1999: 126)

I believe that Islamic culture is not much different; women's bodies have become sacred taboos that are controlled and confined in the name of Islam and tradition. Even more so, as Fatima Mernissi argues, the Islamic view of women as active sexual beings led to more forceful control of women's bodies with claims that women's sexuality is a threat to society (1975).[4] Another exercise of control over women's bodies is the burden of 'honour' and 'shame'. As Deniz Kandiyoti notes, 'Control over female sexuality becomes strikingly evident in the large number of different individuals who see themselves as immediately responsible for ensuring women's appropriate sexual conduct' (1987: 325). Male honour is directly associated with the virtue and purity of females under the domain of his control in the patriarchal family/community structure. Accordingly, women's sexuality and bodies need to be regulated, since any misconduct would bring shame and emasculate male family members.

Similarly, nationalist projects have also manipulated women's bodies in the battle of 'modernism versus Islam'. As Tamara Mayer puts it, 'when nation, gender and sexuality intersect, the body becomes an important marker – even a boundary – for the nation' (2000: 13). The female body as the marker and producer of the nation was manifested in many Islamic countries, such as the cases of Malaysia, Turkey and Egypt in the turn of the twentieth century, where the veiling or unveiling of women became an issue of national identity. The concept of 'modern-yet-modest' (Najmabadi 1991), where women need to preserve the cultural conservatism for the sake of the nation, was advocated repeatedly to marginalize women and confine them to the private space (Aihwa Ong 2003; Deniz Kandiyoti 1991; Lila Abu-Lughod 1998).

In keeping with being 'modest', women's bodies and sexuality are regulated, rules of morality are set and have to be followed to save – using Ayşe Parla's words – 'the honour of the State'.[5] Abu-Lughod explains the parameters of modesty as 'respectful comportment' and 'sexual propriety', which entails the covering of the body and shyness, all of which are a 'fundamental component of a gendered social morality' (2005). Therefore, when women's bodies, which are normally controlled, break the norm and are used as a tool of resistance, they break the mould and become what Marwan Kraidy calls 'performative-contentious model[s] of the public sphere' (2012).

Whereas modesty entails the total covering of the body, nudity is also regulated. Standards of what should be covered and what could be revealed are mainly shaped by culture and cultural norms that define what is acceptable and what is not. The context in which body parts are revealed is another defining factor that enforces frames of categorization of permissible or impermissible nudity. There has always been what can be called 'permissible nudity', that is, nudity within two main frames: pornography and art. These two frames are no threat to any power relation or patriarchal control, to the contrary they enforce the hierarchical relation between male and female, as they objectify the female body whether as an object of sexual stimulation or an object of beauty. As long as the body is represented within the same oppressive system, it is no cause of dispute, in fact, it is a reinforcement of the socially marked divide of the mind and body, as women are reduced to the sexed flesh (body) that submits to the controlling male (mind). That is why when women in Africa expose their breasts in traditional dance, they are never observed as defying any system, yet they are always categorized as primitive: read, 'as no threat to the system'. Unlike, for example, Femen, the 'sextreemist' Ukrainian women's group, who demonstrate naked 'fighting patriarchy in its three manifestations – sexual exploitation of women, dictatorship and religion' (BBC News 2013). As they target politicians and religious institutions, they are a direct challenge to the system. They not only voice opposition, but they break the acceptable framing of nudity: art, pornography or advertisement. In fact, they disrupt the system, as their naked bodies cease to be 'docile' and occupy public space voicing opposition. As Carr-Gomm argues, 'we are fascinated by the naked protest because of its inherently paradoxical nature. Human beings are at their most vulnerable when naked but, when engaged in a protest, are also strangely powerful' (cited in Lunceford 2012: 58). This contradictory state endows them with power that results from the reframing of the nude body, making it a double jeopardy.

The Case of Aliaa Magda Elmahdy: 'The Nude Blogger'

On 23 October 2011, a young Egyptian woman posted a nude picture of herself under the label 'Nude Art'. Though she framed her picture within the permissible frame of art, it still caused a havoc of criticism and stirred up public rage, becoming the central topic of a public debate. However, the debate was not about art, but rather about national identity, the revolution and her political affiliation. Although the context of the Egyptian Revolution tinted all interpretations with a political cause, the fact that Elmahdy's picture broke with the norm of permissible nude art added an extra layer of resentment.

The classical nudes of the Old Masters were a representation of beauty, as they idealized the female figure, 'which stands as a symbol of objectified female beauty' where there 'is no hint of power politics, irregularity or individuality to disturb the gaze' (Carson 2006: 97). These nude women are more or less 'docile bodies' that have been objectified by the gaze of the artist, who represents them as submissive and acquiescing, passively accepting the gaze of the viewer.

Giorgione's *Sleeping Venus* (1510),[6] which has been identified as 'the first female reclining nude in European painting', has been described as:

> Not painted for sexual desire or erotic stimulation, she is depicted as a goddess sleeping and unaware you are peeping in on her. Giorgione has made us the spectators, voyeurs into her private world. He has taken this subject seriously and for the first time the female nude is painted poetry with a new visual language. (Brafford 2005)

However, Elmahdy's picture cannot be conceived as evoking the compliant docile body that is presented for the male gaze. In the realm of classical nude art, Elmahdy is more like Manet's *Olympia* (1863)[7] that is 'no nymph or mythological being; she is a modern Parisian woman . . . a common Parisian whore' (ibid.). It has been argued that the reason *Olympia* was denounced has nothing to do with seductive insinuations but it is about attitude. The woman in *Olympia* is not the passive innocent woman that is the object of the male gaze, instead she is assertive and, most importantly, unlike other nude paintings of the era, she is looking back, boldly returning the gaze. As Berger puts it 'the ideal was broken', as the admirable passive object becomes the defiant agent looking back (Berger 1972: 63).

Nudity in Egyptian art was not much different from that of the European tradition. Mahmoud Said (1897–1964), the prominent Egyptian painter, produced an excellent collection of nude paintings that depicted the same coyness and submissiveness. In spite of the boldness of his paintings and their eroticism, none of his models looks back. They all have their eyes closed assuming the classical poses with darker women replacing the fairer ones. For example, the similarity between The Dreamer (1933)[8] and Sleeping Venus makes the woman in The Dreamer another innocent goddess sleeping, 'unaware you are peeping in on her'.

Like Olympia, Elmahdy's picture is 'trouble', in the sense that she reverses the gaze and challenges the cultural norms and the patriarchal order of control. Both Olympia and Elmahdy mock the viewers by assuming the role of a prostitute (evident from the details of accessories used in the two pictures, such as the red flower and red shoes creating what Laura Mulvey calls the 'to-be-looked-at-ness' of the 'erotic object' (Mulvey 1999). Yet this 'erotic object' is not the seductive pornographic object that is available for sexual gratification and male sexual fantasy, nor is she the unwitting, compliant subject, she is a bold woman looking back implicating the viewer and challenging his control. Thus when Elmahdy, on her blog, questions what the reactions would have been if it were a man posting a picture of a nude woman and states the fact that it would have been acceptable, asserting male control over women's bodies, she implicates the viewer in what has been described as 'the indecent act'. The reversed gaze is reversed power. Therefore, when Elmahdy poses stark naked she not only reverses the gaze, but also reverses the power relation. She is no longer the passive object of male sexual pleasure; instead, she challenges this power relation as she defies the performativity norm that reiterates 'power . . . to produce the phenomena that it regulates and constrains' (Butler 1990: 27).

By publicizing her picture, Elmahdy was not only challenging male control, but she was also defying a conservative mainstream culture that has confined nude art to private galleries and restricted the use of nude models in fine arts schools in Egypt. Mahmoud Said's collection of nude paintings do not lack excellence, yet none of them is shown on any of the official Ministry of Culture websites, but can rather be found only on art auction sites.[9] Mustafa El Razzaz reports that 'with the rise of fundamentalism in the 1970's and 1980's, a series of successive events took place prohibiting the freedom of exhibiting such themes followed by banning of nude models from art schools and rigid censorship of art books containing nude images'. He also notes how Said's nudes, before being removed from display, were placed in a dark room to avoid 'embarrassment' (El Razzaz 2003).

Having shown how Aliaa Magda Elmahdy should be considered a 'critical resource in the struggle to rearticulate the very terms of symbolic legitimacy and intelligibility', a necessary tool for 'democratic contestation' (Butler 1990: 137), it makes us wonder about the rage she stirred up during the Egyptian Revolution, a time when everyone was calling for freedom and democracy. Whereas art historians have identified the reason behind the outrage over *Olympia* as being 'for the first time since the Renaissance a painting of the nude [that] represent[s] a real woman in probable surroundings' (Farwell 1981: 223), the case with Elmahdy is very different. Elmahdy is actually 'a real woman' in a revolutionary context; she was the first woman in the Egyptian context to use nudity for political action. She was not only demonstrating the probability and threat of a reversed gaze, she was a militant body resisting dominant power structures.

The signification of the nude body is culturally bound; in the Egyptian context, the nude body (whether that of a male or a female) is associated with 'humility, and violation of human dignity' (Al Sharif 2011, cited in Mourad 2014). This can only be exemplified by the uproar that surrounded the incident of the 'girl in the blue bra' and the incident of Hamada Saber Ali, a middle-aged man who was also brutally beaten and stripped naked by security forces on 1 February 2012 as he was protesting against Morsi, the Muslim Brotherhood president. The stripping of the woman and the stripping of the man were both seen as the most humiliating of the security forces' brutality.[10] Therefore, placing Elmahdy in the context of the revolution makes her gaze more confusing to the viewer, as it frames the nude body in an unusual frame that does not fit the viewer's beliefs and understanding. As Brett Lunceford notes 'nudity that is strategically employed as a mode of social and political action' is even less acceptable (2012: ix). Hence, the vulnerable naked body becomes more powerful as it disintegrates power relations further.

It is needless to say that any attempt at breaking the norm, let alone subverting a whole system of 'modesty' was disturbing. Besides all the insults, death and rape threats that Elmahdy received from conservative Islamists expressing an ethical point of view, there was a more important criticism from a political viewpoint: the revolutionaries, more so than the Islamists, perceived her as harming their cause and diverting the political debate into a side issue.

In an attempt to place her within the political and revolutionary context, she was rumoured to have been a member of the revolutionary 'April 6 Youth Movement'.[11] However, both the group and Elmahdy refuted this allegation, leaving us to wonder about the drive behind such a radical move at such a critical time. In an interview with CNN, she said, 'I was never into politics . . . I made it clear that I was not part of April 6th Movement after the rumours were spread by remnants of Mubarak's National Democratic Party who wanted to capitalize on the reaction to the photo' (Elmahdy 2011).

True, the liberals, in their fear of losing ground and in attempts at revoking Islamists and counter-revolutionary claims of immorality and atheism, emphatically contested the arguments of Elmahdy being part of the group. Nonetheless, this was the milder side of rejection: people who described themselves as Islamists, on the other hand, had threatened to kill her! The fact remains that her action destabilized the Islamist/secular dichotomy that was/is prevalent in post-revolution Egypt. Whether intentionally or not, Elmahdy confronted both liberals and Islamists with their double standards: she exposed the pseudo-feminist discourse that manipulates women, as it grants them freedom within the confinement of what is perceived to be an acceptable nationalist framework.

Elmahdy had a different political agenda that had nothing to do with nation or the military rule that was exercising violence against the

revolutionaries with an accentuated force against women. Her agenda
revolved around being a woman: 'I am not shy of being a woman in a
society where women are nothing but sex objects harassed on a daily
basis by men who know nothing about sex or the importance of a
woman' (Elmahdy 2011).

She made no attempt at packaging her message in the form of any
public political struggle, nor at joining forces with liberals and feminists who were fighting against the violation of women's bodies by
the military after the incident of the virginity tests. On 9 March 2011,
just a few months before the Elmahdy episode, seven female protesters were arrested by the military, which refused to acknowledge their
political participation and, typical to the military's misogynistic culture, conducted 'virginity tests' in an attempt to prove the protesters'
involvement in prostitution. This incident of bodily invasion brought
the whole issue of women's sexuality and public participation to the
heart of the nationalist struggle. Yet, this was not Elmahdy's struggle:
She was fighting a personal battle that was divorced from the public
fight against the exclusion of women and the regulation of their sexuality. When interviewed about her motives, she said, 'the photo is an
expression of my being and I see the human body as the best artistic representation of that. The powerful colours black and red inspire
me . . . I like being different' (Elmahdy 2011).

As can be seen from the above quote, Elmahdy did not have a public or political agenda that she was fighting for, but, rather, it was all
about her and about reclaiming her own body and her own independence at a time when all of Egypt was fighting for everyone's independence, including women's participation and sexual rights. Whereas
Egyptian women were organizing all-women marches in support of
Sitt el-Banat (the woman with the blue bra, who was stripped and tortured by the army in December 2011), Elmahdy was too focused on
herself. Advocating her freedom of expression and control over her
body, she never mentioned the body of Sitt el-Banat that was being
violated and controlled by SCAF.

Elmahdy, while claiming her identity as a woman in control, made
no effort to include all women; in fact, she disrupted an integral

national identity that is based on a conservative culture. No one can
deny that, as Nancy Fraser states, 'institutionalized cultural values can
be vehicles of subordination' (2007). No one can overlook the atrocities committed, which are still being committed, against women, such
as virginity tests, public rape and continuous organized sexual harassment. Nonetheless, borrowing Bruce Baum's words, 'it is a mistake to
see religious and cultural norms, practices, and identities as nothing
more than expressions of oppressive power . . . Cultural and religious
identities are also basic to how people articulate their ideas of the
good life' (2004). Egyptian and Arab women alike rejected Elmahdy
and described her as an imperialist, as she had violated the integral
self-definition of women that springs from their social and cultural
convictions about gender. The dozens of websites and Facebook pages
with slogans such as 'nudity does not represent me' or 'I do not need
saving' enforce the need to ground resistance and agency within a
cultural context.[12] Lila Abu-Lughod summarizes this problematic situation by questioning the authority to speak for Muslim women, making 'freedom' and 'choice' the key terms in the debates about Muslim
women's rights (2013).

I am not claiming that Egyptian women are submissive and conform to cultural and religious practices as they are played out in a
patriarchal society. Egyptian women are resisting marginalization and
insisting on redefining the nationalist agenda to include women in
the public and political space. They did not attempt to sacrifice their
rights in favour of the nation; on the contrary, they have been trying
to redefine the nation as one that is inclusive, broadening traditional
roles and the concept of cultural authenticity. However, Elmahdy was
not a part of this struggle.

Aliaa Magda Elmahdy, though bold and daring and definitely revolutionary in her own way, cannot be perceived as being part of an
inclusive national feminist revolutionary agenda that calls for the need
for social justice and freedom. As Margalit Avishai and Joseph Raz
note: 'One cannot enjoy the benefits of membership without participation in its public culture' (1990: 452). Her definition of freedom

is very much removed from what many Egyptian activists, including feminists, aspire to. Self-determination in a national context needs to be culturally appropriate, since 'culture determines the boundaries of the imaginable. Sharing in a culture, being part of it, determines the limits of the feasible' (ibid.: 449), and thus Elmahdy's agency lacked the cultural cogency that is necessary for any effective agency.

Elmahdy is very much rooted in a radical western feminism that perceives a universal female existence and erases different cultural values and norms. Deniz Kandiyoti pushes further Ien Ang's 'politics of partiality' in that a feminist political project 'must stop conceiving itself as a natural political destination for all women' (1995: 58) and asserts the need to further distinguish between women in the Middle East based on the differing political and national projects particular to each situation (Kandiyoti 1991). The futility of Elmahdy's agency is similar to the failure of Donna Sheehan's Baring Witness 'No War' pictures formed of nude bodies.[13] Sheehan was inspired by the nude protest of Nigerian women who had demonstrated naked against oil company leaders to put a curse on them. Janell Hobson observes that 'part of the failure of Baring Witness had to do with mistranslation' (2012: 151). Although most West African tradition interprets women's naked protest as a curse that brings shame onto the on viewer,[14] there is no such belief in the United States that would shame the Pentagon into pulling out of Iraq. Similarly, Elmahdy was not sensitive to the cultural meaning of nudity and, thus, the act seems to have been a 'mistranslation' in a reverse direction.

Elmahdy's protest, being extricated from its socio-cultural context, became counterproductive and defeated her purpose. Even when she did get politically vocal by protesting naked against the constitution in Sweden in December 2012, she was not perceived as part of the Egyptian women's resistance, but, as Nicola Pratt, explains: 'El-Mahdi's agency becomes legible to Western media as it is re-presented as resisting the "barbaric Muslim men"' (2013), far from what Egyptian feminists mobilize for.

The Case of Sama El-Masry

Dance as a form of resistance is not a new phenomenon; many oppressed peoples have used it over history. Susan Reed writes:

> In some colonized areas, dance practices posed a genuine threat of political resistance or rebellion, particularly in societies where dance was a site of male collective performance, in which a sense of unity and power was heightened, potentially spawning uprisings against colonial rulers or slave masters. (Reed 1998: 506)

The above described scene is not very different from what Syrian rebels did during the March 2011 uprising, where they performed a *dabkeh* dance, which entails forming a human chain that reflects a 'sense of unity and power'. Neither is it different from the public performance of *Zorba* that took place on the streets of Cairo as part of the Egyptian artists' protest against the MB agenda to Islamize Egyptian culture.[15] The communal, synchronized movements of the dancers become more like a war dance that intimidates and threatens as its collective nature inspires viewers with power and stirs them into action.

The recent Danseurs Citoyens of Tunisia is another example of dance being used as a weapon. Bahri Ben Yahmed, when banned from dancing on the streets by Salafists in March 2012 and told to 'go inside your theatres, the streets do not belong to you anymore!', formed the militant artistic and cultural association to perform on the streets of Tunisia (Pfannkuch 2013). Their first performance as a group was *Je danserai malgré tout*, featuring both men and women dancing a medley of break-dance, belly dancing and folkloric dance to traditional folkloric beats.[16] Though this seemed to take the Tunisian public by surprise, it was only the beginning of reclaiming the streets and all public space back. In an interview with Nawaat (an alternative media website),[17] Yahmed stated the objective of his project is 'to develop for Tunisians, a better understanding of the body and their bodies as subjects operating in space, their spaces' (Nawaat 2014). Thus the dancing citizens resist the hegemonic attempts, reclaiming not only space but also their bodies as uncontrollable by the system.

Dance as a symbol of national identity and culture has always been a threat to any controlling authority. Dance studies 'have explored the "objectification" of dance as national culture' and hence has to be regulated and controlled by the state or the colonizer (Reed 1998: 510). Judith Lynne Hanna shows how state-controlled dance has grown to restore a respectability to traditional dance and dancers and oppose orientalist views, such is the case in Egypt, Iran and Uzbekistan (2010: 220).[18]

African women have also used folkloric dance to subvert both colonial power and patriarchal sexual mores. As mentioned by Bahati Kuumba, in Nigeria there is 'a women's tradition of protest song and dance performance' called 'egwu', which Nigerian women used as a means of resistance against British colonialism as early as 1925 (2006: 117). In the same tradition, Jamaican choreographers subverted 'western dance forms with "body attitudes deemed antithetical to [western] definition"' (Chatterjea 1999 cited in Kuumba 2006).

Conversely, belly dancing has rarely been seen as a form of resistance, but is still deemed dangerous in a different way. The fact that belly dancing is a celebration of women's sexuality and is, to a great extent, erotic, coupled with the Orientalist stereotype of the voluptuous and seductive oriental dancer, framed belly dancers as temptresses who are dangerous to male morality. Egyptian media, no less, has also employed this same image by representing the belly dancer as, to use Reed's words, 'either "pure and pious" – in need of protection from dance – or "fallen and sinful", and therefore either victims or perpetuators of the evils of dance' (1998: 517). The association of dance to sexuality has led to 'the identification of the dancer as a woman of questionable moral status who erotically displayed her body, an unacceptable middle-class norm' (Hanna 2010: 213). The image of the belly dancer in Egyptian popular culture continues to be defamed and is looked down upon as being vulgar and low class.[19]

Another very important factor that cannot be downplayed is the Islamization of culture that prevails in Egypt. Karin van Nieuwkerk explores the impact of Islamization on art to show how the emergence of Islamic piety movements, or the 'new religiosity' that infiltrated middle and upper-middle class in the 1970s and 1980s, led to more confinement on artistic expression in an attempt to create what she terms as 'pious arts' (2013: 239). This shift mainly impacted female artists who were propagated as the 'repentant' artists. Dancers, and especially belly dancers, display their bodies and sensuality, a sin that brings shame and dishonour to women not only from a cultural perspective, but even more so from an Islamist perspective that perceives it as totally *haram* (forbidden). Dance studies have shown that 'prohibitions on and regulation of dance practices are often accurate indices of prevailing sexual moralities linked to the regulation of women's bodies' (Reed 1998: 517). Moral imperatives set by society and the control of religion, as Foucault has shown in 'Sexuality and Power', establishes a type of power that controls individuals by their sexuality (1999: 120). The rise of religious fundamentalisms and their deeply masculinized rhetoric using the discourse of the sacredness of the body, which is, as Susan Brownmiller puts it, a 'tradition of imposed limitation' (1984: 14), led to more confinement of belly dancing, banning it from TV and limiting it to touristic venues.[20]

In the shadows of the repressive Muslim Brotherhood (MB) regime, where the covering of the female body became an issue of both popular and political debate, Sama El-Masry, an unknown belly dancer, making use of the language she knows best, that of the body, invaded the political arena with a YouTube video that mocked the MB and their attempts at regulating morality. Like Aliaa Elmahdy, she kicked up a storm among both liberals and Islamists, but, unlike Elmahdy, El-Masry was embraced by the liberals and revolutionaries, many of whom hailed her as the new militant.

In El-Masry's first YouTube video called 'Thugs' (2012), she dances holding a kitchen knife and a chopper and states that she is not afraid of the Muslim Brotherhood, which she calls a group of thugs that are trying to control women in the name of Islam and political reform. In this skit, with her reference to the failure of the MB's political project, alluding to one of President Morsi's speeches in which he employs the price of mangoes as evidence for prosperity, she highlights the hollowness of the El-Nahda (Renaissance) political project, which focuses on women's sexuality rather than on socio-economic reform. Needless to say, she offended many Islamists, who filed over fifty complaints with the public prosecutor against her, as she had defied the whole Islamist current that was advocating for the veiling of women and their return to the private sphere.

What makes El-Masry's case interesting is her use of belly dancing, the most forbidden of all art forms (which many Egyptians, not only Islamists, see as immoral), as a form of protest. This paradox is further intensified by her parodic performance style which, unlike her other performances that conform to the stereotypical concept of belly dancing, of seductive moves and skimpy dresses, in these videos she dresses conservatively and replaces the seductive looks with funny faces and funny moves. She decodes and deconstructs the stereotypes of belly dancing, eliminating elements of sexuality and enforcing the comic and the satirical. These strategies 'strip the body of its readings' as an object of sexual desire, causing 'de-familiarization whose aim is not necessarily that of seeing the female body differently, but of exposing the habitual meanings/values attached to femininity as cultural constructions' (Doane 1981: 24–25). Therefore, when in one of her skits, 'Ahie' (Oh My) (2012), she dances with a niqab (face cover), she totally reconfigures belly dancing and employs a coercive structure that summons a creative form of resistance. It becomes an act of defiance, making her body a site of that resistance.

El-Masry's popularity rises not only from her continuous insult to and criticism of the MB, criticisms which most liberals uphold, but, most importantly, because she has aligned herself to the popular pulse that was apprehensive of the MB policies. Unlike the elite political analysts that were featured on TV shows, she spoke a language that was familiar to the masses by using slogans from Tahrir or quotes from news headlines, spinning sarcastic songs put to the tunes of familiar folkloric songs, adding complexity to the politics of the parody she employs. As Ryan Claycomb argues: 'The parodic image evokes a cultural image already available to an audience, but signifies through its

difference from the original its otherness from the dominant codes'
(2007: 106).

Therefore, when El-Masry makes fun of political figures such as
Abu Ismail, the prime minister, or even American president Obama,
making use of folkloric tunes, satire is intensified by the conversion
of dominant codes and cultural images. The folksong tunes and cultural symbols she draws upon form a common framework that reflects
a shared popular culture, calling attention to the MB's transgression
from this culture. In spite of the superficiality of the words and obscene
language and the insinuations she uses in these skits, the subversive
irony she uses makes the vulgar acceptable as it becomes like an inside
joke that forms a popular front and alienates the Muslim Brotherhood.

Sama El-Masry is, again, not representative of Egyptian feminists.
Like Aliaa Elmahdy, she has stated that she does not usually give concern to politics, yet she has been insistent on defying the MB, producing over seven skits that criticize their policies regardless of 'the woman
question'. She does not intend for her actions to be emancipatory by
breaking stereotypes or to defy mainstream culture. Nevertheless, her
dual subversion is a complex strategy that should not be overlooked,
though they have gone overlooked by many or dismissed as anything
but subversive. Transforming the sexy into the comic and the folkloric
into the political, she destabilizes all the culturally inscribed givens
about belly dancing and sexuality. Through the politics of her bodily performance, belly dancing ceases to be the erotic expression of
sexuality. Instead, it formulates alternative discourse within which the
divide between mind and body is reconstructed.

However, her popularity, which to my mind was due to the diso-
rientation of the familiar, transformed El-Masry from an unknown
belly dancer into a celebrity, to the extent that she has opened a private
satellite channel that exclusively features her skits. Yet, this new phase
was not as appealing as her YouTube videos; now that the MB are not
in power anymore, her mockery has shifted to revolutionary figures
such as Mohamed ElBaradei and Amr Hamzawy, who were prominent during the revolution. Her obvious support for the new system
reduced her performances to propaganda rather than resistance, as

any oppositional voices were targeted by her satire.[21] Meanwhile, she has started producing skits and songs that support the army, such as 'Handsome Army Spokesperson' (2014), where all funny faces and obscene language disappears to be substituted with red hearts and the flapping of eyelashes.

Conclusion

As Sylvia Burrow rightly states, 'Feminine socialization trains women to view the body as an object of appreciation rather than an instrument of action in the world' (2009: 129). Though both women studied above have used their bodies as instruments of action to break the illusion of the 'abiding gendered self' in the context of the Egyptian Revolution, neither of them has had substantial impact on the progression of the revolution towards democracy and freedom, yet their individual acts should not be ignored. As Alex Shotwell points out, 'in the context of long-term organizing . . . these kinds of onetime experience acquire resonance . . . taken together and narrated [they] become part of the process of placing oneself, as a social being, in relation to history' (2011: 145). These bodies are not 'docile' but rather confrontational and culturally subversive, taking risks that need a lot of courage. However, it is important to explore more deeply the reasons behind their success or failure in specific socio-political-historical contexts, as they become important lessons for us to learn and maybe develop in a different form.

In an informal interview with a few of the Tahrir youths, asking them their opinions of the two women, it was amazing how similar were their responses. All ten interviewed (four males and six females) agreed that Aliaa Magda Elmahdy 'overdid it' and that they could not understand her point. To them, she was a lost cause emulating the West. On the other hand, Sama El-Masry was praised as being 'funny' and 'courageous', as 'pushing the boundaries' and was described by one interviewee as being 'politically aware'.

Though the two women can be considered as examples of feminist agency with purposive strategies, the effectiveness of each is different.

As seen from the responses of the interviewees, Aliaa Elmahdy, in spite of her feminist cause and feminist affiliation to Femen, is alien to Egyptian culture. She has fallen into the trap of the Eurocentrism shown in Western feminism, disregarding the struggles of Egyptian feminists, who are aware of the need to keep their struggle in the public domain and to defend general and inclusive rights, including ownership of their bodies, rather than individualized ones; such is the case with Samira Ibrahim. Yet they are also aware of the need to keep in alliance with a general nationalist project to preserve their newly acquired and highlighted role in the public and political arena. As Ranjoo Seodu Herr puts it, national feminists are 'firmly ensconced in their own culture, not only in the banal sense that their identities are intricately tied to their culture, but also in the sense that their particular feminist agenda makes sense only within their own particular culture [which they] navigate within the parameters set by their culture' (2003: 151). This situation forces the question: What if Elmahdy had posed nude at a different point in Egypt's history? What if Elmahdy had linked her artistic self-expression to the public cause of women's bodily rights? Though I cannot answer for all feminists or liberals in Egypt, I speculate that she would have had much more support. Thus, the fact that Elmahdy is divorced from mainstream culture and national identity puts her out of the realm of Egyptian feminism.

On the other hand, Sama El-Masry, in spite of the complexity of her tactics, her awareness and her belief in 'the woman question' are questionable. El-Masry had used belly dancing as a form of resistance before her political YouTube videos were made. In March 2012, she had threatened to lead a street protest in her belly-dancing suit if her film *Ala Wahda Wa Nos* (*On the Belly-Dancing Beat*) was banned from cinemas. Ironically, the film enforces the stereotypical image of a belly dancer as a fallen woman who was abused and had no alternative but to become a dancer, until she is finally saved and gets a 'respectable' job. This paradoxical situation is in itself indicative that she has no feminist agenda in the traditional sense, albeit using the most feminist of resistance techniques: the female body. Although El-Masry cannot be ingrained in any feminist movement, and in spite of all the questions around her driving force, no one can dislodge her from the cultural repertoire she embodies. El-Masry is no sophisticated intellectual, nor is she a representative of middle-class women that dwell on feminist theories. She is the subaltern agency that springs from the texture of popular culture, making use of what Gramsci called 'spontaneous philosophy' to counter the hegemony of the elite, be they politicians or clergy. She says it simply and without much need for our theories.

Finally, and by way of conclusion, one can say that effective agency has to be in accordance with national and cultural identity. This is why Aliaa Magda Elmahdy, with her radical feminism is rejected by many, while Sama El-Masry is accepted by many. Whereas Elmahdy opposes the 'morality of the people', ironically, El-Masry the belly dancer defends 'the morality of the people' from the controlling attempts of the Muslim Brotherhood. While Elmahdy defies the cultural system, El-Masry makes use of the cultural system to articulate democratic contestation, making her the voice of the masses. She has managed to find space for resistance from within the cultural norms giving voice to the subaltern.

Notes

1. Asmaa Mahfouz is one of the founders of the 'April 6 Youth Movement' and has been known as the initiator of the 25 January Revolution through her video blog calling for people to take to the streets. This, to my mind, is an added factor to the female face of the revolution. Despite holding a prominent place during and right after the revolution, she was systematically pushed to the sidelines. As the situation developed and SCAF came into power she was accused of defaming the army and was detained to be released on bail after Mohamed ElBaradei's interference for her sake in August 2011 (BBC News 2011).
2. See Sutton 1995 and Enloe 2007.
3. 'Embodied subjects' are what Merleau-Ponty (1962) calls the 'the phenomenal body', where the subject's point of view on the world and intentionality of 'being-in-the-world' is the essence, since the body is the expressive space that gives significance to a person's actions.
4. See Fatima Mernissi's discussion of 'Fitna' (1975).
5. Ayşe Parla argues that the state-supported virginity tests enforced on Turkish girls is a surveillance mechanism to control female 'modesty' employed by the modern state (Parla 2001).

6. Giorgione's *Sleeping Venus* can be viewed here: www.backtoclassics.com/gallery/giorgione/sleepingvenus (accessed on 19 June 2013).

7. Manet's *Olympia* can be viewed here: www.google.com/culturalinstitute/asset-viewer/olympia/ywFEI4rxgCSO1Q?utm_source=google&utm_medium=kp&hl=en&projectId=art-project (accessed on 19 June 2013).

8. See www.pinterest.com/pin/452893306250589166/ (accessed 11 January 2015).

9. For example, see www.artvalue.fr/artist—said-mahmoud-1897-1964-egypt-142452.htm (accessed on 20 October 2013).

10. Incidents of stripping prisoners as a means of extra humiliation populate our modern history across cultures, such as the incidents with Iraqis in Abu Ghraib.

11. An Egyptian political group that came to prominence during the revolution.

12. See Gordts 2013; Schemm and Hadid 2013.

13. See www.baringwitness.org/photos.htm (accessed on 28 December 2014).

14. The myth of the curse is based on the belief that if the vagina that grants life is exposed, women are saying: 'We are hereby taking back the life we gave you', cited in International Museum of Women (IMOW), 'The Curse of Nakedness'; available at: www.imow.org/exhibitions/women-power-and-politics/biology/curse-of-nakedness (accessed on 11 January 2015).

15. In June 2013, Egyptian intellectuals, writers and artists started an open sit-in at the premises of the Ministry of Culture to demand the resignation of the MB appointed minister. Public performances, concerts and exhibitions were staged as an integral part of the sit-in.

16. Videos of this performance can be seen here: www.youtube.com/watch?v=4OfWQ2GaVHg (accessed on 29 June 2014).

17. See http://nawaat.org/portail/ (accessed on 29 June 2014).

18. The nationalization of the first folkloric dance company, Reda Troup, in 1961 is the Egyptian example.

19. In her book, *A Trade Like Any Other*, van Nieuwkerk makes the distinction between three contexts for performance that impact the status of dancers: 'the circuit of weddings and saint's day celebrations', being the least in status, followed by 'the nightclub circuit; and, finally, the performing arts circuit, the performances in concert halls and theatres, on radio and television' (van Nieuwkerk 1995: 13).

20. Though traditionally belly dancing used to be an integral part of Egyptian weddings and wedding marches, with the rise of Islamist ideology and sentiments many Egyptians substituted the use of belly dancers with other forms of entertainment. See van Nieuwkerk 2012.

21. The satellite station was closed down after she produced a video making fun of Murtada Mansour, who had announced his intention to run for president and who accused El-Masry of spreading obscenity on an unlicensed satellite channel.

References

Abu-Lughod, L. (1998) 'Feminist Longings and Postcolonial Conditions', introduction in L. Abu-Lughod, ed., *Remaking Women*, Princeton University Press, Princeton.

Abu-Lughod, L. (2005) 'Modesty Discourses: Overview', *Encyclopedia of Women and Islamic Cultures*, Brill Online. Available at: http://referenceworks.brillonline. com/entries/encyclopedia-of-women-and-islamic-cultures/modesty-discourses-overview-EWICCOM_0118a (accessed on 2 September 2013).

Abu-Lughod, L. (2013) 'Topless Protests Raise the Question: Who Can Speak for Muslim Women?', *The National*, 30 November. Available at: www.thenational. ae/thenationalconversation/comment/topless-protests-raise-the-question-who-can-speak-for-muslim-women#full#ixzz35pvcKHwM (accessed on 5 August 2014).

Ang, I. (1995) 'I'm a Feminist But . . . "Other" Women and Postcolonial Feminism', in B. Cain and R. Pringle, eds, *Transitions: New Australian Feminisms*, St. Martin's, New York, pp. 57–73.

Armstrong, A. (2003) 'Michel Foucault: Feminism', *Internet Encyclopedia of Philosophy*. Available at: www.iep.utm.edu/foucfem/ (accessed 13 June 2013).

Avishai, M., and J. Raz (1990) 'National Self-Determination', *Journal of Philosophy*, 87 (9), pp. 439–61.

Baum, B. (2004) 'Feminist Politics of Recognition', *Signs*, Summer, 29 (4), pp. 1073–102.

BBC News (2011) 'Egypt Blogger Mahfuz Quizzed for "Defaming" Military', 14 August. Available at: www.bbc.co.uk/news/world-middle-east-14524094 (accessed on 11 January 2015).

BBC News (2013) 'Femen Activists Jailed in Tunisia for Topless Protest', 12 June. Available at: www.bbc.com/news/world-africa-22881163 (accessed on 17 June 2013).

Berger, J. (1972) *Ways of Seeing*, Penguin Books, London.

Brafford, R. (2005) 'The Nude Reclining', EighthSquare.com. Available at: www. eighthsquare.com/recliningnude.htm (accessed 24 June 2013).

Brownmiller, S. (1984) *Femininity*, Ballantine Books, New York.

Burkit, I. (1999) *Bodies of Thought*, Sage, London.

Burrow, S. (2009) 'Bodily Limits to Autonomy', in S. Campbell, L. Meynell and S. Sherwin, eds, *Embodiment and Agency*, Pennsylvania State University Press, Pennsylvania, pp. 126–44.

Butler, J. (1990) *Gender Trouble: Feminism and the Subversion of Identity*, Routledge, London and New York.

Carrette, J. R., ed. (1999) *Religion and Culture: Michel Foucault*, Routledge, New York.

Carson, F. (2006) 'Feminism and the Body', in S. Gamble, ed., *The Routledge Companion To Feminism and Postfeminism* [e-book], Routledge, London and New York, pp. 94–102. Available at: http://sociology.sunimc.net/htmledit/

uploadfile/system/20100827/20100827023122987.pdf (accessed on 24 June 2013).

Claycomb, R. (2007) 'Staging Psychic Excess: Parodic Narrative and Transgressive Performance', *Journal of Narrative Theory*, 38 (1) (Winter), pp. 104–27.

Doane, M. A. (1981) 'Woman's Stake: Filming the Female', *The New Talkies*, 17 (Summer), pp. 22–36.

Elmhdy, A. (2011) 'Egyptian Blogger Aliaa Elmahdy: Why I Posed Naked', CNN Cairo (interviewed by Mohamed Fadel Fahmy), 20 November. Available at: http://edition.cnn.com/2011/11/19/world/meast/nude-blogger-aliaa-magda-elmahdy/ (accessed on 11 January 2015).

Enloe, C. (2007) *Globalization and Militarism: Feminists Make the Link*, Rowman & Littlefield Publishers, Maryland.

Farwell, B. (1981) *Manet and the Nude*, Garland Inc., New York.

Foucault, M. (1975) *Discipline and Punish: The Birth of the Prison*, Vintage Books, New York.

Foucault, M. (1999) 'Sexuality and Power', in J. R. Carrette, ed., *Religion and Culture: Michel Foucault*, Routledge, New York, pp. 115–30.

Fraser, N. (2007) 'Feminist Politics in the Age of Recognition: A Two-Dimensional Approach to Gender Justice', *Studies in Social Justice*, 1 (1) (Winter), pp. 23–35.

Gordts, E. (2013) 'Muslim Women Against Femen', *Huffington Post*, 4 June.

Hafez, S. (2014) 'The Revolution Shall Not Pass through Women's Bodies: Egypt, Uprising and Gender Politics', *The Journal of North African Studies*, 19 (2), pp. 172–85.

Hanna, J. L. (2010) 'Dance and Sexuality: Many Moves', *Journal of Sex Research*, 47 (2–3), pp. 212–41.

Hobson, J. (2012) *Body As Evidence: Mediating Race, Globalizing Gender*, SUNY Press, Albany, NY.

Irigaray, L. (1985) *This Sex Which is Not One*, trans. Catherine Porter, Cornell University Press, New York.

Kandiyoti, D. (1987) 'Emancipated but Unliberated? Reflections on the Turkish Case', *Feminist Studies*, 13 (2), pp. 317–38.

Kandiyoti, D. (1991) 'Women, Islam and the State', *Middle East Report*, 21 (November/December), pp. 9–14.

Kandiyoti, D. (1996) 'Contemporary Feminist Scholarship and Middle East Studies' in D. Kandiyoti, ed., *Gendering the Middle East*, I. B. Tauris, London, pp. 1–27.

Kraidy, M. M. (2012) 'The Revolutionary Body Politic: Preliminary Thoughts on a Neglected Medium in the Arab Uprisings', *Middle East Journal of Culture and Communication*, 5, pp. 66–74.

Kuumba, B. (2006) 'African Women, Resistance Cultures and Cultural Resistances', *Agenda: Empowering Women for Gender Equity*, 68, pp. 112–21.

Lunceford, B. (2012) *Naked Politics: Nudity, Political Action, and the Rhetoric of the Body*, Lexington Books, Plymouth.

El-Masry, S. (2012) 'Ahie' [video]. Available at: www.youtube.com/watch?v=
iRttQXTNo3Q (accessed 13 August 2014).

El-Masry, S. (2012) 'Thugs' [video]. Available at: www.youtube.com/watch?v=
jo3tdMGkU6U (accessed 13 August 2014).

El-Masry, S. (2014) 'Handsome Army Spokesperson' ('Ya mouthadeth ya helwa')
[video]. Available at: https://www.youtube.com/watch?v=mLZPFdzzsFA
(accessed 30 June 2014).

Mayer, T. (2000) 'Gender Ironies of Nationalism: Setting the Stage', in T. Mayer,
ed., *Gender Ironies of Nationalism: Sexing the Nation*, Routledge, London, pp. 1–25.

Merleau-Ponty, M. (1962) *Phenomenology of Perception*, trans. Colin Smith, Routledge
and Kegan Paul, London.

Mernissi, F. (1975) *Beyond the Veil: Male-Female Dynamics in Modern Muslim Society*, John
Wiley & Sons, New York.

Mourad, S. (2014) 'The Naked Body of Alia: Gender, Citizenship, and the Egyptian
Body Politic', *Journal of Communication Inquiry*, 38 (1), pp. 62–78.

Mulvey, L. (1999) 'Visual Pleasure and Narrative Cinema', in L. Braudy and M. Cohen,
eds, *Film Theory and Criticism: Introductory Readings*, Oxford University Press, New York,
pp. 833–44.

Najmabadi, A. (1991) 'Hazards of Modernity and Morality: Women, State and
Ideology in Contemporary Iran', in D. Kandiyoti, ed., *Women, Islam and the State*,
Temple University Press, Philadelphia, PA, pp. 48–76.

Nawaat (2014) 'Danseurs Citoyens – Entretien avec Bahri Ben Yahmed: La résistance,
par la danse, comme une lutte contre toute forme d'obscurantisme', 31 March.
Available at: http://nawaat.org/portail/2014/03/31/danseurs-citoyens-
entretien-avec-bahri-ben-yahmed-la-resistance-par-la-danse-comme-une-lutte-
contre-toute-forme-dobscurantisme/ (accessed on 8 August 2014). (French).

van Nieuwkerk, K. (1995) *A Trade Like Any Other: Female Singers and Dancers in Egypt*,
University of Texas Press, Austin.

van Nieuwkerk, K. (2012) 'Popularizing Islam or Islamizing Popular Music: New
Developments in Egypt's Wedding Scene', *Contemporary Islam: Dynamics of Muslim
Life*, 6 (3), pp. 235–54.

van Nieuwkerk, K. (2013) *Performing Piety: Singers and Actors in Egypt's Islamic Revival*,
University of Texas Press, Austin.

Ong, A. (2003) 'State versus Islam: Malaya Families, Women's Bodies and the
Body Politic in Malaysia', in R. Lewis and S. Mills, eds, *Feminist Postcolonial Theory:
A Reader*, Edinburgh University Press, Edinburgh, pp. 381–412.

Parla, A. (2001) 'The "Honour" of the State: Virginity Examination in Turkey',
Feminist Studies, 27 (1), pp. 65–88.

Pereira, C., and J. Ibrahim (2010) 'On the Bodies of Women: The Common
Ground Between Islam and Christianity in Nigeria', *Third World Quarterly*, 31 (6),
pp. 921–37.

Pfannkuch, K. (2013) 'Dancing as Resistance', *Your Middle East*, 4 March. Available
at: www.yourmiddleeast.com/columns/article/dancing-as-resistance-video_
13178 (accessed on 28 June 2014).

Pratt, N. (2013) 'Egyptian Women: Between Revolution, Counter-Revolution, Orientalism, and "Authenticity"', *Jadaliyya*, 6 May. Available at: www.jadaliyya. com/pages/index/11559/egyptian-women_between-revolution-counter-revoluti (accessed on 28 December 2014).

El Razzaz, M. (2003) *Fundamentalism and Art Oppression*, Bibliotheca Alexandrina, Alexandria.

Reed, S. A. (1998) 'The Politics and Poetics of Dance', *Annual Review of Anthropology*, 27, pp. 503–32.

Schemm, P., and D. Hadid (2013) 'Muslim Women vs Femen: Topless Protests Inspired by Amina Tyler Seen as Counterproductive by Mideast Feminists', *The World Post*, 4 October.

Seodu Herr, R. (2003) 'The Possibility of Nationalist Feminism', *Hypatia*, 18 (3) (Autumn), pp. 135–60.

Shotwell, A. (2011) *Knowing Otherwise: Race, Gender, and Implicit Understanding*, Pennsylvania State University Press, Pennsylvania.

Sutton, C.R., ed. (1995) *Feminism, Nationalism and Militarism*, American Anthropological Association, Arlington.

FIVE

Framing the Female Body

Beyond Morality and Pathology?

Abeer Al-Najjar and Anoud Abusalim

Introduction

In the 'Arab Spring', the female body enjoyed considerable attention.
At the beginning of the Egyptian Revolution in 2011, revolutionaries
were concerned with supporting the presence of women in Tahrir
Square and hence took measures to guarantee that women did not
experience sexual harassment. On the other hand, officials in Egypt
and Yemen attempted to shame women for their participation in protests, conducting 'virginity tests' on women protesters in the former
and, in the latter, suggesting that their involvement in protests is forbidden in Islam.

A novel phase of concern with the female body in the Arab Spring
was brought to public attention by the posting of nude self-photo-
graphs by an Egyptian woman called Aliaa Elmahdy and a Tunisian
woman called Amina Sboui (later, Tyler). For Aliaa and Amina, as for
many other activists, the collapse of some political leaders in some
Arab countries, including their own, nurtured hopes for an opportunity to change the status quo concerning women's rights and position
in their respective societies. The apparent rupture in the political order

was a source of inspiration for the young women, who wanted to seize the opportunity and capitalize on it to challenge long-standing cultural and social norms guiding women's lives, stories and experiences, especially in relation to their own bodies.

Nudity has frequently been used in different parts of the world to promote social or political concerns, or as a method for protesting and attracting public attention. Protestors around the world have participated in fully or half naked public protests to raise awareness, to express anger and make statements for animal rights, to protest against bull fighting, to protect the environment, to protest against the vulnerability of cyclists on the streets and for community control over social media sites. Around 250 students at the Sao Paulo University in Brazil strolled through their campus naked in a protest against the university's decision to dismiss a student for wearing a short dress (Pietras 2014). In 2005, and as a protest against the US war on Iraq, Hala Al-Faisal, a Syrian visual artist, protested naked in New York with anti-war statements inscribed on her body (Kaysen 2005). She was one of the first Arab females to dare to unclothe publicly, albeit doing so in the United States.

Aliaa and Amina, through publishing pictures of their naked bodies, attempted to stretch the notion of 'freedom', one of the three slogans of the Egyptian Revolution, to include the freedom of women over their own bodies. However, in both cases, the photos triggered heated responses across the Arab world, suggesting that the Arab Spring had failed to generate a revolution in gender and sexual norms.

Against this background, this chapter aims to investigate the degree to which mainstream Arab media developed alternative frames for understanding women's bodies in response to the self-publication of Aliaa's and Amina's respective nude pictures on social media. This, in turn, can shed light on the degree to which the uprisings and political regime changes of 2011 created opportunities to challenge existing gender norms. Towards that end, the first section of the chapter focuses on the different ways in which specific female bodies have been understood in the Arab context, examining the period before 2011. The second section examines the framing of the female body

in reporting of the Arab Spring. Against this backdrop, the third section analyses the ways in which Aliaa's and Amina's actions were
framed and interpreted by the mainstream media. We conclude by
arguing that the mainstream Arab media as well as liberal, leftist and
women activists and commentators were, for the large part, only able
to understand Aliaa's and Amina's nude protests within a moral or
pathological frame, and not within a revolutionary context.

Between Conformity and Rebellion: Understandings of the Female Body before 2011

Nilufer Gole argues that in Muslim contexts of modernity, women's
corporal visibility and citizenship rights constitute the political stakes
around which the public sphere is defined (Gole 1997: 61). Therefore,
women's presence in public is always endowed with a wider socio-
political meaning beyond what she may or may not have intended. In
turn, the understandings of women's agency is often erased and subsumed under the interests of the wider society or of particular political movements. Here, we discuss two different cases, the 'repentant
artists' and what is referred to in the literature as the female 'suicide
bombers', both of which groups attracted widespread discussion in
local and international media.

The 'Repentant Artists', Egypt

Repentant artists became part of the public conversation in the Arab
world during the nineties. The female artists performed their act of
repentance in public, by putting on the veil and refusing to receive
money from their previous films. In this way, they became figures
celebrated in the Islamic media, which viewed the entertainment
industry and its products as a source of moral decadence. However,
opponents of the Islamists viewed these women as 'dupes', who
had been paid by Islamist groups to take the veil. For both supporters
and opponents of the repentant artists, the body and its covering signalled conformity with what was an emerging public sphere that was

marked by Islamization. A consideration of the women's own motivations for veiling, such as a desire to cultivate norms of female modesty
in order to be good pious Muslims (for example, Mahmoud 2005),
was not discussed by the media at this time.

Female 'Suicide Bombers', Palestine

Much of the attention on Palestinian female 'suicide bombers' has
derived from their challenging (whether intentioned or not) of the
binary of 'woman as victim'/'man as defender' (Naaman 2007).
Whilst Palestinians have regarded these women, like their male counterparts, as fighting colonialism, the Western media has sought out
their personal stories in order to 'understand' their motives. Wafa
Idris, the first female suicide bomber in Palestine, used to volunteer in
an ambulance rescuing the lives of compatriots injured in clashes with
the Israeli army, thereby conforming to gendered expectations about
women's contributions to the national cause. This young woman,
who was portrayed as an 'angel of mercy', was the first woman to
commit a suicide bombing or 'martyrdom act', as it is called by Palestinians. Unlike male suicide bombers, whose actions were interpreted in terms of national and/or religious motivations, Wafa's act
of martyrdom was interpreted as a response to her failure to comply
with patriarchal expectations of motherhood. Stories circulated about
Wafa's infertility and her husband's second marriage. Her assumed
alienation from a conservative society where marriage and children
are the norm, thus, made her supposedly more susceptible to persua-
sion by recruiters (Naaman 2007). In other words, like the case of the
repentant artists, the acts of Palestinian female suicide bombers could
not be understood by Western media in terms of their own agency.
Rather, their actions were reduced to a result of manipulation by political groups or an 'emotional' response to personal circumstances.

The Female Body in the Arab Spring

In the survey of the various cases of the understandings of the female
body in the above section, women's acts were either interpreted as

instances of (male) manipulation for political ends or as emotional (that is, not rational) responses. During the Arab Spring, there has been greater contestation over the meanings of the female body, particularly in relation to women's participation in public protests.

Authorities have attempted to discredit women's participation in public protests and dissent, using sexualized terms, claiming that women protesters are 'loose', thus suggesting that they are not motivated by political goals. This moral frame used by the authorities was widespread in the mainstream media. In Egypt, despite the initial optimism of women in the Eighteen Days of the 2011 Revolution, during which they had not been subjected to the harassment that later became the norm in the Egyptian streets, women protesters became the prey of the government under the Supreme Council of the Armed Forces (SCAF). Indeed, the demands of the Egyptian Revolution – bread, freedom, dignity and social justice – were not achieved by Egyptian women, who would be more frequently reminded of their status as women and treated as such rather than as citizens asking for their political rights (Baydoun 2012).

Samira Ibrahim, a 24-year-old, was among several women who were participating in a sit-in in Tahrir Square on 9 March 2011. Samira and the other women in that sit-in were subjected to one of the most horrific episodes of the Egyptian Revolution, that of the so-called 'virginity tests'. According to one writer:

> After the military police evacuated the square, violently dispersing protesters, Samira, along with a number of other women who had been at the demonstration, were beaten, given electric shocks, strip-searched and said they were forced into receiving a 'virginity test', while being humiliated, video-taped and exposed by the military's soldiers and officers. (Mohsen 2012)

Rather than sympathizing with Ibrahim, many in the media questioned her (the victim's) motives for being in Tahrir Square. Samira succeeded in taking her case to the court and a court order was issued to stop this practice, even though the army doctor who performed this forced test upon her was set free later on. It seems that her public and brave decision to face the military alarmed the highly patriarchal society that always wanted to trust that the patriarch knows the best for the people.

Later in December 2011, similar reactions were seen in the media in response to another horrific act. As reported by Mohsen (2012), striking photos and video footage circulated online of a girl being severely beaten and stripped of her clothes by soldiers. The woman, whose face remained covered in the images online, became known to international media as the 'Blue Bra Girl' and, for Egyptians, as *Sitt el-Banat*, the 'Best of All Girls' (Sulieman 2011). Again, the people of Egypt seemed to refuse to believe that the army was capable of inflicting torture on its people and, for them, on its 'weakest link': a woman. Many commentators in the Egyptian media posed the following question as the first response to the attack: 'What was the woman doing there in front of the cabinet offices?' It appeared later that the young woman, who declined to reveal her real identity or her face in fear of the social stigma associated with uncovering her body, is a pharmacist. In other words, the act of unclothing, even when forced upon a woman, is considered shameful and subject to moral judgment and interpretation.

Not only were the motivations of Egyptian women activists questioned. In Yemen, in April 2011, a month after Samira Ibrahim and the others were subjected to virginity tests, President Ali Abdullah Saleh suggested that anti-government protesters in the capital Sanaa were in violation of Islamic law because women were not allowed to mix with men. He engaged in smear campaigns on national TV, implying that women in pro-change demonstrations were 'loose' (Al-Ali 2012). Similar to SCAF, Saleh framed the motivations for women's activism in terms of their sexuality or lack of sexual propriety, thereby discrediting not only their involvement in mass protests but the demands of the protests in general. Yet, there were also alternative, positive framings of women's activism, such as Khadija Al-Salami's film, *The Scream*, which documents the vast sit-in camp that sprang up outside the gates of Sanaa University and the daily lives of the women who demonstrated alongside men until Saleh finally quit under a power transfer deal signed in November 2011 (*The Daily Star* 2013).

Around the time of Samira Ibrahim's case in Egypt and Saleh's accusations in Yemen, Eman Al-Obeidi faced rape by a group of military men in Libya in March 2011. Like Ibrahim, Al-Obeidi decided to go public about her rape. Also similar to Ibrahim, Al-Obeidi's defiance was seen as an act of treason and she was not treated as a victim. Instead, she was labelled as 'mentally unstable' and there were attempts to silence her. As Nadje Al-Ali (2012) argues, the video of women trying to silence Eman as she tried to tell foreign journalists about her ordeal shows that sisterhood is not universal, nor even local. Equally important, the video shows the immense roots of the patriarchal structure in the Arab world, where attempts to defy power and seek protection for the body are not seen as human attempts for justice and freedom, but are regarded as acts of treason, because the attackers, for both Ibrahim and Al-Obeidi, were from the army, an integral part of the patriarchal system.

The story of Zainab Alhusni provides an example of a different type of framing of women's participation in the Arab Spring. Alhusni became a symbol of the Syrian Revolution since she was the first woman to die in Syrian custody after the uprising began in mid-March 2011. Her family said that, according to Amnesty International, Zainab had been decapitated, her arms cut off and skin removed (Huffington Post 2011). The striking difference between the story of Alhusni and the other women discussed above is that Alhusni was the only woman who was treated as a victim, without questioning her actions, after she was killed by the Syrian regime. This illustrates how women's agency is regarded differently depending upon the context, as it intersects with other political dimensions.

The Naked Female Body: The Cases of Aliaa Elmahdy and Amina Sboui

On 23 October 2011, Aliaa Elmahdy posted a nude picture of herself on her blog 'The Diaries of a Rebel'. This picture generated controversy in Egypt and across the Arab world, to say the least. Naturally, Elmahdy's photos are not the first naked photos to be seen in the Arab world; however, her decision to unveil her own images publicly is what generated such a storm. Elmahdy received criticism from many political and social groups in Egypt and even, reportedly, received death and rape threats. Simultaneously, Elmahdy's photo opened the door in the Arab world to publicly discuss the female body in relation to the Arab Spring.

Two years after Aliaa's picture was published, Amina Sboui, a Femen activist in Tunisia posted a photo of her naked upper body on Facebook bearing the slogan, 'My body belongs to me, and is not the source of the honour of anyone' (Ajmi, 2013). In an interview with a commercial TV channel in Tunisia, Amina astutely pointed out that if she had worn a shirt with that slogan, it would not have had any impact (Ajmi, 2013). Amina observed that it was the use of her body that provoked the controversy about her action and not what she wrote on her body. She also told Agence France-Presse that 'everyone has the right to express themselves in their own way, and I chose my way of doing so in the style of Femen' (The Daily Star 2013).

Framing the Female Body

This section sheds light on the public and media responses to the rebellious individual agency of the female body by Amina Sboui, known later as Amina Tyler, and Aliaa Elmahdy (known for using her mother's name Magda as her middle name). Both Aliaa (Egyptian) and Amina (Tunisian) posted nude pictures of themselves online, Aliaa on her blog and Amina on Facebook. Although Aliaa posted her pictures during a revolutionary moment of Egyptian history only a few months after the 25 January Revolution, in November 2011, Amina posted her earliest images more than two years after the Tunisian uprising and after the Islamist Ennahda Party came to power in Tunisia in March 2013.

The nude pictures posted by these young women brought much public and media attention. When she first published her nude pictures,

Aliaa attracted several million visits to her blog (Egyptianpeople.net 2014). However, the women also faced condemnation, including religious fatwas issued against them. Tunisian Islamists were reported to have called for the death of Amina (RT.com 2013), whilst Aliaa had to flee the country. Amina was also prosecuted for engaging in an 'indecent act' publicly (that is, nudity).

What role did the Arab media play in shaping the public's responses to Aliaa's and Amina's acts? Real life is 'dubious enough and ludicrous enough' (Goffman 1974: 2); thus, for our social experiences to remain meaningful they need to be organized in familiar ways, called 'frames'. Framing is the process by which news media and their sources interpret social reality and help members of the public to make sense of, and to form responses to, events. By providing certain frames for social and political issues 'news organizations declare the underlying causes and likely consequences of a problem and establish criteria for evaluating potential remedies for the problem' (Nelson et al. 1997: 567–68). Here, we examine the frames provided in the news media for understanding Aliaa's and Amina's respective public nudity. These cues, mainly through language, help us to understand the larger narrative within which the mainstream media and their news sources frame the acts of public nudity by these young women, whether a 'revolutionary narrative' or a narrative of women's rights or freedom, as suggested by the women themselves in their statements (discussed below).

Despite the complexity and diversity of the female experience in Arab countries, it is common to treat and frame the female body as a 'social', 'tribal' or 'familial' possession. The society/tribe/family decides how women should dress and behave. In many Arab/Muslim societies, women's bodies can even be subjected to socially justified and accepted violence by their husbands or male family members if women transgress expected gender behaviour (Douki et al. 2003). By posting naked pictures of themselves on the internet, both women rebelled against the socio-political order through claiming ownership over their bodies.

The Self and the Collective: Nudity as Resistance

The two women framed their publicizing of their nude pictures as a protest against social and political injustices and inequality and as a cry for freedom. Aliaa wrote on her blog next to her nude picture 'Nude Art' and Amina wrote *Jasadi melki wa lays sharaf ahad*, 'my body belongs to me and is nobody's honour' in reference to the traditional view of the female body as a source of honour or dishonour to the family and especially to male relatives. Amina described her behaviour as a 'protest move' commemorating both International Women's Day and the establishing of a Femen office in Tunisia (CNN Arabic 2013).

In doing so, both women clearly presented an unfamiliar, bizarre and hence a newsworthy story to the news media and public in Egypt and Tunisia. This was largely due to the way they used their bodies to deliver their social and political statements. Hence, their bodies did not conform to the dominant cultural narrative about the female body in their respective societies, that is, as an object to be exploited and exposed by men for pleasure and commercial purposes, as in the case of the popular media use of the female body in advertisements, films and music videos. It was not accepted that the female body could be used to tell a social or political story. In publishing their own naked images in this way, they claimed their bodies as their 'property' (Simmel 1950: 322–44) and their liberty to unclothe to send a public message.

Even more significantly, the women desexualized their bodies. Aliaa states in her blog that these images are a protest against the sexual harassment that Egyptian women face daily in the streets and for which they are held responsible by society: 'even if we "girls" are naked, nobody has the right to attack or harass us' (Anees 2011). In other words, Aliaa challenged the culturally dominant narrative in Arab countries and Arab media, to some extent, regarding the sexual harassment of women in which women are blamed for being sexually harassed or even raped, as we discussed in relation to the stories of Eman Al-Obeidi, Samira Ibrahim and others.

As noted above, media representations of the female body (re)produce 'dominant cultural narratives' in which the female body is to be exploited for purposes of profit or pleasure (Moore and Kosut 2010: 345). In this way, the mainstream media functions as a social institution that contributes to maintaining dominant cultural norms. In turn, the only socially legitimate women's voices and agency are those that conform to the dominant cultural rules and norms, which reinforce and perpetuate the dominant collective narratives. Aliaa and Amina published the photographs of their own bodies in defiance of the rules and expectations of a patriarchal society, in which women's bodies are controlled (Hassib 2011). Consequently, their actions did not contribute to the dominant understanding of the position and ownership of the female body and, as such, were marginalized as extreme, immoral and pathological.

Liberal Frames and Responses

Makarim Ibrahim (2011a) notes that nudity, full and partial, is present in Arab popular culture, in TV, magazines, arts and on the internet. Hence, one would think that it was not the nudity of these women that made their stories so shocking and provocative to the public, it was the message or the ways in which the public understood their nudity. In popular culture, nude images are viewed by the public within three 'familiar and bounded frames: art, pornography and information' (Eck 2001: 603). When the public attempts to make sense of nude images, two issues are of significance: the 'context' within which the image is 'situated' and its classification or category. 'Classification' is particularly vital to decreasing doubts people face when their 'worldview' is defied by a cultural item (Eck 2001).

The fact that Aliaa's and Amina's nude bodies were not commercialized or sexualized was a source of social concern. The pictures were not situated in an advertisement or a music video or any other popular culture format that would suggest commercialized or sexualized bodies (Mikdashi 2011). Both Aliaa and Amina chose their respective parents' homes as the context for taking their nude photographs, a location that does not seem to provide an appropriate context for sexualized or pornographic material. They made political and social statements through situating and labelling their nude pictures within then current national conversations about women's rights and revolutions, using the spaces opened up by the revolutions and cyberspace to extend the interpretation of freedom to include the freedom of the female body to appear publicly, to unclothe and be free from social and the male control. Hence, the provocative dimension of their behaviour concerned the ways in which their nude pictures were contextualized, which transgressed the usual classifications of naked female bodies in popular culture.

The purpose of posting their nude pictures was to exercise their individual agency to participate in the revolutionary moment, alongside their male and female counterparts in their countries. Many other women, such as Samira Ibrahim, chose a different modality of agency, such as taking to the streets, in order to make their socio-political statements. When Samira Ibrahim stood up against the sexual abuse perpetrated against her and others by SCAF, she also capitalized on the same moment of socio-political rupture to reject any military subjugation of women's bodies. Yet, whilst many leftists and liberals supported Ibrahim's struggle against the military, they rejected Elmahdy's actions.

Many liberals claimed that Aliaa's posting of her naked image next to slogans for women's freedom and in support of the revolution, was an attack on them and even a conspiracy against the Egyptian revolutionaries to decrease their popularity. Her action was interpreted as undermining their political and social capital. After news about Aliaa's membership of the April 6 Youth Movement spread on the internet, the latter circulated a press release denying that Elmahdy had ever been a member of the group. Tariq Al-Kholi, the then spokesperson of the movement, was quoted in *Al Arabiya* asserting that 'None of the members of the movement has this "loose" characteristic (*ebaheyah*) that Aliaa has. This girl is nothing but an agent of the old security system which is used to defame the 6th of April movement and its youth before Egyptian and Arab public opinion, after all its successes and contributions to the Egyptian revolution' (Kabaisi and Slaiman 2011) (italics added). She was also condemned for causing 'a huge damage to all liberals' (Al-Mehwar TV 2011). Meanwhile, blogger Ramez Abbas argued that Aliaa's pictures aborted any possibility of building a civil state in Egypt (Al-Bawaba 2011).

In addition, pictures of Aliaa and Amina were perceived as threats to the ethics and values of Arab and Muslim societies in their respective countries. The moral question has been central to all public understandings, critiques and condemnations of these actions. *Al Arabiya*'s reporters from London and Cairo stated that, because of what they called 'Aliaa's liberation revolution', the 'Arab wall of modesty is collapsing, with many other Arab females announcing their intention of taking similar steps' (Kabaisi and Slaiman 2011).

It seems that very few people in Egypt and Tunisia could openly support or show understanding of a person who attaches freedom to the human body and to the female body in particular. Perhaps paradoxically, such an association was perceived as a threat to the mobilization of the public in support of freedom and human rights. Even when not openly disputing a woman's right to control her body, or publicly acknowledging the importance of the message communicated through it, many liberals still made moral judgments about Aliaa's actions. A few of them found her nude pictures to be 'cheap and debasing' (Ibrahim 2011b) and an 'extreme' method (Hassib 2011) for promoting freedom, including freedom for women. Tunisians were reported to be unfamiliar with 'Tunisian women posting their nude pictures online' and rejected Amina's conduct, calling it 'immoral' (*Cawalisse* 2013) and a 'shock to the Tunisian public' (Euronews 2013). This absolute moral framing of their behaviour made it very challenging for competing frames to emerge, especially within the Arabic-speaking public commentary. However, it is important to note that a few commentators acknowledged the non-pornographic nature of these images, despite the dominant view of sexualizing the nude female body (Ibrahim 2011a) let alone the act of publicly undressing.

The alternative frame provided was the psychologically troubled. Amina was described by her aunt in a YouTube video as 'unbalanced' and 'mentally ill'. Her actions were labelled as 'pathological' as well as 'shameful' and that she had damaged her father's 'pride as a man'

(Tapson 2013). A Tunisian TV presenter asked Amina on Tunisian television if she visited a psychiatrist (Didymus 2013). Similarly, Sayed Al-Qemani, characterized by the Egyptian media as a 'liberal scholar, writer and strong critic of political Islam', and whose writing was quoted by Aliaa in her blog, stressed in a television interview that 'he is not responsible for Aliaa's actions or for the behaviour of millions of readers'. As a 'liberal' he added, 'he can't hit Aliaa or curse her or anything of that sort'. For him, the young lady must have a 'psychological problem' (Al-Mehwar TV 2011). The same frame is used also by a female Jordanian commentator Hanan Al-Shaikh, who questioned Elmahdy's merit, reason and psychological stability (Al-Shaikh 2013). Although, Al-Qemani's statement seemed more aware of Aliaa's message and of his own limitations speaking about Aliaa's body, he suggested that her parents were somehow responsible for her behaviour and hence the use of her body, thereby failing to acknowledge her message regarding women's ownership over their own bodies.

Frames and Responses from Women

Taking into consideration the issue of sisterhood and women's solidarity, this section explores the level of public support Amina and Aliaa enjoyed from women in their own countries and beyond, who are subjected to similar circumstances and experience the same power structures. For the freedom cry of Aliaa and Amina to have any meaning and relevance, there must exist a recognition of their message. Even if other women did not agree on the technique of undressing the body, an acknowledgement of the statement or the meaning of the act would have made the moves by Amina and Aliaa less marginalized and would have enabled an alternative public framing for their actions to emerge.

Despite the sweeping condemnation of Amina's nude pictures, she did receive more public support than Aliaa. A few Tunisian women posted their naked pictures online in solidarity with Amina, especially after she was reported to have disappeared after her first posting in March 2013. Tunisian film director Nadia Alfani, posted a picture of the upper half of her body, half-naked, holding a paper over her breasts, on which was written *karama*, 'dignity', with *hurriya*, 'freedom', written on her forehead and 'for Amina' on her arm (iNewsArabia 2013). Elmahdy gained less support, yet some individuals publicly expressed understanding. Makarem Ibrahim wrote that Elmahdy 'unclothed on the internet to challenge the taboos of her eastern society which imposes covering up on her' (Ibrahim 2011b). One Egyptian blogger, critical of the responses of both 'liberals' and 'leftists' in Egypt to Aliaa's pictures, understood the publishing of nude pictures as a way of claiming ownership of her body and taking it back from the 'public to the private space' (Hanibaael 2011).

Yet, condemnations rather than support were more audible and visible in the Arabic-speaking media. Largely, women seem to have missed or ignored the message that Aliaa and Amina meant to deliver through their use of their nude pictures. One of the female presenters on Al-Mehwar Television (an Egyptian private channel) appeared embarrassed when speaking about Elmahdy. She repeated that 'I don't know how to deal with this [story]'; '[I] am only bringing this story up because it is so strange and alien to us [Egyptians]' (Al-Mehwar TV 2011). Clearly, the presenter was scared of discussing this matter and bringing it to her viewers, hence she dealt with it as a source of dishonour that should be hidden from the public using the absolute morality frame.

The denunciation and disowning of Amina's images came also from Tunisian women and women's organizations. It was reported in the media that 'Tunisian women rejected her [Amina's] action and denounced it claiming that she is not a representative of Tunisian women and that her pictures are derisory' (Cawalisse 2013). In addition to the condemnation and disowning that Amina faced during her trial in May, protestors also demonstrated to voice their anger and cursed her (Euronews 2013). It should also be noted that the interpretation of women undressing in Tunisia and Egypt is complicated by the histories of colonialism and Orientalism, where European colonizers sought to unveil Muslim women to demonstrate the 'progressiveness' of the colonial project and the 'backwardness' of Arab-Muslim culture.

Conclusion

This chapter aimed at exploring the degree to which the Arab Spring enabled the emergence of new framings and understandings of women's agency and female bodies in public spaces. The chapter began by considering the framings of women's agency before the Arab Spring, taking the widely discussed cases of the 'repentant artists' and female 'suicide bombers'. We found that women's agency and control over their own bodies was undermined in media and public debate, as these women were either portrayed as 'manipulated' by the male leaders of political/religious groups or as motivated by emotions and personal problems. The notion that women may use their bodies to make a political statement was, for the most part, ignored.

Throughout the Arab Spring, women used their bodies to make political statements, in defiance of the authorities but also of patriarchy. Despite the support and solidarity that they received from other revolutionaries, nevertheless the authorities attempted to discredit women's participation in public protests by labelling them as 'loose'. Moreover, the media, for the most part, also questioned the motives of women participating in protests, even when they were victims of sexual abuse and harassment, such as in the cases of Samira Ibrahim, the 'Blue Bra Girl' and Eman Al-Obeidi. In other words, despite women's massive presence in public protests, the Arab Spring failed to encourage new framings of women's agency to emerge in mainstream Arab media.

Perhaps the biggest controversy over women's bodies was that of the nude self-photos posted on social media by Aliaa Elmahdy and Amina Sboui (Tyler). Both Amina and Aliaa placed their nude or partially nude photos within two contexts simultaneously, that of cyberspace and the revolutionary space. The cyberspace, or internet, with its wide audience did not encourage any artistic framing or understanding of these images. Meanwhile, for the most part, commentators failed to frame the acts as revolutionary or even to associate the women's narratives with the revolutionary ideals of freedom and equality. Hence their actions were largely condemned in the media and placed either within a moral or pathological frame. Their acts were rarely placed in the broader frame of the Arab Spring and there was a lack of alternative or competing frames provided by the mainstream media and personalities.

Despite the various responses from the public and the media to the utilization of the female body to resist the political and social order, the Arab public largely failed to acknowledge that a woman's body is her 'personal property'. Reactions to Aliaa and Amina illustrated the extent to which the female body continues to be a source of honour or dishonour to the family, the tribe, the nation and even to a political movement, as in the case of the April 6 Youth Movement. Even those seeking to resist the political status quo, such as the April 6 Youth Movement and other 'liberals', viciously condemned and rejected the women's actions.

This chapter argues that it was not nudity itself that brought public outrage and moral judgment. This condemnation was a product of the non-conventional combination of the message and the medium, in that political and social messages were communicated through uncovering the human body. These women converted the female body from a 'tool of repression' to 'an assertion of power', as the Syrian-American photographer Mallorie Nasrallah has argued (Namazie 2012). A lack of recognition of the socio-political message intended by the women's nudity hindered any serious debate about the message itself.

References

Ajmi, S. (2013) 'Does Tunisia Need Femen?', openDemocracy, 3 June. Available at: www.opendemocracy.net/sana-ajmi/does-tunisia-need-femen (accessed 30 June 2013).

Al-Ali, N. (2012) 'Gendering the Arab Spring', Middle East Journal of Culture and Communication, 5, pp. 260–31.

Al-Bawaba (2011) 'The Nude Revolution Between Aliaa AlMahdi and Samira Ibrahim', 17 November. Available at: www.albawaba.com (accessed on 11 January 2015).

Al-Mehwar TV (2011) '90 Minutes', 17 November. Available at: www.youtube.com/watch?v=L7Hwe_chWAg (accessed on 30 June 2013). (Arabic).

Al-Shaikh, H. (2013) 'Aliaa Al-Mahdi and the Unclothing Against Mursi', *Al-Quds Al-Arabi*, 3 January. Available at: http://issuu.com/mrkezcom/docs/quds_03_01_2013/1 (accessed on 29 June 2013). (Arabic).

Anees, A. (2011) 'In Defense of Aliaa Magda Al-Mahdi', *Al-Hewar Al-Mutamaden*, 18 November. Available at: www.ahewar.org/debat/show.art.asp?aid=283924 (accessed on 29 June 2013). (Arabic).

Baydoun, A. S. (2012) 'Not a Female But a Citizen: On the Representations of Women in Arab Intifadas', *Kalamon*, Summer (7). Available at: www.kalamon.org/articles-details-157#axzz36b8GSRY6 (accessed on 29 June 2013). (Arabic).

Cawalisse (2013) 'Amina's Breasts are Nude Again on the Internet and the Tunisian Women Disown Her', 3 May. Available at: www.cawalisse.com/21269/05/21/14 (accessed on 29 June 2013). (Arabic).

CNN Arabic (2013) 'Women Campaign to Unclothe in Solidarity with the Tunisian Amina', 22 April. Available at: http://archive.arabic.cnn.com/2013/entertainment/3/23/tunisia.femen/index.html (accessed on 30 June 2013). (Arabic).

Didymus, J. T. (2013) 'Tunisian Amina, 19, in Psych Ward for Posting Topless Femen Pics', *Digital Journal*, 24 March. Available at: http://digitaljournal.com/article/346342 (accessed on 29 June 2013).

Douki, S., F. Nacef, A. Belhadj, A. Bouasker and R. Ghachem (2003) 'Violence Against Women in Arab and Islamic Countries', *Women's Mental Health*, 6 (3), pp. 165–71.

Eck, B. A. (2001) 'Nudity and Framing: Classifying Art, Pornography, Information, and Ambiguity', *Sociological Forum*, 16 (4), pp. 603–32.

Egyptianpeople.net (2014) 'In Pictures: Extraordinary Number of Visits to See Aliaa Al-Mahdi', 25 February. Available at: www.egyptianpeople.net/default_news.php?id=172725 (accessed on 1 June 2014). (Arabic).

Euronews (2013) 'New Accusations to the Activists' 30 May. Available at: http://arabic.euronews.com/2013/05/30/tunisian-femen-protester-faces-new-charges on (accessed on 30 June 2013). (Arabic).

Goffman, E. (1974) *Frame Analysis: An Essay on the Organization of Experience*, Harvard University Press, Massachusetts.

Gole, N. (1997) 'The Gendered Nature of the Public Sphere', *Public Culture*, 101 (1), pp. 61–81.

Hanibaael (2011) 'Aliaa Al-Mahdi: The Freedom of the Body on the Face of Patriarchy', 24 November. Available at: http://hanibaael.wordpress.com (accessed on 30 June 2013).

Hassib, M. (2011) 'Commentary: Revolutionary Blogger: To Strip or Not To Strip?', *Caravan*, 27 November. Available at: https://academic.aucegypt.edu/caravan/story/commentary-revolutionary-blogger-strip-or-not-strip (accessed on 29 June 2013).

Huffington Post (2011) 'Syria: Zainab Al Hosni Believed To Be Killed In Custody', 23 September. Available at: www.huffingtonpost.com/2011/09/23/syria-zainab-al-hosni-died-custody_n_977550.html (accessed on 29 June 2013).
Ibrahim, M. (2011a) 'A Woman's Revolution in Egypt. Freedom and the Culture of Nudity of Aliaa Al-Mahdi', Global Arab Network, 23 November. Available at: www.globalarabnetwork.com/culture-ge/culture-studies/6383-2011-11-23-214034 (accessed on 30 June 2013). (Arabic).
Ibrahim, M. (2011b) 'Freedom and the Culture of Revolution of Aliaa Al-Mahdi', Al-Hewar Al-Mutamaden, 19 November. Available at: www.ahewar.org/debat/show.art.asp?aid=284060 (accessed on 30 June 2013). (Arabic).
iNewsArabia (2013) 'Director Nadia Al-Fani Unclothes in Support of Amina', 25 March. Available at: www.inewsarabia.com (accessed on 29 June 2013).
Kabaisi, K., and M. Slaiman (2011) 'April 6th Movement Declares No Connection with An Egyptian Who Published Her Completely Nude Photos on the Internet', Al Arabiya, 15 November. Available at: www.alarabiya.net/articles/2011/11/15/177270.html (accessed on 29 June 2013).
Kaysen, R. (2005) 'The Naked Truth About the Power of Protest Today', The Villager, 75 (12), 10–16 August. Available at: http://thevillager.com/villager_119/talkingpoint.html (accessed on 29 June 2013).
Mahmoud, S. (2005) The Politics of Piety: The Islamic Revival and the Feminist Subject, Princeton University Press, Princeton.
Mikdashi, M. (2011) 'Waiting for Alia', Jadaliyya, 20 November. Available at: www.jadaliyya.com/pages/index/3208/waiting-for-alia (accessed on 29 July 2013).
Mohsen, H. (2012) 'What Made Her Go There? Samira Ibrahim and Egypt's Virginity Test Trial', Al Jazeera, 16 March. Available at: www.aljazeera.com/indepth/opinion/2012/03/201231613129201850.html (accessed on 29 July 2013).
Moore, L. J., and Kosut, M. (2010) 'Bodies in the Media', in L. J. Moore and M. Kosut, The Body Reader, New York University Press, New York.
Naaman, A. (2007) 'Brides of Palestine/Angels of Death: Media, Gender, and Performance in the Case of the Palestinian Female Suicide Bombers', Journal of Women in Culture and Society, 32 (4), pp. 933–55.
Namazie, A. (2012) 'Nothing is Sacred: I Carry it With Me Wherever I Go', Free Thought Blog, 4 December. Available at: http://freethoughtblogs.com/maryamnamazie/2012/12/04/december-2012-i-carry-it-with-me-wherever-i-go/ (accessed on 30 June 2013).
Nelson, T. E., R. A. Clawson and Z. M. Oxley (1997) 'Media Framing of a Civil Liberties Conflict and its Effect on Tolerance', American Political Science Review, 91 (3), pp. 567–83.
Pietras, E. (2014) 'Naked Protests: From Topless Bike Rides to Nude Hikes and Animal Rights Campaigns', The Mirror, 29 May. Available at: www.mirror.

co.uk/news/weird-news/naked-protests-topless-bike-rides-3622081 (accessed on 30 June 2013).

RT.com (2013) 'In a Video: Femen Movement Announced Nudity Jihad in Protest of Islamists' Rule', 4 April. Available at: http://arabic.rt.com/news/612048 (accessed on 30 June 2013). (Arabic).

Simmel, G. (1950) The Sociology of Georg Simmel, trans./ed. K. Wolff, Free Press, New York.

Sulieman, M. (2011) 'A Controversy in Egypt over the Truth of the Dragging and Unclothing of the Prime Ministry Girl', Al Arabiya, 21 December. Available at: www.alarabiya.net/articles/2011/12/21/183779.html (accessed on 30 June 2013). (Arabic).

Tapson, M. (2013) 'Topless Jihad', Mark Tapson [blog], 12 May. Available at: http://marktapson.blogspot.ae/2013/05/topless-jihad.html (accessed January 3 2015).

The Daily Star (2013) 'Opinions in Tunisia Divided over Topless Feminist Amina', 6 June. Available at: www.dailystar.com.lb/News/Middle-East/2013/Jun-06/219575-opinions-in-tunisia-divided-over-topless-feminist-amina.ashx (accessed on 30 June 2013).

SIX

Women's Bodies in Post-Revolution Libya

Control and Resistance

Sahar Mediha Alnaas and Nicola Pratt

Introduction

Several authors have demonstrated how the reshaping of gender identity and gender relations is integral to political transformation processes (Alvarez 1990; Al-Ali 2005; Waylen 2007; Al-Ali and Pratt 2009; Al-Ali 2012, amongst others). In this chapter, we examine the understudied case of Libya where, in 2011, an uprising and armed conflict supported militarily by NATO succeeded in overthrowing the 42-year-old regime of Muammar Gaddafi. We discuss the appropriation and instrumentalization of Libyan women's bodies as the markers of both Muammar Gaddafi's Jamahariya and the Islamized post-Gaddafi Libyan state. We not only identify the transformation in gender discourses and practices that have emerged in the post-Gaddafi period, but also explore how newly emerged political forces seek to control women's bodies as part of a struggle over authority and power in the 'New Libya'. In effect, women's bodies have become a battlefield, with implications for women's ability to be active in the public sphere. Yet, women are not only victims of the transition process; our chapter also highlights women's agency in resisting their marginalization from post-Gaddafi political processes through their bodily performances in the public sphere. Departing from much of the scholarship on women and political transformations, which focuses on the presence or absence of women in formal political institutions, we explore the significance of women's agency in the public sphere more broadly, particularly with regard to subverting and resignifying religious and nationalist norms.

This chapter is based on extensive fieldwork in Libya conducted by Sahar Mediha Alnaas in the period between December 2012 and March 2014. Sahar interviewed 27 female members and 5 male members of the General National Congress (GNC) in addition to conducting 89 interviews with political party members and leaders, founders and members of women's groups, members of the National Transitional Council (NTC), female and male activists, and friends and family members. In addition to consuming local media, she also observed and attended public demonstrations, conferences, workshops, seminars, political party meetings and women's social gatherings.

The first section of this chapter discusses the appropriation and instrumentalization of women's bodies between pre- and post-revolutionary Libya. The next section examines efforts by post-revolutionary political actors to control women's bodies as part of exercising their authority in the New Libya and the implications of this for women's presence in the public sphere. The third section highlights women's efforts to resist their marginalization in the public sphere through their bodily performances. The chapter concludes by reflecting on the need for studies of political transformations to examine women's agency beyond formal political institutions.

Appropriation and Instrumentalization of Women's Bodies: From Gaddafi's Jamahariya to the New Libya

As part of his 'revolutionary ideology' of 'Jamahariya' (state of the masses), Muammar Gaddafi promoted women's participation in the public sphere and women were encouraged to enter professions such as the judiciary, law, university teaching and medicine (Spellman-Poots

2011). Legislation was amended to give women greater rights, such as Article 10 of a 1984 law allowing women of 20 years or older the freedom to marry without the permission of a male guardian and regulating polygamy or Article 21 of the Green Charter in which forced marriage was prohibited (Freedom House 2005). In addition, the Libyan regime ratified a number of international conventions on women's rights, including CEDAW (United Nations 2011) in 1989 (albeit with reservations).[1] Gaddafi also used his female bodyguards and police to present an emancipated image of Libyan women to the international community.

However, undoubtedly, this 'progressive' attitude towards women was part of the regime's efforts to legitimize itself internationally and to promote its ideology domestically. In reality, Libyan women were not 'emancipated' by Gaddafi. Despite women having equal political rights, the participation of women at the legislative level in the General People's Congress between 1969 and 2006 was 11 per cent and in the executive branch, or General People's Committee, during the same period it did not exceed 2 per cent (Al-Obeidi 2007). Libyan women's political participation was used instrumentally for the state's propaganda and personal interest. Meanwhile, the authoritarian nature of Gaddafi's regime limited political participation to women and men who were ideologically and politically affiliated with Gaddafi and his regime.

In addition, the considerable presence of women in the judiciary and legal profession was not reflected in the general status of women in Libya, especially with regard to the application of women's rights legislation. Indeed, the despotism of Gaddafi often led Libyans to turn increasingly towards the private sphere of family and tribe, thereby sidestepping state legislation. This trend was exacerbated during the sanctions years, when Gaddafi empowered tribal leaders in order to maintain his rule (Spellman-Poots 2011).

Like other nationalist discourses (Kandiyoti 1991; Yuval-Davis 1997), Gaddafi promoted women's participation in public as a symbol of the country's modernization, whilst controlling women's sexuality in the name of Libya's 'Islamic identity'. For example, women accused of *zina* (sexual relations outside of wedlock), even if they were victims of rape, would be remitted by the People's Prosecutor to the so-called Bayt Al-Ijtima'i (a facility for 'social rehabilitation'). Contrary to all the conventions and international agreements regarding women's, children's and human rights signed and ratified by Libya, such women and girls would be subjected to compulsory 'virginity tests' and would be denied education, work and even the right to object or appeal against their sentence (Human Rights Watch 2006).

Like other Arab countries, Libyan society experienced the spread of Wahhabi teachings via audio cassettes and, later, via satellite channels, which displaced the indigenous Sufi Islam.[2] As a result of this type of Islamization, increasing numbers of women began wearing the headscarf and informal restrictions were placed on personal freedoms in general and on women's conduct, body and sexuality in particular. Arguably, many of those participating in the Islamization trend were resisting Gaddafi's regime and its instrumentalization of women for its 'modern' image. However, in the 1990s, Gaddafi was obliged to make peace with political Islam, thereby opening up Libyan society further to Islamization, or the spread of a particularly conservative interpretation of Islam originating in Saudi Arabia.[3]

During the 17 February 2011 Revolution, women participated in many ways to topple the Gaddafi regime (see, for example, Hilsum 2012). However, in spite of their crucial and full participation in the revolution and on the front line, Libyan women were portrayed mainly as the mothers, sisters, wives and daughters of the revolutionary fighters. Libyan media was filled with images of Libyan women cooking for their sons, brothers and husbands on the front line or of mothers encouraging and inspiring their sons to fight. Women were also presented as the victims of the war and stood in for the 'weak' and 'vulnerable' Libya in need of 'masculinist protection' (Young 2003) by the militant Libyan male. Messages from women would be sent with food to the revolutionary fighters to encourage them and to remind them to fight for and protect their 'womenandchildren' (Enloe 1990). The 'mother of the martyr', umm *al-shaheed*, or 'mother of the revolutionary', umm *al-thuwar*, was regularly celebrated in the media throughout and after the 17 February Revolution and these terms were used in many revolutionary songs. Images and video clips of Libyan women saying goodbye to their dead sons were played repeatedly on Libya's Al-Ahrar TV channel.

The celebration of particular types of femininity, namely, the domestic and nurturing roles of women, can be contrasted with the celebration of a militarized masculinity within the revolution. It is worth noting that before the revolution of 17 February, many young Libyan men would do anything to escape compulsory military service, without feeling ashamed or emasculated for doing so. Indeed, the military was considered to be feminized by Gaddafi, since women participated in it (Al-Raya 2012). By contrast, Libyan men fighting against Gaddafi were praised as the ideal citizens for their courage and patriotism and they were regularly portrayed on TV and through social media. After the ousting of Gaddafi, those who fought against the regime were automatically awarded first class citizenship and promised a share in the new government (Libya Almostakbal 2011). In comparison, women in the New Libya have experienced systematic efforts to marginalize them within political transition processes. Moreover, whilst Western military intervention to help topple Gaddafi was welcomed by opponents of the previous regime, these same political actors now reject any Western influence with regard to issues of women's rights, as discussed further below.

The Political Transition in Post-Gaddafi Libya: Women's Bodies as Battlefields in the Political Struggle

On Libya's first 'Liberation Day', on 23 October 2011, marking the overthrow of the Gaddafi regime, after months of fighting by Libyan revolutionaries, Mustafa Abdul Jalil, then head of the National Transitional Council (2011–2012), announced that the restrictions on polygamy introduced by Gaddafi were against shariah and would be ended (McConnell and Todd 2011), much to the consternation of many of the women who had participated in the revolution (Hilsum 2012). The following year, on 10 August 2012, during the handover

of power ceremony from the Transitional Council to the elected
General National Congress (GNC), Salah Baadi, an Islamist GNC member, walked out in protest that the ceremony host, Sara Elmesallati,
did not cover her hair, leading Abdul Jalil to order Elmesallati to leave
the stage (Grant 2012). Both of these events are examples of how
Libyan women's bodies, their conduct and sexuality are appropriated
and controlled for the purpose of symbolically marking the Islamic
identity of the New Libya, asserting its sovereignty vis-à-vis the West,
whose military air power was crucial in the victory of the revolutionaries, and differentiating the New Libya from the Libya of Gaddafi.

Abdul Jalil's statements and actions should also be interpreted in
light of Libya's fragmented political field and struggle for power and
resources amongst competing groups.[4] Two opposing blocs have
emerged from this fragmented field: the National Forces Alliance
(NFA), which is a coalition of groups considered to represent 'an economically privileged class and prominent families', that seeks to draw
a line under the past and restore stability (Lacher 2013: 11); and a second coalition of groups, of which the Muslim Brotherhood is the larg-
est, which were either the former opposition and/or led the armed
struggle against the former regime and seek to exclude all those associated with the former regime from public life (Lacher 2013: 11–12).

As in other situations, the control over women's bodies (whether
discursively or physically) becomes an important element in the exercise of power over particular communities (Al-Ali and Pratt 2009: 93).
In effect, women's bodies are instrumentalized by competing political
actors to display or prove their Islamic credentials to underwrite their
claims to authority in the New Libya. The campaign against CEDAW,
discussed next, is an example of how political actors attempt to consolidate their authority by claiming sovereignty over women's bodies
and their sexuality in the name of religion.

The Campaign against CEDAW

After the fall of Gaddafi's regime, a campaign against CEDAW (Convention on the Elimination of All Forms of Discrimination against Women,

which Gaddafi had signed in 1989) and the UN recommendations to end violence against women issued in March 2013 (CSW 2013) was initiated, organized and led by political Islamists in Libya. These comprised the Muslim Brotherhood (MB) and its Justice and Construction Party, the Salafist members of the GNC, the Loyalty to the Blood of the Martyrs Bloc (*Kutlat al-wifa li-damm al-shuhada*) within the GNC,[5] Dar Al-Ifta headed by the Grand Mufti al-Sadiq al-Ghriani, and some civil society organizations funded and sponsored by Islamists, such as the Pen Movement (*Harakat qalam*), a women's group in Tripoli.[6] In line with their party's political platform, the female GNC members of the Muslim Brotherhood's Justice and Construction Party have lobbied against CEDAW and the UN recommendations to prevent violence against women. They argue that total equality, *musawat*, between men and women contradicts Islamic teachings and that gender relations should be based on complementarity, *takamul*. They construct a dichotomy between gender equality and gender complementarity rooted in notions of 'authenticity', whether according to Islamic teachings, innate gender characteristics or national values.

On 9 March 2013, even before the UN had released its recommendations on ending violence against women, Dar Al-Ifta organized a conference entitled, 'Libyan Women: Where To?' (*Al-mar'a al-libiya ila ayn?*). The conference, which was well attended, focused on the UN's 15 March recommendations and CEDAW. In his opening speech, the Grand Mufti described both UN documents as 'evil' and 'un-Islamic'. He criticized the notion of gender equality, since men have guardianship over their female relatives, or *wilayah*,[7] and declared that men have a unilateral right to divorce without a court order. He refused to recognize marital rape, claiming that a man has the right to have sexual intercourse with his wife without her consent. He opposed women's right to choose what to wear and, instead, strongly advocated for the *niqab* and the *hijab*. He asserted that a woman's sexual conduct and reproductive rights should be decided by her male *wali* (guardian) and her family.[8] He affirmed that women can acquire their rights only through shariah. At the end of his speech, he urged women to demonstrate against such conventions and documents and to show the world that Muslim women are 'chaste women' (Tanasuh Foundation 2013).

Indeed, the Pen Movement (*Harakat qalam*), led by Khadija El-Saadi, the daughter of Sami El-Saadi, a former member of the Libyan Islamic Fighting Group (LIFG), organized a demonstration to protest against the UN documents. El-Saadi explained her objections to the UN document, not on the basis of male superiority within Islam but on the basis of innate gender differences. In an interview on YouTube, she said:

> I came out on this demonstration after I read the UN convention against violence against women and found that the document itself is violence against our God-given nature . . . If you read it, you would see how it does not discuss violence against women in any of its articles, instead the whole convention is founded and based on total equality between men and women. I reject equality, but I am for justice and fairness, because equality is not always just; if God wanted us to be all equal he would have made us all women or all men. We women give birth; can men give birth too? Impossible, because we are different, physically and psychologically, and all psychologists agree that women are psychologically different. Of course our rights overlap at certain points and in many other areas they do not. And I see this as just to me as a woman. I do not see it as discrimination because if a man is attacked a woman will not be able to protect him, because of our nature. Men are stronger, physically, and even psychologically, they are inherently stronger. (Benhurraa 2013)

The rejection of CEDAW and the UN declaration against violence against women goes beyond political Islamist groups. Almost all the women that Sahar interviewed refused to advocate for CEDAW. When asked if they would join a demonstration held on 14 March for Women's Dignity Day against domestic violence and to demand the implementation of CEDAW, most women's groups and organizations refused to join because of their belief that the UN Convention does indeed contradict Islam. One member of the GNC for the National

Forces Alliance told Sahar, 'We are Muslims and we cannot accept what the West accepts for women'.[9]

On the 21 March 2013, Sahar attended a workshop on CEDAW, organized again by Dar-el-Ifta, at which Islamic jurists and clerics spoke. In the discussion, terms such as 'women's freedom' and 'gender equality' were interpreted as encouraging women to abandon their morals and religious values and become 'loose' women. Among those attending the workshop was the Chair of the Human Rights Committee in the GNC and a member of the National Forces Alliance (NFA). She reassured the panelists and the audience that the GNC had not agreed to accept the UN document and would not do so. When Sahar asked her if she had read the 15 March recommendations or CEDAW, she answered that she did not have time to do so. Despite having read none of the documents, she still adhered to the clerics' reading.

In this campaign against CEDAW, we see that certain political actors (both men and women) attempt to construct a consensus about what constitutes 'authentic' gender norms according to notions of religion, national identity or biology. These notions are explicity or implicitly embedded within binaries of local/foreign, authentic/alien, natural/unnatural and/or male/female, which function to reassert/reconstruct Libyan sovereignty in the face of much interest and intervention by Western countries in the wake of the 17 February Revolution. Simultaneously, these discursive moves also delegitimize notions of gender equality and women's sovereignty over their own bodies as undermining of Libyan political sovereignty. These efforts to forge consent amongst Libyan citizens is, simultaneously, buttressed by threats and intimidation (from both male and female Islamists) against the few members of the GNC and women activists who resist such conservative gender norms and openly support CEDAW and UN human and women's rights conventions. Such acts operate to discipline the wider community not only to comply with 'authentic' gender norms but, in the process, to submit to the political authority of the respective political actors.[10] In the following sections we examine further coercive practices against women's bodies in state institutions and public spaces.

Women Members of the General National Congress (GNC)

An example of how Western intervention has sought to promote
gender equality is the case of the electoral system. As a result of international pressure, the election system chosen by the National Transitional Council for the first post-revolution elections ensured women
were included on the party list of all political entities, resulting in
women winning thirty-two seats, plus one seat as an independent, in
the GNC (HNEC 2012).[11] Of these thirty-three seats, seven were won
by women members of the Muslim Brotherhood's Justice and Construction Party and twenty-four were won by women members of the
NFA, considered to be the more 'liberal' or 'moderate'.[12]

Despite constituting 16.5 per cent of parliament, women parliamentarians face a range of coercive practices, from silencing to
intimidation. Almost all female members of the GNC complained in
interviews that the head of the GNC would cut short their speeches by
turning off the microphone whilst they are speaking or ignore their
indications to speak during the GNC assembly. Yet, he would allow
male members to speak, even if their intervention was irrelevant to
the topic discussed.[13] As one woman member of the NFA said, 'People
think we cannot talk, but the fact is that we are not allowed to talk'.[14]

Women parliamentarians also face open intimidation and threats
by male parliamentarians. For example, on 8 January 2013, in a live
TV broadcast of a GNC parliamentary session, Mohamed al-Kilani, a
member calling himself a '*salafi* brother', insulted the female members of the GNC and blamed them for the failure of parliament. He
stated that women and men should never mix in public and that God
will never bless their work as a result. He described women as dressing 'immodestly' and applying make-up, thus creating a distractive
environment for the male members of parliament. His statement was
received with applause.

Al-Kilani's statement did not come as a surprise to women in the
GNC, as they had been receiving regular messages from him and
other Salafist GNC members concerning the way they dress. Yet, most
women parliamentarians have chosen not to confront the religious

political forces within the GNC. They cite a lack of knowledge of Islamic jurisprudence and the fear of blasphemy accusations, which would lead to their exclusion from the political arena, as a reason for their silence. Consequently, no woman responded to Al-Kilani at the time of his speech.[15] However, a few days later, on 12 January, a woman member of the GNC read out a joint response by women members to the *salafi* brother's insult, requesting that he advise them in private and not in public the next time he had an opinion relating to their attire. Such a response was disappointing and unsatisfactory to many women outside the GNC, who expected more from those who are supposed to represent them.

By contrast, following the statement of the women GNC members, Najia Ba'yo, a female member of the GNC for the NFA, decided to confront Al-Kilani directly. Ba'yo did not witness the *salafi* brother's intervention but, after learning about it from her colleagues, tried to talk to the him and so sat next to him in the parliament hall, where-upon he turned to her and ordered her to leave and not sit next to him, threatening to hit her if she did not move. When she reported the incident to the second deputy head of the GNC (who is a member of the Justice and Construction Party), she was insulted and accused of 'provoking' him. When Sahar interviewed Najia, she was collecting signatures from other members of the GNC to support a complaint against the second deputy head of the GNC. She managed to collect only 28 signatures out of the 200 members. No investigation was ordered and not much attention was paid to the fact that the *salafi* brother had insulted and threatened her.

The experience of female GNC members embodies a dilemma for women in the public sphere in the New Libya. Despite their participation in the revolution against Gaddafi, their presence in parliament is largely thanks to 'international pressure' to promote gender equality, rendering them symbolic targets for male political leaders seeking to demonstrate their authority and Libyan sovereignty, as well as promoting their conservative gender agendas. In this context, it is not surprising that some women in the GNC seek to conform with notions of gender complementarity and reject UN conventions on gender equality in order to 'bargain with patriarchy' (Kandiyoti 1988) and secure their presence in the public sphere.

Violence against Women in Public Spaces

The violence against women in Libya did not decrease with the overthrow of Gaddafi. Indeed, the increase in violence against women during the six months of the uprising in 2011 was only a forewarning of what would follow. The assassination, intimidation, abduction, torture and rape of women and women activists reported since the overthrow of Gaddafi has become a serious issue for women, particularly those who are known for their activism and advocacy for women's issues, but also professional women.[16] Most of these crimes remain unpunished at the time of writing and it is not clear who the perpetrators are: militias linked to political Islamist groups or remnants of the former regime. Women are particularly vulnerable in light of the breakdown in law and order after the fall of Gaddafi and rivalry between different centres of power to consolidate their respective authority.

For example, Magdulien Abaida, an outspoken feminist and critic of the growing power of the Grand Mufti Sheikh Sadiq al-Ghriani, told Sahar that she was kidnapped on 9 August 2012 from a workshop that she was running in Benghazi on women's rights in the constitution. She was held for five days, during which time she was tortured and told that she would be killed if she ever again criticized the Mufti. She was forced to leave Libya through the Tunisian border and travelled to the UK, where she sought political asylum.[17] In another example, on 13 February 2013, Aicha el-Moghrabi, a university lecturer, was being driven home in a university car, by the university driver, when she was stopped by armed groups at a checkpoint. She was humiliated, harassed, insulted and threatened with guns for not wearing the headscarf and for being in a car with a man who was not a *mahram*.[18] On 14 February 2013, Sana el-Mansouri, a TV presenter, was stopped by an armed group at Benghazi Airport, where she was insulted, humiliated, subjected to interrogation at gunpoint and harassed for not wearing the headscarf and for advocating for women's rights. On 4 June 2013, a Libyan lawyer Hanan Mustafa and her father were both attacked and severely beaten in front of Zarouk courthouse in Misrata. She was representing a Norwegian mother whose son had allegedly been kidnapped by his Libyan father. While the attack took place, none of the court police guards or people who witnessed the incident intervened to help Hanan. Furthermore, when she called for help from passers-by, some men told her that she should have covered her hair first.[19] More generally, sexual harassment in the streets, universities and workplace has been accompanied by a widespread public campaign for a mandated 'Islamic dress code', supported by the Grand Mufti. Leaflets with images of what is claimed to be the Islamic dress for women have been disseminated in public offices, universities, hospitals and on the internet since the overthrow of Gaddafi's regime.

These incidences of violence against and harassment of professional women, women's rights activists and women who do not wear a headscarf should not be considered as merely an unfortunate consequence of the deterioration in the security situation. These acts constitute a symbolic and strategic move to discipline women's behaviour more generally in the New Libya as well as delineating a break with the 'state feminism' of the Gaddafi regime (Spellman-Poots 2011) and underwriting the authority of new political actors and their gender agendas.

Women's Resistance to Patriarchy in the New Libya: Between Confrontation and Compliance

Most studies of women and political transformations focus on women's organizing to influence or involvement in political institutions. As discussed above, women's involvement in political institutions and their influence over women's rights measures is shaped by the power struggle between dominant political actors. On the one hand, the majority of women in parliament comply with the discourses and practices of dominant political actors, including opposing UN documents such as CEDAW as being against Islam or alien to Libya. For some women, such as members of the Muslim Brotherhood, this attitude may reflect their own ideological beliefs. For others, it could be considered a non-confrontational strategy to maintain their presence in parliament and the public sphere more broadly, recognizing the limits of their power against conservative Islamist political forces. On the other hand, a small number of women openly challenge the political Islamists and their conservative gender norms, but risk being silenced or completely excluded from the public sphere by these same actors.

In between compliance and confrontation, we find many Libyan women trying to maintain their presence in the public sphere, not through recourse to binary categories of gender equality or complementarity or advocacy of universal women's rights instruments, but rather through recourse to their religion or national identity and belonging. Below we discuss three different initiatives and efforts by Libyan women, which involve resignifying nationalist and/or religious discourses to present counter-discourses against conservative Islamist forces.

Women and Sport

Hadia Gana, a ceramics artist from Tripoli, started riding her bike with Houd Elghali, another Libyan artist from Zwara, immediately after the overthrow of Gaddafi in 2011. She would ride in the streets of Tripoli early Friday mornings to avoid harassment. More women, mainly artists to begin with such as Rim Jibreel, and other activists, joined Hadia and soon a Facebook page was created under the name, 'Friday's Bike'.[20] Pictures of Libyan women riding their bikes were regularly posted on the page and page visitors posted encouraging comments. While riding their bikes in the streets of Tripoli, people would cheer and smile to Hadia and the women with her as a sign of support and encouragement. On one occasion a woman told them that she wanted her daughter to join them. On another occasion, the municipal council and the head of the police force in Tripoli offered to close some streets for the bike group every Friday morning to allow people to cycle or walk in a car free zone.

Friday's Bike was the first of its type in the history of Libya. Conventionally, women's bike riding has been regarded as 'against culture and religion' on the basis that it contradicts norms of female modesty. Hadia told Sahar that she began riding her bike and encouraging other Libyan women to join her in order to forge a new relationship with her city and claim her presence in the Libyan public sphere:

> I ride my bike everywhere I go abroad, why not in Libya? I want
> to have a different experience with the streets of Tripoli. I want to
> have a different relation with the public sphere as a woman with no
> restrictions and gender barriers.[21]

Hadia and others in the Friday bike group believe that, as human beings and equals to men, they too have the right to ride their bikes in public. In doing so they challenged conservative social norms about women riding bikes as well as claiming a space for women in the public sphere. The group stopped due to the outbreak of fighting in May 2014.[22]

Lawyer and human rights activist Azza Maghur,[23] a member of Friday's Bike and well known for her activism and advocacy for human rights and women's rights in Libya since the 1990s, built on the success of the bike group by organizing another sporting event in May 2012. The event was called 'Women and Sport', but included both men and women participants, and was an attempt to create a weekly sporting event for women to encourage them to exercise in public and to resist being confined to the private sphere. Two hundred women attended and participated alongside many men. The day was a huge success, during which many businesses donated water and drinks and the police force secured the event with the permission of Tripoli County Council.

Azza believes that sport has the power to transcend the gender binary and bring men and women together in the public space as equals. She considers that sport can bring the best out of people and that people are more relaxed and less tense while exercising, thus challenging conservative gender discourses through sports will be less confrontational. Unfortunately, Azza received a serious death threat and was forced to cancel the project after the first week.[24]

Through Friday's Bike and Women and Sport events, women activists have sought to construct a new relationship between women and the public sphere on the basis of women's legitimate place in public space. In the process, they have subverted existing gender norms about women and exercise, not through recourse to dichotomous discourses of equality versus complementarity or through citing UN documents. Rather, women have embodied their right to be in the public sphere by acting in public spaces.

Women and National Dress

As mentioned previously, since the fall of Gaddafi, there has been a campaign for a mandated Islamic dress code, which is considered to be a long black loose dress and long black headscarf that covers the shoulders and chest. Salafists and some other political Islamists claim that this costume is the only 'authentic Islamic dress'. In resistance to this campaign and the spread of the black dress, in March 2013, a group of Libyan women and men decided to start Farashiya National Day, inspired by a similar initiative in Tunisia. The *farashiya* is a white sheet traditionally worn by Libyan women in public.[25] The women and men who participated in the 13 March demonstrations in Tripoli and Benghazi characterized the black dress as a Wahhabi costume, belonging to the Gulf countries, not to Libya. They argued that Libyans have their own modest national costume that reflects their history and identity. Embracing other countries' national costumes would thus mean losing their identity as Libyans. Moreover, the demonstration took place in Martyrs' Square in Tripoli and Tahrir Square in Benghazi, both places being spaces particularly associated with the uprising against Gaddafi.

In this form of resistance, women use their bodies, considered by political leaders as markers of the nation, to subvert the conservative gender discourses of radical political Islamists. This may appear initially ironic, as the *farashiya* completely covers the woman's body except for

one of her eyes. We can consider this a strategic use of national culture
that validates the 'authenticity' of the *farashiya*, as rooted in Libyan tradition, against efforts by political Islamists to impose a 'foreign' dress
code on women. By demonstrating in Tahrir and Martyrs' Squares, the
activists also reinscribed the *farashiya* with revolutionary legitimacy,
thereby resisting the claims to authority of political Islamists in the
New Libya.

Women and the Political Arena

As discussed previously, women in politics have faced intimidation
and threats as a means to silence their voices and marginalize their
concerns in the New Libya. Unlike the women members of the GNC,
who have backed away from confronting hostile political actors
using religious discourses, one woman, Amal Bilhaj, decided to use
religious arguments to justify her participation in politics. Bilhaj, the
founder of the Free Communication (*al-tawasul al-hur*) development
organization and a representative of the Libyan Centre for Peace,
decided to stand as the first Libyan women candidate for prime minister. She told Sahar:

> We fought hard to have a voice and constitutional rights but
> were only given 6 seats out of 60 seats on the constitutional
> committee . . . Having only 6 seats on the constitutional committee
> shocked me and made me think that I need to do something. Even
> my family did not know what I was going to do. But before I put
> forward my candidacy, I went to Al-Azhar in Egypt and Al-Zituna
> Mosque in Tunis to seek advice from religious scholars to make
> sure that I was not doing something against my religion, especially
> the *hadith* that prohibits women from holding any high decision-
> making position. All the advice I got encouraged me and I found
> nothing in Islam against women leaders. I know I will not be the
> prime minister, at least not now . . . Women were used during
> the revolution and the first elections in 2012. Afterwards they
> were systematically excluded from the public sphere and sent back
> home. Because of that I want to challenge and break the norm and
> encourage other women to do the same.[26]

172 PART TWO

Amal's recourse to religion to resist efforts by certain political actors to marginalize women from the public sphere can be considered a tactical move to legitimize her participation in politics, as well as an affirmation of her own religious beliefs. Amal, and others before her (Badran 1996), subvert the conservative gender discourses of political Islamists in order to secure their presence in the public sphere.

Whilst dominant political actors seek to control and discipline women's bodies in public in order to display or prove their authentic Islamic credentials, underwrite their claims to authority in the New Libya and assert Libyan sovereignty, simultaneously women in the above examples disrupt these efforts through their bodily performances in public (whether riding a bicycle, wearing a certain type of dress or standing as a candidate for prime minister). Moreover, they legitimize their presence in public not through recourse to universal human rights or women's rights conventions, but through resignifying dominant religious and nationalist discourses and notions of national 'authenticity'.

Conclusion

As markers of nations and political communities, the redisciplining of women's bodies and reconfiguration of gender relations has been central to the political transition process in Libya. During the 42 years of Muammar Gaddafi's rule, women's presence in public was promoted as part of the regime's 'revolutionary ideology', even whilst women's sexuality was controlled as part of the regime's claims to 'Islamic identity'. During the seven months of the uprising against Gaddafi, women were celebrated as the wives, mothers and sisters of those who took up arms against the regime.

Since the fall of Gaddafi, politicians, state institutions and non-state militias are engaged in disciplining women's bodies in order to mark the new Libya from the old Libya and assert national sovereignty in the wake of Western military support against the former regime. They fight their political battles on the bodies of Libyan women and central to these battles is women's behaviour in public as well as new controls on women's sexuality, justified by conservative readings of Islam. Campaigns against CEDAW and for obligatory 'Islamic' dress for women and the silencing of women parliamentarians and women professionals through intimidation and violence are all part of controlling and disciplining women's bodies. Women's bodies are instrumentalized to mark the New Libya and its 'Islamic identity' as well as sites where competing political forces display their 'Islamic credentials' to underwrite their claims to authority and to discredit Western intervention in Libyan affairs to promote 'gender equality'.

Despite these challenges, women find ways to maintain their presence in the public sphere as a necessary means of ensuring their continued participation in building the New Libya. Their agency goes beyond dichotomous discourses of equality versus complementarity or authentic versus foreign gender norms and involves resignifying and subverting dominant discourses. In effect, Libyan women's bodies are not only objects of discipline and control but also 'sites of dissent and revolution' (Hafez 2014: 172).

Much of the existing literature on women, gender and political transformations tends to focus on women's engagement with political institutions (constitutions, laws, legislatures and so on) and the degree to which the latter recognizes 'women's interests'. The case of Libya demonstrates that political institutions have yet to become welcoming to women and the relatively small number of women who attempt to engage with them face significant challenges in the form of intimidation, threats of violence and delegitimization. However, current literature on political transformations has generally ignored the significance of women's agency in the public sphere more broadly. Our chapter illustrates that women attempt to shape political transformations through their bodily performances in the public sphere, by resignifying religious and nationalist discourses in order to reimagine women as equal citizens in the New Libya.

Notes

1. These reservations were: 'Article 2 of the Convention shall be implemented with due regard for the peremptory norms of the Islamic *Shariah* relating to determination of the inheritance portions of the estate of a deceased person, whether female or male . . . The implementation of paragraph 16 (c) and (d) of the Convention shall be without prejudice to any of the rights guaranteed to women by the Islamic *Shariah*' (Libyan Arab Jamahariya 1995).
2. The Sanussia Order was a Sufi missionary order first established in Mecca in the early nineteenth century and which spread to eastern Libya, where it gained political legitimacy during the Italian occupation of Libya through its resistance to the occupation. King Idriss Sanussi ruled Libya from 1950 until 1969. For more on the history of the Sanussi family, see Martin 1986; Sammut 1994; Takeyh 2000.
3. For further discussion of the relationship between the Gaddafi regime and political Islam, see Takeyh 1998.
4. For further details of Libya's post-revolution political environment, see Lacher 2013.
5. The Martyrs Bloc was formed at the end of January 2013 'to pursue the specific goals of ensuring the election of a Constitutional Committee and the direct election of provincial governors and mayors, as well as push for the law of "political exclusion" (*al-'Azl al-Siyasi*), which would bar Gaddafi-era officials from positions in politics, business, administration and the security organs' (Lacher 2013: 12).
6. For details of the Egyptian Muslim Brotherhood's objections to the UN recommendations to end violence against women, see Hoda Elsadda 2013.
7. *Wilayah* in the mainstream interpretation of Islam is the power held by male members of the family over female members.
8. The Grand Mufti, in general, advocates for a mandated 'Islamic dress code' for women (Dar Al-Ifta 2012; Eshahed 2013; *Al Arabiya* 2013a), as well as for total sex segregation in public spaces, including schools, universities and the workplace. In addition, al-Ghriani urged the Ministry of Social Affairs to prohibit the marriage of Libyan women to non-Libyan men, for fear of 'the spread of the Shi'i sect' in Libya (*Al Arabiya* 2013b).
9. EI, interview, 16 January 2013.
10. For Antonio Gramsci, hegemony is exercised through consensus backed by coercion (Gramsci 1971: 261). In this case, rival political groups seek hegemony over one another through forging a consensus backed by coercion.
11. Such an election system is known as the 'zipper quota' or 'zebra list', in which women make up fifty per cent of all party lists and would be positioned at the top of the party list. Article 15 of the election law mandates that candidates should alternate genders on the lists and that half of all the lists of a party must have a female at the top. Only two-fifths of the Congress's 200 members were

elected through party lists, with the remaining three-fifths elected as independent constituency representatives (HNEC 2012).

12. The description of the NFA as 'liberal' is a misnomer. As a coalition, it includes some individuals who may be considered liberal. However, many NFA members are committed to shariah as a basis of legislation (see Lacher 2013: 10–11).

13. FB, member of NFA, interview, 24 February 2013.

14. ZT, interview, 28 February 2013.

15. When Sahar asked the female members about this incident, they said that most of them left the GNC Assembly before the *salafi* brother had made his comments and the only two female members who witnessed the incident were shocked and did not feel they could reply without discussing the matter with the rest of the female members.

16. On 25 June 2014, Salwa Bugaghuis, a lawyer and activist, was shot dead in her house after returning from the polling station, having cast her vote in the 2014 parliamentarian elections. On 17 July of the same year, Friha Barkawi, a member of parliament, was shot dead in her car.

17. Interview, 10 June 2013.

18. In Islam, a *mahram* is the son, brother, father, grandfather, uncle or husband of a woman.

19. Interview, 20 February 2014.

20. See www.facebook.com/pages/Fridays-bike/326642487433615?fref=ts (accessed 21 June 2014).

21. Interview, 23 June 2014.

22. On 19 May 2014, General Khalifa Hifter launched the 'Dignity Operation' ('*amaliyat al-karama*) to fight the political Islamist group Ansar Al-Shariah, allegedly responsible for the assassination of over 500 army members and activists in Benghazi.

23. Azza Maghur is a lawyer and expert in constitutional law, who enjoys great respect from her male colleagues and many politicians because of her knowledge and professionalism. In February 2014, she was appointed as the only woman among 14 men to the 17 February Committee to draft the new constitution.

24. Azza Maghur, interview, 20 March 2014.

25. According to one blogger, lamenting Libyan women's abandonment of the traditional *farashiya* in favour of the black *abaya* and/or *niqab*, the garment 'is a white sheet, often woven out of silk that is worn in such a way that it covers the whole body, usually leaving only one eye peeking out. It's a useful garment that can be used as a quick cover up when a woman wants to go out and also offers protection from the hot north African sun'. Interestingly, one of the respondents on her page remarks that the *farashiya* is not in fact a traditional North African garment but was introduced to the region by the Ottomans (KhadijaTeri 2010). Nevertheless, the *farashiya* is certainly considered today to be 'authentic' Libyan dress for women.

26. Interview, Tripoli, Libya, 20 February 2014.

References

Al-Ali, N. (2005) 'Reconstructing Gender: Iraqi Women between Dictatorship, War, Sanctions and Occupation', *Third World Quarterly*, 26 (4), pp. 733–52.

Al-Ali, N. (2012) 'Gendering the Arab Spring', *Middle East Journal of Culture and Communication*, 5 (1), pp. 26–31.

Al-Ali, N., and N. Pratt. (2009) *What Kind of Liberation? Women and the Occupation of Iraq*, University of California Press, Berkeley.

Al Arabiya (2013a) 'Masadir Libiya tanfisihat wa thiqat 'an muraqabat al-malabis al-dakhiliya al-nisa'iya', 13 May. Available at: http://arabic.arabianbusiness. com/society/culture-society/2013/may/13/331378/#.UhPunpM1iP8 (accessed on 14 May 2013). (Arabic).

Al Arabiya (2013b) 'Libyan Women Should be Banned from Marrying Foreigners: Grand Mufti', 28 March. Available at: http://english.alarabiya.net/en/News/middle-east/2013/03/28/Libyan-women-should-be-banned-from-marrying-foreigners-Grand-Mufti.html (accessed on 28 March 2013).

Alvarez, S. E. (1990) *Engendering Democracy in Brazil: Women's Movements in Transition Processes*, Princeton University Press, Princeton.

Badran, M. (1996) *Feminists, Islam and Nation: Gender and the Making of Modern Egypt*. Princeton University Press, Princeton.

Benthurraa (2013) 'Fatat harakat qalam tarud 'ala al-'amaniyat' [video]. Available at: www.youtube.com/watch?v=ZKHLj7VkOe8 (accessed on 15 March 2013).

CSW (Commission on the Status of Women) (2013) 'The Elimination and Prevention of All Forms of Violence Against Women and Girls: Agreed Conclusions'. Available at: www.un.org/womenwatch/daw/csw/csw57/CSW57_Agreed_Conclusions_(CSW_report_excerpt).pdf (accessed on 15 March 2013).

Dar Al-Ifta [online] (2012). Available at: http://ifta.ly/web/index.php/2012-09-04-09-55-16/2012-10-16-13-04-01/905-2013-01-22-13-47-30 (accessed 21 June 2014) (Arabic).

Elsadda, H. (2013) 'A War Against Women: The CSW Declaration and the Muslim Brotherhood Riposte', *openDemocracy*, 3 April. Available at: www.opendemocracy. net/5050/hoda-elsadda/war-against-women-csw-declaration-and-muslim-brotherhood-riposte (accessed on 13 June 2014).

Enloe, C. (1990) 'Womenandchildren: Making Feminist Sense of the Persian Gulf War', *The Village Voice*, 25 September.

Eshahed (2013) 'Infirad mufti Libya yatlub manhahu al-raqaba' la al-malabis al-dakhiya li-l-nisa'. Available at: www.eshahed.com/site/main/view_news/14883 (accessed on 1 June 2013). (Arabic).

Freedom House (2005) 'Women's Rights in the Middle East and North Africa – Libya', 14 October. Available at: www.refworld.org/docid/47387b6dc.html (accessed 19 June 2014).

Gramsci, A. (1971) *Selections from the Prison Notebooks*, trans./ed. by Quinton Hoare and Geoffrey Nowell-Smith, Lawrence and Wishart, London.

Grant, G. (2012) 'Jalil in Headscarf Controversy as First Row Erupts at National Congress', *Libya Herald*, 9 August. Available at Shabab Libya: www.shabablibya.org/news/jalil-in-headscarf-controversy-as-first-row-erupts-at-national-congress (accessed on 13 June 2014).

Hafez, S. (2014) 'The Revolution Shall Not Pass through Women's Bodies: Egypt, Uprising and Gender Politics', *The Journal of North African Studies*, 19 (2), pp. 172–85.

Hilsum, L. (2012) 'Is That What We Fought For? Gaddafi's Legacy for Libyan Women', *openDemocracy*, 6 April. Available at: www.opendemocracy.net/5050/lindsey-hilsum/is-that-what-we-fought-for-gaddafis-legacy-for-libyan-women (accessed on 13 June 2014).

HNEC (The High National Elections Commission) (2012). Available at: http://hnec.ly/?lang=en (accessed on 2 May 2012).

Human Rights Watch (2006) *Libya: A Threat to Society? Arbitrary Detention of Women and Girls for 'Social Rehabilitation'*, Human Rights Watch, New York.

Kandiyoti, D. (1988) 'Bargaining with Patriarchy', *Gender and Society*, 2 (3), September, pp. 274–90.

Kandiyoti, D. (1991) 'Identity and its Discontents: Women and the Nation', *Millennium: Journal of International Studies*, 20 (3), pp. 429–33.

KhadijaTeri [blog] (2010) 'Throwing Tradition to the Wind', 10 April. Available at: http://khadijateri.blogspot.co.uk/2010/04/throwing-tradition-to-wind.html (accessed on 8 June 2014).

Lacher, W. (2013) *Fault Lines of the Revolution: Political Actors, Camps and Conflicts in the New Libya*, SWP Research Paper, German Institute for International and Security Affairs, Berlin. Available at: www.swp-berlin.org/fileadmin/contents/products/research_papers/2013_RP04_lac.pdf (accessed on 13 June 2014).

Libya Almostakbal (2011) 'Al-thawar fi libya yutalibuna bi-timthil bi nisba 40% fi-l-majlis al-intiqali', 27 December. Available at: www.libya-al-mostakbal.org/news/clicked/16804 (accessed on 4 January 2014).

Libyan Arab Jamahariya (1995) 'Declarations, Reservations and Objections to CEDAW'. Available at: www.un.org/womenwatch/daw/cedaw/reservations-country.htm (accessed on 13 June 2014).

McConnell, D., and B. Todd (2011) 'Libyan Leader's Embrace of Sharia Raises Eyebrows' CNN Online, 26 October, http://edition.cnn.com/2011/10/26/world/africa/libya-sharis/ (accessed 13 June 2014).

Martin, B. G. (1986) *Moslem Brotherhoods in Nineteenth-Century Africa*, Cambridge University Press, Cambridge.

Al-Obeidi, A. (2007) Remarks made to Al-Mu'tamar al-Awal li-l-Siyassat al-'Ama fi Libya (the First National Conference for Public Policy in Libya) [online], Garunis University, Benghazi. Available at: http://archive.libya-al-mostakbal.org/Libya%20Internet/June2007/libya_alyawm170607p5alabeedi.htm (accessed 4 January 2015).

Al-Raya (2012) 'Harisat al-Gaddafi: Juwari fi haramlik al-a'aqid', 20 April. Available at: www.raya.com/site/topics/article.asp?cu_no=2&item_no=

637897&version=1&template_id=47&parent_id=42 (accessed on 4 January 2014).

Sammut, D. (1994) 'Libya and the Islamic Challenge', The World Today, 50 (10), pp. 198–200. Available at: www.jstor.org/stable/pdfplus/40396547. pdf?acceptTC=true (accessed on 12 June 2012).

Spellman-Poots, K. (2011) 'Women in the New Libya: Challenges Ahead', openDemocracy, 23 December. Available at: www.opendemocracy.net/5050/kathryn-spellman-poots/women-in-new-libya-challenges-ahead (accessed on 13 June 2014).

Takeyh, R. (1998) 'Qadhafi and the Challenge of Militant Islam', The Washington Quarterly, 21 (3), pp. 159–72.

Takeyh, R. (2000) 'Qadhafi's Libya and the Prospect of Islamic Succession', Middle East Policy, 7 (2), pp. 154–64.

Tanasuh Foundation (2013) 'Mu'atamar al-mara' ila 'ayn: kalimat al-Sadiq al-Ghriani' [video]. Available at: www.youtube.com/watch?v=DyJAet2-1sI (accessed on 9 March 2013).

United Nations (2011) Convention on the Elimination of All Forms of Discrimination Against Women. Available at: www.un.org/womenwatch/daw/cedaw/cedaw.htm (accessed on 19 November 2011).

Waylen, G. (2007) Engendering Transitions: Women's Mobilization, Institutions and Gender Outcomes, Oxford University Press, Oxford.

Young, I. M. (2003) 'The Logic of Masculinist Protection: Reflections on the Current Security State', Signs: Journal of Women in Culture and Society, 29 (1), pp. 1–25.

Yuval-Davis, N. (1997) Gender and Nation, Sage, London.

PART III

Gender and the Construction of the Secular/ Islamic Binary

SEVEN

Islamic Feminism and the Equivocation of Political Engagement

'Fair is foul, and foul is fair'

Omaima Abou-Bakr

Introduction

The recent rise and fall of the Islamist rule in Egypt calls for reflection, not just on the role of Islamic feminist ideas in society, but also on the shifting political grounds and questions of ethical and principled opposition. The presentation of this subject does not take the approach of the usual secular/Islamist binary or a criticism of secular liberalism, but is rather focused on a critique of any feminist movement, be it secular or Islamic, that allows itself to be co-opted and silenced by corrupt political regimes. I attempt to conceptualize and articulate an ethical politics for the Islamic feminist trend, not necessarily or not only defined by its contrast to secular or liberal feminism in Arab context. The Islamic feminist orientation in Egypt so far has been mainly concerned with areas of discourse and religious knowledge, critiquing patriarchal interpretations and advocating feminist justice within and through Islam. In other words, it began as a theological and knowledge project with definite potential of being a useful resource for legal reform for women, but lacked a strong activist dimension. Therefore, I argue that if Islamic (not 'political Islamist') feminists wish to

grow and develop into a conscientious social and activist movement –
especially in this region at this historical juncture – they need to take
stands vis-à-vis the politics and ethics of both the religious establishment and the ruling regime.

This chapter, in its first part, will discuss the general issue of the
precarious relationship between feminists and the state, especially
in the modern Egyptian context, and, in its second part, will look
into the moral ambiguities associated with Islamic feminism's political stands. A quick look at the background of modern European state
feminism provides not necessarily a perfect standard to emulate, but
an opportunity to think about the differentiation that democratic or
non-democratic contexts create in relation to a feminist movement's
ability to voice opposition freely. A situation in which women bargain
with the state, at the expense of ignoring fundamental violations and
corruptions and only for limited and gender-specific gains, constitutes
an ethically distorted form of state feminism.

Women's Movements and the State

A number of studies have been recently produced to outline a theory
of state feminism, perceived generally as women's activism – in pursuit of change and reform on the ground – working in collaboration
with policy makers and state agencies (Adams 2007; McBride and
Mazur 2010). Women's policy agencies are state-based institutions or
councils established to promote women's rights and gender equality.
State feminism as an overarching concept was introduced in 1987 by
Helga Hermes in the course of studying the Scandinavian model of
the proactive role of the welfare state, taking measures to incorporate
female citizens as effective participants in public life. Hermes defines
state feminism as 'a variety of public policies and organizational measures, designed partly to solve general social and economic problems,
partly to respond to women's demands' (Hermes 1987: 11). Since the
1990s, researching the application of this notion became increasingly
focused on the specific work of these government structures and state
actors and on analyzing 'whether the structures are actually effective

in making the state more inclusive of women and their interests'
(McBride and Mazur 2010: 5). These studies in general argue two
main points: using the criteria of women's inclusiveness and gender
mainstreaming to measure and judge the acceptable performance of
the state in this area; and, at the same time, maintaining that wom-
en's movements can be more successful when they forge alliances in
strategies and policy goals – a 'successful agency-movement alliance'
(McBride and Mazur 2010: 5).

Joyce Outshoorn (1994), who first coined the label 'femocrats'
to describe those individuals working in bureaucratic and state agencies to promote women's rights and improve their conditions, gives
a general positive assessment in her analysis of the phenomenon by
maintaining that feminist bureaucracies are on the whole equipped
to transform the goals of the women's movement to actual concrete
public policies. Yet, even within the general tendency of the literature on the subject to view the state–movement alliance as useful and
impactful, the issue of whether the women's movement can be autonomous at times and in alliance with governments at other times is
raised (Outshoorn 2010). Acknowledgement of the changing political contexts and specific national environments becomes an essential
factor in studying the diverse state and governmental machineries in
considering both the opportunities and challenges for agencies and
women's movements to co-operate and mobilize (Outshoorn and
Kantola 2007).

In other words, theorizing state feminism as a successful phenomenon depends on a specific political and social context that can allow
for women's movements to maintain independence and free determination of the extent and scope of alliance with governments and
regimes. Hence, we find other research that casts doubt on the traditional positive outlook of the complete success of state feminism
(especially as it had originated within the Nordic welfare state model)
by referring to the uneasy relationship between official femocrats and
activists, one that can be characterized by confrontation and competition rather than co-operation (Valiente 1997). This precarious relationship or tension between 'women working from inside and outside

government' is expressed succinctly by Marian Sawer (within her general assessment of welfare public policies versus market rationalization in three specific countries):

> Women's policy machinery is the daughter of the women's movement and there is an in-built tension in this relationship. Women's policy units are accountable to government and not just to the women's movement, meaning that conflicts of interest and perspective are inevitable. Femocrats must demonstrate loyalty to government in order to be credible in their policy advice; policy brokering involves compromises even if this leads to accusations of co-option. (Sawer 1996: ii)

The above references are samples of empirical studies conducted to gauge the impact and success of state feminism across Europe and as part of the apparatus of diverse established Western democracies. They focus on specific measures and policies undertaken by the state within the 'process of making democracies more democratic' (McBride and Mazur 2010: 3). Not only so, but they also suggest that such feminist government action points to a significant political and social development of making states more overtly feminist (Mazur 2002). The situation in a country like Egypt – pre and post the January 2011 Revolution – is different, more complex and unstable.

State Feminism in Egypt

The relationship between women's movements and the state in the Arab region, and in Egypt in particular, is complicated by a modern history of colonialism and national struggle for independence. Ellen Fleischmann (1999) gives a comprehensive overview of the history and political environment of the modern emergence of a women's movement in Egypt in the first half of the twentieth century. She outlines three consecutive stages: first, the 'awakening' period or the beginning of public and intellectuals' attention to women's issues around the turn of the twentieth century, also marked by the formation of women's organizations and spread of women's journals; second, women in the arena of the nationalist movement for independence and the struggle against British colonial power; third, the period of state policies in advancing formal gender equity in education and work in the public sector. Her analysis shows, however, that there seems to be a historical pattern that characterizes national struggle movements and the building of independent states following libera-tion: newly established governing regimes or states tend to sideline women's specific demands and inclusiveness and do not automatically grant women their due rights, even as acknowledgement of their roles within the struggle for emancipation.

Indeed several scholars specializing in studying the evolution of women's movements in the Arab region or the greater Middle East had noticed this historical irony of women serving the cause of national-ism, only to be forsaken by it later (Baron 1991: 272). Both Deniz Kandiyoti (1991) and Anne McClintock (1991) have also revealed in their writings the falseness of women's assumptions that achieving the goal of a strong, independent and modern national state leads natu-rally to their emancipation and equal citizenship rights. Further, the expectation of the state being the source of active implementation of progressive gender policies may be a misplaced trust on the part of women. Analysis of the attitude and policies of states like Turkey and Iran – at the peak of both regimes' modernization and secularization projects in the first half of the twentieth century – shows that the state, in encouraging women's rights and public participation, is never a disinterested party. States in this context of consolidating ideologies and regimes tend to use women's cause as a political tool or card to demonstrate to the outside world the face of a 'modern, democratic, inclusive' state, while bargaining with the local women's movement for an exchange of interests and gains.

It was Mervat Hatem (1994) who focused her analysis on this para-doxical relationship that has existed between the women's movement and the Egyptian state since the 1950s. In this case, 'state feminism' has been both a blessing and a curse: overall, women may have ben-efitted from state policies in promoting education, work and public participation, as part of its nation-building citizenry project, but it has been at the expense of women's autonomy. During Nasser's regime (1952–1970), the state adopted policies similar in some ways to the Scandinavian welfare state model in supporting women's inclusiveness in its social, economic, political, health and educational programmes, as working citizens in the service of the state's progress. Women were given the right to vote, to be part of the labour force, to be appointed in office and various other government positions in the public sector. However, Hatem's (1999) comparative research has also shown that this 'type' of state feminism (for example, in Turkey) – when post-colonial regimes adopt a top-down totalizing, modernizing project or aim to enforce its political legitimacy – links women's rights to the changing political interests of the state and determines the priorities and demands of women for them. Hence, in their sole reliance on the state for formal gender equity policies, especially in the public sphere, the women's movement tends to lose its independence and control over its own agenda of more reform in other spheres.

Another drawback of this kind of state–movement association in the specific case of a country like Egypt, as it moved from Nasser's era to that of Sadat (1970–1981) and Mubarak (1981–2011), is the price of possible co-option. Though the state's withdrawal from welfare services and other social support through its adoption of the free economy policy since 1974 led to its encouragement of non-governmental and charity organizations to work as alternative civil institutions to official policies, it was still wary of these NGOs' potential political confrontation. Heba Raouf (2001) monitors the developments in the relationship between the women's movements and feminist organizations (designated by her as clearly secularist) and the state during the 1990s in particular, the decade that witnessed the two major United Nations conferences on women – the ICPD (International Conference on Population and Development) and Beijing. Raouf argues that Islamist women's activism is more authentic and grassroots, whilst the elitist and secularist feminist activists engage in a bargaining game with the government. From this pro-Islamist perspective, her analysis shows that government crackdown on Islamists and its public hostility to their discourses created a 'golden opportunity for the secularists to attack Islamists harshly on the issue of women, to appear as supporters of women's rights, and to accuse the Islamists . . . of being the major threat to the women's cause' (Raouf 2001: 250). Anxious for the state's approval of their agenda, major women's associations and groups would not wish to confront or oppose the regime: 'This automatically put the main bulk of secularists and feminist circles on the side of the government, yet the price was that they had to keep silent about the violations of human rights committed by the state in the process' (ibid.). In this context, Raouf views the formation of the National Council of Women (NCW) by a presidential decree in the year 2000 and the appointment of well-chosen names for its members as a measure of allocation of power – a tool of bargaining and rewarding the supporters and allies of the state.

While that view is characterized by generalization and exaggerated bias against *all* non-Islamic women feminist activists, it nevertheless directs attention to the potential trap of a close association with the regime, particularly when it is authoritarian and undemocratic. This inherently flawed dimension of a women's movement–state collaboration (mainly in the form of the NCW operating directly under the auspices and supervision of Suzanne Mubarak) increased the public perception of this movement as an ally of a corrupt and oppressive regime, hence undermining its legitimacy, relevancy and support. That is why this form of 'state feminism' proved its fragility upon the ousting of Mubarak by the January 2011 Revolution and became vulnerable, during the following transitional period, to reactionary voices calling for withdrawing some of the legal gains achieved during the previous regime.

'Combating the shadow of the First Lady syndrome' is how Hoda Elsadda (2011) expressed a major obstacle to be faced by women's rights activists in the period immediately following the January Revolution. As a result of the above-mentioned situation, what has developed throughout the past decade is 'a prevalent public perception that associates women's rights activists and their activities with the ex-First Lady, Suzanne Mubarak, and her entourage – that is, with corrupt regime politics in collusion with imperialist agendas' (Elsadda 2011: 86).

Yet, Elsadda rightly refutes this false assumption by carefully outlining how such legislative changes were in fact the direct outcome of a long process of women activists' struggles, separate from the First Lady's desire to appropriate women's issues for her public image and from the more officially publicized activities of the NCW's femocrats.

Though I have been posing the association and collaboration with corrupt states or regimes as problematic and as given to abuse, to discredit any reform efforts by the majority of women activists is the other side of political manipulation, which is also rejected. Elsadda documents the situation that immediately arose beginning April 2011 of calls to rescind the specific legal changes that had been passed in the preceding decade within Personal Status Law to improve some legal positions of women in marriage and divorce procedures. Such calls came from both the Islamist and non-Islamist camps at the time by politicians aiming to invalidate women's gains and even malign the whole feminist movement under the pretext of voicing due attacks on the fallen regime and righting situations after the revolution. The article goes on to show that, despite the efforts of women's rights activists in the complicated domain of legal reform, the visible outcome at the very end of this process would still be determined by the First Lady's endorsement and political leverage (Elsadda 2011: 93), in effect hijacking the issue. Public antagonism and complete rejection of the NCW on the part of independent women activists may have not been possible at the time of Mubarak's rule, yet most harboured the awareness that the Council 'competed with existing women's organization, sought to appropriate women's activism and work, and tried to monopolize speaking on behalf of all women' (ibid.).

During the transitional period of the control of the Supreme Council of the Armed Forces (SCAF) in 2011, and in the spirit of revolutionary changes, there were calls by women activists to restructure and democratize the NCW to transform it from an institution run by state-appointed officials or bureaucrats to an entity representing civil society demands. Yet despite the public debates over this and the new suggestions of reformulating the state's relationship with women activists and NGOs, the developments of this turbulent year and a half (until mid-2012), which included the rise of criticism and outcries of women against the violent practices and aggression of SCAF's policies towards women protestors and demonstrators, put an end to this endeavour. Nevertheless, '[t]his push to explore new forms of organization indicates that the state's institutional relationship to women – one that has allowed the former to dominate the latter in exchange for some concessions – has been significantly challenged' (Hatem 2011: 38). It is true that since the January Revolution, 'activist Egyptian women have expressed a clear desire to distance themselves from the institutional and political legacies of state feminism' (ibid.: 41), yet I argue that this was clearer during the time of SCAF's governments and the one-year term of Mohammed Morsi's rule, but not in the period following the 3 July military intervention.

Women's groups and activists did not refrain from voicing opposition and dissent against both SCAF's violations of human rights and use of oppressive measures and the Muslim Brotherhood's push for policies based on a conservative, regressive gender ideology. During the latter's rule, even the NCW of the time dissociated its campaign of women's rights promotion from the ideas and policies of the existing government and the presidential institution's attempts to impose its agenda. This confrontation was clear during the 57th United Nations Commission on the Status of Women (CSW) in March 2013. Though the head of the NCW, Ambassador Dr Mervat Al-Tellawi, would traditionally represent the Egyptian government in this international forum, President Morsi dispatched his appointed presidential assistant for political affairs, Dr Pakinam Al-Sharqawi, to head that year's delegation and deliver an official speech on women's issues from the new regime's perspective, in a move that was clearly meant to pull the rug from under the CSW delegate and to undermine its representational status. Dr Al-Tellawi did not attend the talk so as not to be considered in automatic agreement with Al-Sharqawi's views. However, Al-Sharqawi went ahead to announce that Egypt was joining a cross-regional coalition of seventeen countries protesting the unconditioned passing of the UN declaration on violence against women on account of respecting and preserving cultural and religious specificities. Al-Tellawi's position was unambiguously defiant, as she ignored this intended official policy by the Egyptian government and announced that the CSW delegate would nevertheless join international consensus on the UN document that sets global standards for action to prevent violence against women. That year's theme of violence against women was particularly relevant to the growing problem of violence and sexual assaults on women demonstrators, which had developed during the reign of SCAF and continued under Morsi's rule. Women activists and initiatives were very outspoken in exposing this phenomenon as a systematic state policy (perpetrated by the police and security forces in control of the streets and public spaces) to intimidate women and end their participation in street protest movements (Abd Al-Hamid and Ahmad 2014; Langohr 2014). Al-Tellawi even included in her paper that she presented at a panel in the CSW a clear condemnation of these violent practices, calling them 'a new political weapon . . . to assault them and frighten them from taking part in demonstrations' (Al-Tellawi 2013: 3).[1] When the Muslim Brotherhood and the International Union for Muslim Scholars released a very strong statement denouncing the UN declaration for going against Egyptian cultural and religious values, the NCW responded promptly to refute these claims and women activists were also public in criticizing and rejecting this path of the Egyptian state's official policy in undermining women's activism towards more equal rights.

The purpose of the above account is to highlight the difference between the actions of the NCW and the women's movement during SCAF's rule and the MB's regime, which manifested resistance to state control over the women's cause in both periods, and after. A shift took place following the 3 July 2013 military intervention. In a well-publicized and widely covered international press conference held by the NCW, headed by Al-Tellawi, Sakina Fouad (the newly appointed president's councillor on women's affairs), and Tahani al-Gibali (ex-vice president of the constitutional court, known for her support of SCAF's policies, hence previously criticized by various women groups and activists), the main objective of the event was clearly political. Held less than a week after the government's 14 August 2013 violent disbanding of the Rabia sit-in camp, the conference, in a very hasty and premature move, presented the speakers as the sole representatives of the women's movement's position, speaking in the name of all Egyptian women (Ramadan 2013). They expressed total support and approval of the regime, especially justifying the actions of the armed forces and the 'national' police in the latest Rabia mass killings. Ironically, Al-Tellawi is quoted commenting on the just-ousted Muslim Brotherhood (MB) regime that 'women were treated *brutally* [emphasis added] by the MB'. The speakers also lambasted the West for their criticism of the Egyptian government's violent acts and measures against a huge sector of the Egyptian people. An official NCW statement was issued and read by Al-Tellawi, entitled 'Women Against Violence and Terrorism', in which full support of the armed forces and police was emphasized and a demand was made in the name of 'the Egyptian woman' to put the MB on the international list of terrorist organizations.

This early press conference would initiate a new stage in the relationship between various women activists and groups and the new military-backed Egyptian government/regime. With the exception of a few opposition feminist and human rights groups, as well as a small number of conscientious women activist figures, I am claiming that there is a noticeable shift, or rather a turning back, to the previous pre-January Revolution situation of the NCW and its associates and collaborators keeping silent about the state's violations of human rights and participating in its 'illiberal democracy'. In a position paper produced recently by three independent NGOs (The Women and Memory Forum, The Egyptian Initiative for Personal Rights, Nazra for Feminist Studies) for a joint presentation at the 58th United Nations CSW of March 2014, this issue of the independence of women's and civil society's NGOs vis-à-vis the state was briefly but succinctly raised. It was noted, as an example, how, despite the increase in reports of sexual assaults and torture perpetrated by members of the police and security forces and in the police detainment centres, the NCW completely ignored the outcries of the few activist groups about it and refrained from issuing any statements that might implicate the deliberate practices and policies of the Ministry of the Interior. This raises questions about the political biases of the NCW, its association with the state's 3 July regime and its dissociation from the urgent concerns of the women's movement. During an official signing of a protocol of co-operation between the NCW and the Ministry of the Interior in September 2013, in which the latter announced intent to set up a special unit of human rights to combat violence against women, Al-Tellawi thanked both the current and previous interior ministers, refusing to put the responsibility of returning security only on the police's shoulders. She went on to praise the police, saying that it 'came back to the people; the gap between the police and the people ended after the revolution of 30 June' (Al-'Issawi 2013). This affirmation was not based on evidence on the ground, rather on a pre-intent to declare unconditional and unjustified support for the authority and practices of the security forces.

Another example mentioned in the report is the role played by the NCW in campaigning and mobilizing women across the country to vote in support of the new 2014 constitution, thus influencing and directing them towards a set political goal, instead of undertaking the responsibility of raising awareness on the importance of political participation and free choice based on understanding and analysis. Hence, the fact that the NCW continues to be a state-sponsored institution under the direct auspices of the presidency seriously undermines its independence, especially in the area of political engagement and decisions. A negative result seems to be the NCW functioning mainly as a propaganda tool for the regime, rather than supporting women in their lived realities and crises, as well as protecting them against any form of abuse – domestic, public, institutional or state. During a conference held by the NCW on 24 May 2014 to publicize the success of the presidential elections and women's participation, Al-Tellawi created an overly dramatic scene when she dismissed two attending members of the EU Election Observation Mission, rejecting their report as reflecting animosity towards Egypt, accusing them of falsifying and interfering in Egypt's internal affairs – 'You are out of the Middle East' (El-Banna 2014). The audience cheered this demonstration of a patriotic act against 'Western conspirators', in accordance with the dominant political climate.

As breaches of human rights, violent practices by the police, reported torture, random arrests and illegal measures by the prosecution authorities continued in 2014, there were no references to this situation by the NCW during the 58th United Nations CSW in March 2014. The defiance and independence that characterized the NCW's position during the previous year – going against the Egyptian state government at the time – was considerably softened to a general campaign against conservatism everywhere, in a noticeable evasion of the more relevant and pressing issues (Lederer 2014). While the council is indeed pursuing goals that will benefit women and help promote their rights and is duly participating in international policymaking to implement reform, it has also reverted to its old comfortable position of a state-loyal institution that will not criticize oppressive practices, even if they are against women's and men's human rights as well as democratic and political freedoms. In a newspaper article, Dr Neveen Mos'ad, a political science academic, column writer and a prominent member of the NCW, records and comments favourably on Sisi's symbolic meeting with the Council during his short presidential campaign. After presenting what she describes as an objective summary of the dialogue – which did not touch on any of the reports at that time of random arrests, collective mistreatment in police stations and sexual violence in police custody – she ends the article by a brief recommendation directed at the candidate 'to invest in education, then you'll find every mother standing behind you' (Mos'ad 2014).

If such deliberate overlooking of defective discourses and policy malfunctions can be justified as a political necessity at this stage, an ethically empowered Islamic feminist position should take a different approach. The principles of both feminism and Qur'anic moral imperatives require an honest critical outlook on forms of injustice, based on achieving a high level of moral conscientiousness and practice. In this regard, the Qur'an states: 'O you who believe, stand firmly for justice, as witnesses for God, even if it means testifying against yourselves, or your parents, or your kin, and whether it is against the rich or poor, for God prevails upon all. Follow not the lusts of your hearts, lest you swerve, and if you distort justice or decline to do justice, verily God knows what you do' (Q 4: 135) (Quoted in Abou El Fadl 2002: 14).[2] Rejection of injustice and political hypocrisy and deception is important, even if it means at the least refraining from directly aiding and participating in these 'silent' state institutions.

Islamic Feminism and the Changing Political Context

During Mubarak's reign, especially in the last ten years before the January 2011 Revolution, the state-adopted public political campaign was a call for 'the renewal of religious discourse', with the implied message that it was the Islamist ideology that prevented a complete enlightened modernization of civil society. This meant that the authorities did not see a threat in views that adopted a 'moderate', non-resistant and non-politicized Islamic discourse, as they were focused on restraining MB aggressive ideology of Islamic polity and governance. Hence, feminist researchers working in the field could, and did, present apolitical treatments of women's issues in Islam, and so were perceived and categorized as conveniently 'enlightened' and 'safe'. However, the situation was always ambiguous and uncomfortably vague: security and state authorities kept a close watch on human rights and women's NGOs – in addition to journalists, academics, writers and public figures – to monitor the religious component in their activities and ideas that could potentially cross the line from moderate and tamed to open criticism of state policies. Hence, the state cautiously tolerated views calling for the reform of women's conditions based on 'enlightened' religious arguments, as long as they played a part in undermining political Islam.

The trend that self-identifies as 'Islamic feminism', working for the production of an alternative gendered Islamic knowledge that can play a part in the reform of religious discourses and cultural practices, found itself in an equivocal situation following the rise of political Islamism to power and rule. From the beginning, this project of criticizing theological patriarchy, contesting religious justifications of gender hierarchy and developing gender justice and equality values within Islam's worldview has been about carving an oppositional, intermediate space between fundamentalist secular rejection of religious referencing altogether and religious conservatism. In Egypt, this brand of feminist work, though based on religious arguments and study, has never been a part of political Islamism or the MB's project. Its researchers did not participate in the ideological activism or subscribe to the gender ideas of the Sisters – that is, the active women of the Muslim Brotherhood. As an example, while a pro-MB organization like the International Islamic Committee of Women and Children (*Al-Lagnah al-islamiyah al-'alamiyah lil-mar'ah wa-l-tifl*), headed by Camilia Helmy, promoted the typical conservative views of gender hierarchy, male leadership and anti-feminist sentiments, another group – Women and Civilization – conducted research on women's issues in Islam with the goal of exploring an Islamic, feminist epistemology and a discourse that is critical of both patriarchal interpretations of Islam and secular perspectives. I expressed this newly developed ambiguity of Islamic feminism at the time:

> Today it finds itself in a slightly shifting situation with the Islamic Freedom and Justice party in power. Using 'Islamic-based' arguments and emancipative concepts may have qualified as a form of resistance in the previous context, but now this orientation can be easily perceived as in alignment with the new 'state feminism' or rather the conservative Islamist gender ideology that has characterized MB thought. (Abou-Bakr 2013: 1)

The concern was for this trend of Islamic feminist thought to be falsely perceived as identified with MB Islamist discourses, not as independent feminists with a distinct political and an intellectual stance. The question raised was how they could maintain this independence so as not to enforce the hegemonic claims of the new ruling regime or be used by competing political camps in a game of power struggle. It was a dilemma that necessitated clarifying and stressing a unified oppositional and resistant position:

> To be an Islamic feminist researcher is not to subscribe to right-wing political projects, or to gender-biased interpretations of Islam, or to 'superficializing' *shari'ah*, or to the neo-orientalist

and 'modernist' discourses, or to the Enlightenment-Dark Ages
paradigm, or to the Islamic-civil polarization, or the 'righteous
Salaf' versus the corrupt present. Perhaps more than ever, this is
the time for an alternative self-conscious movement that bridges
the gap between research and knowledge building, on one side,
and activism and public engagement, on the other. (Abou-Bakr
2013: 2)

The statement was meant to combine research and knowledge production interests with a rejection of political opportunism and a compromise of values.

With yet another drastic shifting of political situation and environment, Mohammed Morsi was ousted and MB rule abruptly ended. It is
true that conservative gender views of the MB and outrageous literalist
Salafist discourses (such as condoning female circumcision and under-
age marriage of girls, undermining feminist demands for equality and
combating domestic violence, and blaming women demonstrators
for street and police harassment) have greatly offended and incensed
women – including Islamic feminists – necessitating resistance. However, with the increase in popularity and adulation of General Abdel
Fattah El-Sisi, leader of the ousting, he began to be cast in the public
media as a super-male saviour of Egypt – in turn, cast as a damsel in
distress – carrying her off either on his knight's white horse or as a fly-
ing Superman. These cartoon images were furthered by a number of
newspaper columns and panegyric poems foregrounding this aspect
of masculinity with unmistakable sexualized insinuations, such as references to Egypt's pregnancy by the 'star' of his heroism and Egyptian
women's offering themselves in marriage – or even as concubines –
to him. It is interesting how this constructed 'masculine' image by
the politically biased mainstream media has served also to reinforce
a form of militarized patriarchy. In the 15 January 2014 issue of Al-
Watan – a pro-army, widely circulated newspaper – a headline of the
major story covering the constitutional referendum the previous day
described the long lines of women for the ballots (with special army
forces securing voting centres) as 'Queues of Women in the "Shadow"
of Army Men'. The use of the colloquial Egyptian dill directly alludes

to the much-criticized folk saying: '[living in] the shadow of a man is better than the shadow of a wall'. The saying is understood in popular culture as an endorsement of patriarchal protection, needed under any circumstances for naturally helpless women.

Mistaking this elision of patriarchy and militarism for an inter-preted 'expression of female agency' is an example of feminist analysis gone awry. In a related article, the phenomenon of women 'ululating, clapping and challenging the red lines of female propriety by dancing in broad daylight in public' is read as displays of agency, 'uninhib-ited and unrestrained by patriarchal mores' (Tadros 2014). However, these actions have always been part of very traditional cultural expres-sions of communal celebrating among large sectors of society. This problematic reading does not consider that women dancing and sing-ing to the tune of the notorious song produced immediately after 3 July to glorify the military for its ousting of President Morsi and the MB rule is also a reflection of anti-feminist personality cult revolv-ing around a super-male military hero. A feminist consciousness and perspective should not sacrifice an ethically consistent outlook on political engagement for superficial or temporary outcomes. To avoid a double-standard position, its critique ought to extend to religious and military patriarchy alike. Interestingly, no feminist analysis came forward on Sisi's remarks in media interviews before his presidency regarding the traditional image of women as mainly the mothers and homemakers, whose contribution is signalled by 'turning the lights off' after their kids and not being bothered by the serious public issues of their husbands' work, which of course reinforces the belonging of women to the domestic domain rather than their being equal citizens.

The Politics and Ethics of Islamic Feminism

Does ethics have a place in the political engagement of feminists? I think it should. If feminism's primary mission has always been resist-ing patriarchal authoritarianism and gender injustice, it is also quite pertinent and even more fitting to maintain its opposition to state dic-tatorship and injustices by ruling regimes. If feminism developed out

of exposing and rejecting exclusionary practices, it ought not to yield
to a moral complacency that justifies concern for women's conditions
only and ignores the larger frameworks of monopoly, state violence
and despotism. As a conscionable movement, it can thus be distinguished from a history of institutional patriarchal practices of political
opportunism and authoritarianism. Furthermore, ethical feminism in
that sense should also consider class issues and the needs of poor, marginalized and disempowered women.

Islamic feminist thought is equipped with a holistic worldview of
'lived ethics' that can potentially enrich it to be a principled, consistent oppositional movement against all forms of *zulm* (injustice). In his
study of the tradition and system of ethics in Islam, Amyn Sajoo demonstrates that the ethical perspective is not an abstraction or a purely
philosophical reflection, but 'the practical unfolding of moral principles: ideals and their implications are set forth within the bounds of the
relationship among the individual, society, and the divine' (2004: 2).
Sajoo presents a reading of Muslim ethics as a model in which religious or faith-based ethics is grounded in the lived experiences of
the community (*ummah*) and the moral choices of its individuals and
groups. The 'reasoned accounts of right and wrong' (Sajoo 2004: 4)
are played out on the social canvas and the public. He discusses the
corpus of the leading ethical texts in the classical age of Islam, which
envisioned an integration of personal moral traits (*akhlaq*) and social
refinement (*adab*) for a social purpose and a moral critique of politics.

This kind of social ethics that has a role in public life and polity is
what distinguishes Muslim understanding from the liberal approach to
the public sphere. While the first transcends 'normative rule-making
and compliance' as well as 'instrumental reason that denies the sacred
on the basis of an ideological construction of rationality' (ibid.: 43), the
latter 'privileged an amoral rationality in which ethical norms function
as surrogates either for 'appropriate conduct' (denying any judgment
on the basis of the good), or 'rational conduct' (denying any role for
the sacred)' (ibid.: 44). Sajoo's critique and analysis of liberal praxis is
that, in effect, it reduces the moral content of ethics to mere 'professionalism', polite manners and formal law-abiding conduct. On the other

hand, a religious grounding of social ethics in the public domain is 'not only the handmaiden of the rule of law, but the underlying ethos which gave birth to those entitlements that privilege human dignity and which we now cherish as human rights' (Sajoo 2004: 85).

Both Saba Mahmood and Charles Hirschkind, each through the examining of different social phenomena in Egypt during the 1990s, had argued that the ethical is also political in many ways and that Islamic ethos or sensibility as a motivation does not necessarily mean militant political action or that it is defective from the liberal-progressive perspective towards the notion of free agency. Hirschkind's active 'ethical listening' constitutes the goal of seeking a transformation of the moral being, towards a more perfect moral character as a Muslim. He maintained that cassette sermons are meant to cultivate a certain religious sensibility embedded in ethical and social considerations and that the phenomenon is 'part of a complex ethical and political project whose scope and importance cannot be contained within the neat figure of the militant or terrorist' (Hirschkind 2006: 6). Mahmood has also argued that a proper grasp of the mosque movement's ethical agency and pedagogical nature yields a different interpretation of political agency as well:

> The political efficacy of these movements is . . . a function of the work they perform in the ethical realm – those strategies of cultivation through which embodied attachments to historically specific forms of truth come to be forged. Their political project, therefore, can only be understood through an exploration of their ethical practices. (Mahmood 2005: 35)

While I agree with the above views of valorizing the ethical dimension and its role in a newly conceived 'political' domain, their emphasis is more on private, individual piety and the improvement of moral behaviour/religious conduct that do not necessarily inform public stands or voice objection to public corruptions and injustices.

The above discussion means to link an operational level of ethical principles and the political engagement of feminist activism. It is hoped that Islamic feminism, in particular, sees itself as currently positioned to face the 'unethical' patriarchy and political compromises of religious institutions as well as the state's undemocratic policies and constant attempts at the co-option of both the women's movement and the religious establishment. Khaled Abou El Fadl expresses this intricate relationship succinctly:

> I eschew politics when it is unlawful and eschew law when it is not moral. To the extent that politics is not subject to law, it is reprehensible, and to the extent that law is not subject to morality, it is reprehensible. Reason and compassion, disciplined and guided by the search for the Divine Will, must constitute the essential unity which forms the backbone of politics, law, and morality ... Politics without law is nothing but opportunism, and law without morality is nothing but despotism, and morality unless guided by the Divine Will risks becoming nothing more than a concession to whim. (Abou El Fadl 2006: 84)

Just as Islamic feminists refused to align themselves with the previous MB regime and gender ideology, they should continue their resistance in linking the struggle for gender justice against patriarchal monopoly with opposition to state persecution and violence. Criticism of MB conservative and self-righteous paternalism must continue with criticism of a militarized, masculinist despotism. An Islamic feminist vision is able to underline the convergence of both theological and political authoritarian patriarchy through conceptualizing and invoking specific, relevant ethical tenets: resisting all forms of *zulm* (injustice), *istikbar* (pride) and *baghy/tughian* (transgression) for the pursuit of a holistic *'adl* (justice). These are more than simply the equivalent Arabic words for these meanings, as the systematic recurring of each in specific moral contexts throughout the Qur'an forms together a thematic and conceptual cluster of an Islamic ethos and imperative. The major Qur'anic (favourable) narrative of Queen Sheba's success, cited often by Islamic feminist interpreters to legitimize women's political rule, can also be used in juxtaposition to the Pharaoh's despotic rule to craft a model for an Islamic feminist stance that rejects this male form of political autocracy – from a Qur'anic point of view – while validating women's leadership.[3] A full analysis of the political nuances of these two narratives is beyond the scope of this chapter, but one can find embedded the above-mentioned Qur'anic concepts and themes that can be applied to both political tyranny and patriarchal injustice directed at women. Amina Wadud, for example, in developing the 'Tawhidic paradigm' (oneness/unicity of God in Islam) as a governing, foundational principle in undoing gender hierarchy, reconstructing gender justice and gender relations within Islam, has already referred to its extension to other realms: 'Thus, the overarching concept *tawhid*, or the unicity of Allah, forms a trajectory organizing Islamic social, economic, moral, spiritual, and political systems' (Wadud 2006: 29).

Conclusion

This chapter has presented a critique of the strategy of an unconditional alignment of the women's movement with the state, particularly in the present equivocal Egyptian context of questionable politics. More than just a reservation about the general idea of the state as itself a patriarchal institution either marginalizing or instrumentalizing women, feminists should be wary of the ethical deficit in their activism. If, as presented at the beginning of the chapter, Nordic state feminism is ultimately about the 'process of making democracies more democratic' – enhancing established democracies by increasing women's inclusion and gender mainstreaming, a state feminism that results in legitimizing 'illiberal democracy', hence making an oppressive state more oppressive, ought to be rejected. In its turn, an Islamic feminist current can adopt an ethically informed politics through taking stands that do not condone either state despotism or the religious establishment's hypocrisy and co-option by that state. In the current Egyptian context, those who voice open criticism of some of the state's policies or Al-Azhar, for example, can be easily accused of treason, agency to Western conspiracies, MB membership or terrorism.

In Shakespeare's *Macbeth*, in which the themes of moral vagueness and personal choices complicated by deception and self-deception run through the play, wrong can be easily mistaken for right, and

deliberate equivocation can be the means to detract from a fixed ethical criterion. The Witches' evil trap is mainly based on a web of moral
confusion, where appearance and reality do not correspond (hence
the telling utterance 'fair is foul, and foul is fair'). Thus, the Porter
admits through his imaginary Hell's gate the 'equivocator, that could
swear in both the scales against either scale' (*Macbeth*, Act II, iii), one
who evades a moral commitment. And, in the Qur'an, a major characteristic of the unethical, double-dealing *munafiqin* (hypocrites) is the
fact that they waver (*mudhab-dhabin*) between two positions, not making a sincere, principled commitment to either (*la ila ha'ula' wa-la ha'ula'*:
belonging to neither one group nor the other) (Q 4: 143).

Notes

1. Al-Tellawi's paper was entitled 'Prevention of Violence Against Women in
   Constitution and Nation-Building Processes' (2013). For press reports on these
   events, see: 'Egyptian Delegation to UN Status of Women Commission Criticized'
   (www.dailynewsegypt.com/2013/03/10/egyptian-delegation-to-un-status-
   of-women-commission-crticized/); 'NCW Responds to Muslim Brotherhood
   Statement' (www.dailynewsegypt.com/2013/03/14/ncw-respons-to-muslim-
   brotherhood-statement/); 'NCW Reflects on the UN Declaration on Violence
   Against Women' (www.dailynewsegypt.com/2013/03/21/ncw-reflects-on-
   the-un-declaration-on-violence-against-women/).
2. For a simplified presentation of the Qur'an's basic ethical obligations and general moral thrust, see Abou El Fadl (2002), especially pp. 13–23.
3. For a very useful discussion of the traditional debate over this story and its significance to contemporary Islamic feminist issues, see Reda (2013).

References

Abd Al-Hamid, D., and H. Ahmad (2014) 'Women as Fair Game in the Public
    Sphere: A Critical Introduction for Understanding Sexual Violence and
    Methods of Resistance', *Jadaliyya*, 9 July. Available at: www.jadaliyya.com/
    pages/index/18455/women-as-fair-game-in-the-pblic-sphere_a-critical
    (accessed on 29 July 2014).
Abou-Bakr, O. (2013) 'To Be or Not to Be . . . A Muslim Feminist in the Arab
    (Islamic) Spring', *AMEWS E-Bulletin*, 1, pp. 1–2.
Abou El Fadl, K. (2002) *The Place of Tolerance in Islam*, Beacon Press, Boston.
Abou El Fadl, K. (2006) *The Search for Beauty in Islam*, Rowman & Littlefield Publishers,
    New York.

Adams, M. (2007) 'National Machineries and Authoritarian Politics', *International Journal of Politics*, 9 (2), pp. 176–197.

El-Banna, R. (2014) 'Talawy Dismisses EU EOM Members out of NCW Conference', *The Cairo Post*, 31 May. Available at: www.thecairopost.com/news/113055/news/talawy-dismisses-eu-eom-members-out-of-ncw-confernce (accessed on 11 January 2015).

Baron, B. (1991) 'Mothers, Morality, and Nationalism in Pre-1919 Egypt', in R. Khalidi, ed., *The Origins of Arab Nationalism*, Columbia University Press, New York, pp. 271–88.

Elsadda, H. (2011) 'Women's Rights Activism in Post-Jan 25 Egypt: Combating the Shadow of the First Lady Syndrome in the Arab World', *Middle East Law and Governance*, 3, pp. 84–93.

Fleischmann, E. (1999) 'The Other "Awakening": The Emergence of Women's Movements in the Modern Middle East, 1900–1940', in M. Meriwether and J. Tucker, eds, *Social History of Women and Gender in the Modern Middle East*, Westview Press, Boulder, CO, pp. 89–139.

Hatem, M. (1994) 'The Paradoxes of State Feminism', in B. Nelsen and N. Chowdhury, eds, *Women and Politics Worldwide*, Yale University Press, New Haven, CT, pp. 226–42.

Hatem, M. (1999) 'Modernization, the State, and the Family in Middle East Women's Studies', in M. Meriwether and J. Tucker, eds, *Social History of Women and Gender in the Modern Middle East*, Westview Press, Boulder, CO, pp. 63–87.

Hatem, M. (2011) 'Gender and Revolution in Egypt', *Middle East Report*, 261, pp. 36–41.

Hermes, H. (1987) *Welfare State and Woman Power: Essays in State Feminism*, Norwegian University Press, Oslo.

Hirschkind, C. (2006) *The Ethical Soundscape: Cassette Sermons and Islamic Counterpublics*, Columbia University Press, New York.

Al-'Issawi, M. (2013) 'Bi-l-suwar tawqi' awwal birutukul ta'awun qawmi al-mar'a wa-l-dakhiliya', *Al-Youm Al-Sabi'*. Available at: http://tinyurl.com/lnk6zka (accessed on 5 April 2014).

Kandiyoti, D. (1991) 'Identity and its Discontents: Women and the Nation', *Millennium*, 20 (3), pp. 429–43.

Langohr, V. (2014) 'New President, Old Pattern of Sexual Violence in Egypt', *Middle East Research and Information Project*, 7 July. Available at: www.merip.org/mero/mero070714 (accessed on 20 July 2014).

Lederer, E. M. (2014) 'AP Interview: Egyptian Fights for Women's Equality', *The Guardian*, 21 March. Available at: www.theguardian.com/world/feedarticle/11256185 (accessed on 11 January 2015).

Mahmood, S. (2005) *Politics of Piety*, Princeton University Press, Princeton.

Mazur, A. (2002) *Theorizing Feminist Policy*, Oxford University Press, Oxford.

McBride, D., and A. Mazur, eds (2010) *The Politics of State Feminism: Innovation in Comparative Research*, Temple University Press, Philadelphia.

McClintock, A. (1991) 'No Longer in a Future Heaven: Women and Nationalism in South Africa', *Transition*, 51, pp. 104–23.

Mos'ad, N. (2014) 'Observations on the Meeting with Al-Sisi', *Al-Shorouk*, 17 April.

Outshoorn, J. (1994) 'Between Movement and Government: "Femocrats" in the Netherlands', in H. Kriesi, ed., *Yearbook of Swiss Political Science*, Haupt, Bern/Stuttgart/Vienna, pp. 141–65.

Outshoorn, J. (2010) 'Social Movements and Women's Movements', in D. McBride and A. Mazur, eds, *The Politics of State Feminism*, Temple University Press, Philadelphia, pp. 143–63.

Outshoorn, J., and J. Kantola, eds (2007) *Changing State Feminism*, Palgrave Macmillan, New York.

Ramadan, R. (2013) 'Al-Talawi: Al-Gharb Yuda'm al-Ikhwan wa yutanasun haquq al-mar'a', *Al-Youm al-Sabi'*. Available at: http://tinyurl.com/o2pn7qb (accessed on 5 April 2014).

Raouf, H. (2001) 'The Silent Ayesha: An Egyptian Narrative', in J. Bayes and N. Tohidi, eds, *Globalization, Gender, and Religion*, Palgrave, New York, pp. 231–57.

Reda, N. (2013) 'From Where Do We Derive "God's Law"? The Case of Women's Political Leadership: A Modern Expression of an Ancient Debate', in O. Abou-Bakr, ed., *Feminist and Islamic Perspectives: New Horizons of Knowledge and Reform*, The Women and Memory Forum, Cairo, pp. 119–35.

Sajoo, A. (2004) *Muslim Ethics: Emerging Vistas*, I. B. Tauris, London and New York.

Sawer, M. (1996) 'Femocrats and Ecorats: Women's Policy Machinery in Australia, Canada, and New Zealand', Occasional Paper, United Nations Research Institute for Social Development, Geneva.

Tadros, M. (2014) 'Egypt's Constitutional Referendum: The Untold Story', *openDemocracy*, 17 January. Available at: www.opendemocracy.net/5050/mariz-tadros/egypts-constitutional-referendum-untold-story (accessed on 29 January 2014).

Al-Tellawi, M. (2013) 'Prevention of Violence Against Women in Constitution and Nation-Building Processes', 5 March. Paper presented at the Fifty-Seventh session of the UN Commission on the Status of Women, 4–15 March, New York. Available at: www.un.org/womenwatch/daw/csw/csw57/panels/panel1-paper-el-tallawy.pdf

Valiente, C. (1997) 'State Feminism and Gender Equality Policies', in F. Gardiner, ed., *Sex Equality Policy in Western Europe*, Routledge, London, pp. 127–41.

Wadud, A. (2006) *Inside the Gender Jihad: Women's Reform in Islam*, Oneworld, Oxford.

EIGHT

Islamic and Secular Women's Activism and Discourses in Post-Uprising Tunisia [1]

Aitemad Muhanna

Introduction

This chapter explores the construction of an Islamic[2]/secular feminist binary in Tunisia and the historical and contextual reasons behind its amplification in post-uprising Tunisia. The research analysis draws upon empirical data collected from a large number of female political figures and women activists working in civil society organizations (CSOs) which mostly emerged after the Tunisian uprising. The research participants were from two sites: Tunis, the capital, and Kasserine, an interior poor region located in the middle-west of Tunisia. They include Islamic women activists, secular feminists and female leaders belonging to different political parties, human rights and feminist organizations, in addition to independent academics, researchers and activists.

This research demonstrates that the Islamic–secular feminist binary in Tunisian society is artificially constructed and does not reflect the actual gender politics adopted by the two self-identified groups. The de facto division between Islamic and secular women activists and organizations is not based on two different ideological orientations (that is, Islamism versus feminism). Rather, it is influenced by multiple political, social, cultural, geographical and, more importantly, subjective factors reflecting the different individual experiences and histories of women leading these organizations. Both Islamic and secular women's groups and organizations appear not to be homogeneous. There is a wide range of diversity in their interpretation of gender and gender politics and their understanding of women's equal rights responding to the fluid and unstable political power relations, regardless of different ideological orientations. Gender politics as a result remains contingent and unpredictable, reflecting changes in the political equation of power in post-uprising Tunisia.

The research also validates that ideological divergence between the Islamic and secular feminist women's groups, and within each group, has encouraged the different women's groups to learn from each other's experiences, and that each group should question the limitation of its discourse in relation to the other. Women, through their involvement in the process of social and political change, engage with and negotiate the different intersectional factors (religious, political and socio-economic) that subordinate women. They learn how to be critical of the actuality of gender and gender relations in their own context. Among Islamic women, the continuous encounter between their ideal Islamic beliefs and the fluid socio-political structure has inspired them to rethink and restrategize their discourses to be responsive to the emerging socio-economic and cultural challenges of the post-uprising context.

I use the reductionist Islamic/secular classification of women activists and their organizations, as defined by research participants, not to describe a reality but as a methodological instrument to examine the historical, political and socio-cultural factors of the de facto institutional division and how it influences the negotiation of women's rights issues and the empowerment of women. The haphazard Islamic/secular classification also enables me to understand how Tunisian women negotiate dominant political and social relations beyond gender relations. It also helps to understand how the ideological, political and institutional disparities override what could be considered common gender interests. The assumption of the existence of common gender interests is problematic, as it ignores divisions on the basis of class, race, religiosity and politics. The research also examines how ideological and political disparities endanger the co-optation of the women's movement by the state and its key political players and hinder the capacity of both Islamic and secular feminist women's movements to represent women's constituency and to claim for gender equality (Molyneux and Razavi 2003: v).

This chapter begins by discussing the historical context for women's rights in Tunisia, which constitutes an important element informing the current construction of an Islamic–secular feminist binary. I then discuss the current discourses on women's rights in post-revolution Tunisia, highlighting the existence of a spectrum. Following this, I explore the objectives of different women's activism, demonstrating the existence of common goals despite the different ideological orientations.

Historical Context for Women's Rights in Tunisia

Habib Bourguiba was the first president of Tunisia after independence and ruled from 1957 to 1987. He pursued a secular modernist and socialist model of governance, making revolutionary reforms to the Code of Personal Status (CPS), including abolishing polygamy, creating a judicial procedure for divorce, requiring marriage to be based on the mutual consent of both parties and obliging wives who had a source of income to contribute to the family's expenses. In addition, he granted women equal rights to education and participation in the workforce. Bourguiba's CPS established a strong social and legal framework for gender equality in Tunisia and helped Tunisian women to move out of the domestic sphere and to participate effectively in all sectors of the public domain (Murphy 2003).

Despite the rejection by some Islamist scholars of the CPS reforms, Bourguiba and his supporters, including clerics, presented the CPS as not opposing the shariah and as a liberal interpretation of Islamic law (Charrad 2001); that is, he kept the shariah frame of discourse. He tried to generate support from all Tunisians, conservatives and modernists, by leaving more deep-rooted elements of shariah-based law untouched, such as unequal inheritance codes. Bourguiba also created a distance between the Tunisian people and their Arab-Islamic history and traditions, which were considered by him to be the major obstacle to modernity (Mezran 2007: 114). Although Tunisians owe Bourguiba the creation of an institutional basis for an independent modern nation state and for women's liberation through egalitarian gender laws and regulations, he was not concerned about democracy and civil society institutions, including women's organizations, which remained constrained by Bourguiba's political patriarchy (Gilman 2007: 98).

Zine El Abidine Ben-Ali's ruling model followed the same ideological and political path as Bourguiba's. He controlled all society institutions, including the Ministry of Religious Affairs and the mosques, banning hijab in public and state institutions. The two presidents attempted to popularize an image of Tunisian modernity as progressively linear, secular and inherently supportive of women's rights (Gray 2013). For example, school enrolment increased from 5 per cent in 1956 to 98 per cent in 2003 for both boys and girls. With the government policy of family planning, the fertility rate was 7.2 children per family in 1966; it declined to 2.03 in 2007 (Gataa 2009: 222). A woman's right to abortion was legalized in 1973 and the number of abortions officially reported tripled (Arfaoui 2007). In terms of women's inclusion in senior professional positions, official statistics prior to the Tunisian uprising indicated that 30 per cent of judges, 70 per cent of pharmacists, 40 per cent of doctors and 40 per cent of university teachers were women, and women's participation in the labour force increased to reach 27 per cent in 2011 (Labidi 2012). Despite the positive gender discrimination policies adopted by both the Bourguiba and Ben-Ali governments, women's integration into the political structure remained limited both at the national and local levels.

A gender equality discourse was used by Ben-Ali as a means to legitimize his authoritarian regime nationally and internationally (Goulding 2009) and the state played a central role in introducing laws and legislation regarding women's rights (Murphy 2003). The feminist movement in Tunisia remained either restricted, or co-opted, by state political agendas and interests. During the Ben-Ali era, any women's groups that did not support the agenda of the government, whether Islamic or secular feminists, were often targeted by the authorities or co-opted into the larger state-sponsored feminism. It was only women who belonged to Ben-Ali's ruling party or, as described by Goulding (2009: 72), 'who subscribe to the "state-sponsored" brand of feminism', who were promoted by the regime because they spoke his language and served his masculine politics. Meanwhile, his socio-economic policies marginalized the majority of the Tunisian population, particularly rural women living in the poorer, interior regions (Taymoumi 2008; 2013). For example, before the uprising, nine out of every ten jobs created in Tunisia were on the coast, creating a considerable socio-economic gap between interior and coastal regions (Hopmann and Zartman 2012: 9–12).

Despite the repressive nature of Ben-Ali's regime, feminist organizations in Tunisia such as the Association of Tunisian Democratic Women (ATFD) and the Association of Tunisian Women for Research and Development (AFTURD) were able to lobby the government for further legal reforms. They called for a number of radical changes that Ben-Ali was reluctant to implement in order to avoid social conflict, especially with the Islamists, such as the abolition of all reservations to the Convention on the Elimination of All Forms of Discrimination against Women (CEDAW) and the elimination of Islamic inheritance law. They also lobbied for better protection for women by penalizing rape in general and rape within marriage. In 1998, these feminist organizations succeeded in pressuring the government into issuing a new law that provided single mothers the right to claim child maintenance from the biological father of their child and, in 2004, sexual harassment was made punishable (Fitoussi and Baron 2012).

Nevertheless, the impact of Tunisian feminist organizations' work remained limited to legal change and was concentrated in major cities and their discourse was characterized as elitist, used only by highly educated middle-class women with little popular constituency. Operating within an authoritarian state forced some independent feminist organizations to co-operate with the state feminist organizations and, as stated by many research participants, even to accept funding from government institutions to work within the government's feminist agenda. As argued by Murphy (2003), during the Ben-Ali era, Tunisia did not experience effective independent feminist movements through which women could challenge the authoritarian structure of the government regarding its gender policies.

From the early 1970s, state feminism was also criticized by the Islamist movement (later Ennahda). The movement called for a reform of the CPS by restricting divorce rights and abortion, and reintroducing polygamy. Some Islamists argued that the CPS caused huge problems within Tunisian families, leading to increasing rates of divorce and the 'distorting' of family values (Boulby 1998). While Islamist conservative voices against equal rights for women were repressed by the regime, radical feminist leaders and organizations fell into the trap of the undemocratic regime, which tried to co-opt them to legitimize its human rights violations against the Islamists. Alhough a number of individual secular feminists, such as Khadija Arfaoui, Radhia Nasraoui and Sihem Bensedrine, faced persecution and imprisonment by Ben-Ali because of their struggle for human rights, some feminist organizations allied with the regime against the Islamist threat to women's rights and the modernity of Tunisia.

Before the Tunisian uprising, there was a consensus among a large number of feminist leaders that the Islamist project and its patriarchal culture were the main threats facing women's equal rights in Tunisia, with little attention given to the historical, structural and institutional causes of women's disempowerment, including the state's neo-liberal socio-economic policies, corruption and clientelism, and the oppressive police and security system. After the uprising, the political and ideological divisions between Islamist and secular political parties exacerbated the hostility between Ennahda women's representatives and the representatives of feminist CSOs and constructed an Islamic–secular feminist binary. Although each group homogenizes the other, in reality there exists a spectrum of positions among them – ranging from the radical to the more pragmatic interpretations of women's rights, as discussed below.

Discourses of Women's Rights in Post-Uprising Tunisia and Dynamics of Women's Activism

Tunisian women's activism and women's rights discourses are by no means mirroring the Islamic–secular division in post-uprising Tunisia. There are multiple and diverse discourses of women's rights across the National Constituent Assembly (NCA), the government and the CSOs. There is also a divergence among both Islamic and secular feminist groups with regard to their understanding of women's rights and empowerment. I identify three major discourses on women's human rights and women's empowerment in Tunisia: radical democratic feminism; pragmatic democratic feminism and Islamic women's activism. Moreover, the terms 'democracy' and 'secularism' and their relation to Islam are used differently by the representatives of the three discourses. The representatives of the first two identify themselves as democratic and confine democracy to secularism, with the first discourse adopting the radical French model of secularism that rigidly rejects the inclusion of religion into state politics (Hopmann and Zartman 2012). Meanwhile, moderate Islamic women activists represent the pragmatic discourse of Ennahda and emphasize that Islam is compatible with democracy and international civil and political rights, without necessarily naming themselves as 'secular'.[3] Thus, combining the term 'democratic' with 'feminism' here is based on how the research participants define themselves, but does not necessarily mean that all secularists are democratic, or vice versa.

Radical Democratic Feminism

The radical feminist movement is represented in the active leading feminist institutions working during Ben-Ali's era, essentially ATFD and AFTURD in addition to the female members of the Tunisian League for the Defence of Human Rights (LTDH), the members of the women's committee in the Tunisian General Labour Union (UGTT), and some female members of the newly emerged secular Coalition for Women of Tunisia (CWT). Radical feminists in Tunisia represent an older generation of feminist activists. Most of them align with liberal or leftist/socialist ideologies, and are largely influenced in their feminist education and experience by the French model of second wave feminism from the 1970s, which targeted patriarchy as represented in dominant male culture, religion and state structures as being the major cause of women's oppression and subordination, and they consider the legalization of gender equality as the most effective means against women's oppression (Cavallaro 2003), regardless of Tunisian cultural particularity and diversity. Radical feminists have remained powerful after the uprising due to their long experience of feminist activism and their strong institutional network with regional and international funding organizations and women's coalitions. From my research, I identified three main points of consensus amongst radical democratic feminists: a strong belief in the universality of women's rights and opposition to cultural specificity; a strong opposition to the Islamist political project and denial of any possibility of reconciling (political) Islam with women's rights; and a denial of any possibility of effective women's agency within the framework of (political) Islam.

Despite the increasing religious trend, which is also associated with the expansion of extremist Salafism and the resulting public debate over the cultural identity of Tunisia and the Tunisian people, radical feminists have not addressed the possibility of reconciling universal feminist principles with local cultural values and practices. Rather, they continue to advocate for full gender equality including equal inheritance between men and women and the rights of single mothers,[4] which, for the majority of Muslim Tunisians, contradict Islam, which prohibits women to have children outside of an Islamic marriage contract. Some radical feminists in Tunisia, including some socialists, the latter of which would be expected to be critical of a capitalist market economy whether it is led by a secular or Islamist ruling party, have identified Islam and its patriarchal attitudes as the major cause of women's subordination. This has historically distracted the attention of the feminist movement in Tunisia (liberal and socialist feminists) away from struggling against the state's neo-liberal socio-economic policies that marginalize the majority of poor Tunisian women.

In an interview conducted in March 2013, Ahlem Belhadj, the president of ATFD, stated that democratic feminists have to continue advocating for the universality of their rights and should not respond to cultural relativism or multiculturalism. Cultural specificity for radical feminists always justifies the violation of women's rights in the name of religion and tradition. Belhadj explained Tunisian women's rejection of some articles in CEDAW, such as equality of inheritance, as a lack of awareness among poor and illiterate women in rural areas. In order to popularize universal women's rights, Belhadj recommended 'to better educate and mobilize poor and uneducated women in interior regions and to organize them to cooperate with us to defend their equal rights in the constitution'.[5] However, I have found that the women who stand against the withdrawal of reservations to CEDAW are not actually illiterate poor rural women who are not familiar with, or interested in, the elitist feminist and human rights language. Rather, those who support reservations to CEDAW are highly educated Islamic women, who have developed their own discourse of women's rights within their Islamic framework.

Despite the changing context in post-uprising Tunisia, Belhadj and other radical democratic feminists dehistoricize and decontextualize women's rights by focusing on universal measures of gender equality and on the legalization of equal rights without any critique of the discursive frame of the 'universal human rights' doctrine and its ignorance of cultural particularity (Abu-Lughod 2013). As Abu-Lughod (2013) argues, Tunisian women, like women in other parts of the world, shape their desires, interests and understanding of their world in reference to their social and historical context, and also to their belonging to particular communities with their particular beliefs and moral ideals. Thus, universal rights for women must include women's desires, interests and underline their particular cultural and religious attitudes, as long as these attitudes and values are chosen freely and willingly by them. Despite their notable achievements of legal reforms for women's rights, nevertheless radical feminists in Tunisia have failed to localize and contextualize their understanding of universal women's rights and feminism and, thus, they have historically been accused by a large segment of the Tunisian population as being part of Westernized elites speaking a language that is not relevant to Tunisian society.

Their advocacy of universal rights leads radical feminists to dismiss efforts to reinterpret Islam to be compatible with their understanding of feminism. For example, in an email conversation in April 2014 with Bochra Ben Hamida, a leading democratic feminist and a human rights defender, she declined to comment on the possibility of reconciling an Islamic culture-centred approach with feminism, claiming that this issue is not part of the concerns of the Tunisian women's movement. In addition, radical feminists believe that women's rights are not compatible with the Islamist political project. Belhadj argues that the male leaders of Islamist parties and clerics intend to curtail the women's rights provided by the previous secular regime (in the CPS), albeit with some of these codes based on shariah. For radical democratic feminists, CEDAW is the only legal safeguard to prevent Islamist politicians from using their political power to violate women's equal rights.

Belhadj's scepticism towards the Islamists reflects her observation of the Ennahda conference held in March 2013, when some female members of Ennahda argued against CEDAW without a single objection from anyone in Ennahda. Radical feminists have continued to state their fears that Ennahda will not constitutionalize gender equality in accordance with universal international laws. Yet, Ennahda's female and male leaders have declared that they consider the CPS to be the legal framework for women's rights in Tunisia, as it does not contradict shariah.[6] Moreover, Ennahda adopted gender parity electoral rules and supported the constitutionalization of gender equality in the national constitution. Radical feminists' disregard of the pragmatic gender agenda of Ennahda serves a singular strategic political objective: defeating the Islamist political project and what they believe to be its patriarchal interpretation of Islam with regard to gender norms.

Their rejection of any possibility of reconciling Islam and women's rights also leads radical feminists to deny any feminist agency for Islamic women activists. For example, Belhadj does not see any possibility for Tunisian Islamic women to change the patriarchal culture of their male leaders. Meanwhile, Ben Hamida excludes Islamic women activists from the history of the Tunisian women's movement, ignoring the historical fact that, during Ben-Ali's time, Islamists (men and women) were oppressed and not allowed to participate in any form of activism. They also dismiss the idea that religion and religiosity could empower Tunisian Muslim women more broadly or that poor Tunisian women may prefer to bargain with patriarchy (Kandiyoti 1998) rather than to resist it in order to achieve social and political power, as well as individual and family security and stability in a situation of prolonged economic deterioration and poverty.

Pragmatic Democratic Feminism

From within the radical feminist movement, an increasing number of women have rethought the radical liberal and leftist feminist discourse and shifted towards a more pragmatic one. While not yet a mainstream view among secular feminists, the pragmatic trend has become noticeable. Their number has rapidly increased among the political opposition, female academic scholars, women activists in youth and development CSOs, and among some female members of the less radical secular political parties such as Nidaa Tunis and Aljoumhouri. The pragmatic discourse is characterized by its desire to reconcile feminism with religion and local traditions; to rethink the historical relationship between feminism and the state; and to develop a women's movement independent of political parties.

According to Radhia Belhaj Zekri, former president of AFTURD, there is currently a sharp contestation between the radical and pragmatic approaches in the democratic women's movement over the relationship to religion. Belhaj Zekri explained why democratic feminists should engage with religion:

> Tunisian progressive feminists should deal with religion in a resilient and tactical way, as a sign of respect to Tunisian society. We need to encourage the good tradition against the discriminatory one, and we also need to encourage the reinterpretation of religion, in order not to leave the Islamists to manipulate the field of religious interpretation.

Other pragmatic secular feminists representing AFTURD emphasize that secular women's organizations have to work on the ground and stop focusing on abstract universal concepts that are not relevant to the social and cultural context of Tunisia. For example, Nedra Hweiji, a lawyer, secular feminist activist and member of a secular women's organization called Musawat wa Tanasuf (Equality and Equity), said:

> I think the only two issues that create tension between Islamic and feminist women's groups are: homosexuality and inheritance. I myself do not see the two issues are problematic in the Tunisian society. Most Tunisian women do not ask to constitutionalize the rights of homosexuals and equal inheritance right. As a lawyer, I find unequal inheritance is not a substantial issue that undermines women's equal rights in Tunisia. It can be legally sorted out by people's awareness to distribute their inheritance before they die, and this is what actually happens among educated people living in urban areas in Tunisia. Rural poor women are more concerned about the inheritance right as it is stated in Islam.

Pragmatic feminists, such as Dalenda Largueche, the former director of the Center for Research, Studies, Documentation and Information on Women (CREDIF),[7] believe that it is necessary to develop a shared feminist agenda with Islamic women activists:

I know that there are a number of conservative Islamists within
Ennahda who are against equal rights for women ... However, I
am against the few radical feminists who are against dialogue with
Islamists. We, genuine feminists, have to encourage the moderate
female figures in Ennahda to crystallize a moderate feminist view of
Islam that criticizes the patriarchal interpretation of Islam. I believe
that some members of Ennahda go towards more pragmatism and
the democratic feminist movement has to avoid further tension, but
to encourage dialogue.

For other pragmatic feminists, it is essential that Tunisian feminists
develop a new agenda based on a reconsideration of the history of
state feminism. One woman, a lecturer in Gender and Women's Studies, told me:

We Tunisian secular women have to admit that we did not actually
struggle to gain our rights. All our rights that we have been
enjoying were granted to us by dictators, Bourguiba and Ben-Ali.
This may be the reason why we blinded our eyes to the bias and
oppression practised against Tunisian Muslim women who were
tortured by Ben-Ali in the name of modernity and gender equality.
This is the time that we have to assess our feminist history and to
develop a new collective feminist approach that attracts women in
interior regions.

Nevertheless, some feminists continue to demonstrate mistrust of the
Islamists and emphasize the need to build a women's movement that
is independent of all political parties. Professor Amel Grami, a secular
gender scholar specializing in Islamic and Gender Studies in a Tunisian
university who used to be an activist in AFTD and AFTURD, described
the contestation between the secular feminists and the Islamic women
as a battle of political positioning and repositioning. She said: 'What
secular feminists in ATFD and AFTURD do is a political resistance
[representing the politics of leftist parties which advocate for a secular
civil state] rather than a resistance for a feminist agenda (focusing on
the actual needs and problems of Tunisian women)'. She emphasizes
the importance of having an independent Tunisian feminist agenda to

challenge the extremist Islamist threat against women's equal rights. Although Grami talked about Islamists as a homogeneous ideological group, mixing the radical Salafists such as Hizb El Tahrir[8] with Ennahda moderate members, she emphasized that women have to work together on common prioritized issues such as poverty, children's rights and domestic violence. However, Grami thinks that Tunisia has not yet developed a mature liberal interpretation of Islam or Islamic feminism. This is despite evidence that Islamic women activists are engaging dynamically with secular and religious norms, as discussed later in this chapter.

Islamic Women's Activism

Islamic women are clear in defining the relationship between their political agenda – representing Islamist political parties or political Islam – and their gender agenda. For Islamic women, the priority is given to their political Islamic identity, not to their gender identity, and they act accordingly. They exercise their power not for the sake of gender equality but to mobilize and advocate for a political and social Islamic discourse, including social justice and the empowerment of women. In addition, a considerable number of female Ennahda members, MPs and civil society activists invest in their party's instrumentalization of women's political participation to achieve their own political manoeuvring. They frequently mentioned in their interviews that they would not be able to learn politics from outside their Islamist political party. Islamic women's activism is characterized as opposed to the universality of women's rights; an emphasis on the family unit for achieving women's rights; and an understanding of women's rights within an Islamic framework.

Islamic women criticize the universalization of women's rights within the framework of CEDAW, claiming that each society has to shape its understanding of rights in a way that respects its culture and religion and responds to its specific socio-economic context. For example, Islamic women support reservations to CEDAW in relation to the issue of single mothers, which, according to their reading of

Islam, implies disrespect for women. A member of Ennahda explained her view by saying:

> Secular women think that we are against the protection of the rights of single mothers. This is not true. Our approach towards single mothers is that this social phenomenon is not a free choice taken by women. There are around 2000 cases of single mothers in Tunisia, mostly from the most vulnerable families. It is true that we do not call for constitutionalizing equal rights for single mothers. Women have to be supported to marry and to have a connected family and to live in dignity. We need to work together to reduce this social problem by providing poor women with the material and technical resources that they need to avoid being vulnerable. We also need to protect the rights of the children of single mothers and reintegrate single mothers in the society. Our society has become so much individualized by the previous regimes. We Islamic women focus on the family as a cohesive unit, where we prioritize women to become well-educated and well-equipped to transfer good virtues for their children: boys and girls. Responding to secular women's criticisms, focusing on family does not mean that we call for women to go back to their homes. On the contrary, we advocate against women's illiteracy and exclusion because this is the reason why they are unable to better educate their children.

Islamic women activists work within their local communities to revive what they view as the 'distinctive cultural identity' of Tunisian society that is centred on family connectedness and intimacy against the 'alien, standardized, Western, individualistic gender norms'. The major 'alien gender norms' that Islamic women resist are those related to freedom of sexuality and social practices that contradict their perception of Islamic morality, such as immodesty in clothing, prostitution, sexual relations before marriage, homosexuality[9] and drinking alcohol in public. These alien Western norms, from an Islamic women's point of view, have spoiled the Tunisian family, which is the central unit for creating a society based on Islamic virtues. For example, Islamic women explain the high rate of divorce in Tunisia[10] as being the result of men's lack of responsibility and commitment to religious virtues and their inclination towards opportunistic individualism.

The interviewed Islamic women also emphasized that non-Islamic gender norms and practices are not only a by-product of a lack of religiosity, but, more importantly, are produced by poverty and social marginalization of both men and women living in interior regions. For example, Naima from Kasserine spoke about poor women who are forced to work as prostitutes and thinks that those women are forced to take this path for economic reasons in order to earn an income. If they were offered an opportunity of earning with dignity, they would not be prostitutes. As described by one of the Islamic research participants: 'Islam calls for social justice by which human dignity of men and women is equally respected and none lives in material and spiritual deprivation'. However, there is a belief that the message of Islam has been somewhat distorted and misunderstood as a result of social conditions and rigid cultural traditions.

Interestingly, the narratives of poor women interviewed for this research are critically supportive of the Islamic women activists' discourse, without necessarily being framed or defined as Islamic. Poor women do not understand their equal rights in the same way as Tunisian feminists do. One of the common phenomena discussed by young single unemployed women is that equal rights given to women in Tunisia have made men lazy and more reliant on their wives' incomes, or they go searching for working women to marry. For them, this is a reason why the age of marriage for women has increased and their choices of marriage have decreased. Another issue of concern to women is the increasing rate of divorce among couples in Tunisia. Poor women's narration of their understanding of gender and gender relations reflects their actual social problems, and thus it defines the form of activism and feminism they can embrace (Badran 2009). For example, they showed an interest in reviving family relations based on traditional values and religious virtues of family connection that would make Tunisian men responsible for their families and children.

Although most of the Islamic research participants represented the moderate understanding of Islam, the researcher managed to interview three young women wearing *niqab* (a veil covering the face except for the eyes), who are categorized by Ennahda women as 'Salafists'. The three women emphasized that their decision to cover their face is purely their free choice, aiming to realize themselves as ideal Muslims. They all decided to put on the *niqab* as a symbol of their religious identity after the revolution. Either consciously or unconsciously, wearing the *niqab* can be seen as a resistance to secular politicians and feminist groups who seek to exclude shariah from the constitution and governance. It can also be a sign of resistance against Ennahda, which, from their point of view, has provided too many religious compromises to satisfy the secular opposition. They want to show their distinctive Islamic identity.

Hayat is a 24-year-old woman from Kasserine. She narrates her story about the *niqab* by saying:

> The niqab does not undermine my sense of freedom. In contrast, I feel freer now and more motivated to participate in public activities, especially for educating poor children. I developed two project ideas and I am trying to search for some funding to implement them.
> But, who is going to support such projects for a woman who puts a niqab? We, women with niqab, are excluded, as we are considered by those in power as conservative and wanting to bring the society backward.

One could consider these as being 'conformist autonomous' young women (Bucar 2010), who use their religious beliefs to enhance their autonomy and to exercise their agency to achieve their goals in life. Their number is still small but is likely to grow because of increasing poverty and youth unemployment, and also due to the continuous exclusion of young people in general and those in poor regions in particular from public life. The term 'conformist' should not be equated with obedience and submission. The three women interviewed emphasized that they struggle against the structural socio-economic causes of their exclusion by their persistent search for a job to achieve their economic independence, and by their engagement in public religious educational activities. They also struggle to convince their parents of their choice to put on the *niqab*, as well as to gain societal recognition for their newly emerged religious identity and practice. Young women's inclination towards conformist/conservative Islamist beliefs may be a good lesson for radical feminists who need to better contextualize women's exercise of agency and see it as always dynamic and never taking a linear, singular form (Mahmood 2005).

Although this research illustrates diverse interpretations of Islam among Islamic women (between conformist and moderate Islamic women), this divergence does not undermine the argument that both groups exercise their individual power and autonomy to construct their own desired gendered subject. They show a dynamic learning capacity resulting from their interaction with the social and political world around them. Through social interaction, the ideal moral values of Islamic women, whether conformist or moderate, are reconstructed according to the experiences of women's everyday life and their desires for social recognition and valuation (Moore 2007). Divergence among Islamic women activists and between Islamic women and secular feminists appears to motivate Islamic women to further question the limits of traditional gender norms in order to meet their ideological, social, economic and political goals.

Ideological Differences but Common Goals to Defend Women's Equal Rights

Most participants representing different CSOs, whether Islamist or secular, asserted that the motive for their activism within their organizations is to serve their local communities, particularly to empower poor women to challenge their problems of poverty, unemployment, domestic violence, illiteracy and lack of awareness of their rights. Yet, each group uses a different discourse in presenting its activities. Secular CSOs use the legal and human rights approach, whilst Islamic women's organizations frame their activities in terms of humanitarian and development work. In a focus group (FG) conducted in Kasserine with 15 Islamic and secular women's organizations, there was evidence of ideological conflict between the two groups but also much overlap in the actual activities and pragmatism of these organizations.

For example, Fatima, who represents Doustourna, a secular human rights network, and also works with a secular women's organization based in Kasserine called Tigar, was aggressive towards the Islamists at the beginning of the discussion, reflecting her fears that the Islamists would change the CPS. She went on to describe the work of her organization:

> We are a human rights-based organization concerned to contribute to the draft constitution and to constitutionalize women's rights. We also work on campaigns aiming to bring material support to families in need, especially children. We also work on environmental campaigns and against the exploitation of female workers.

With regard to development work, Fatima disagreed with Islamic organizations, which, she believes, only focus on charity work. For her, charity turns Tunisian women into beggars for material support. She argues that women's organizations have to build women's capacity to achieve their economic independence. Yet, Tunisian Islamic women activists in Kasserine, similar to their secular feminist counterparts, use the Arabic term *tamkeen*, which they define as a process of enabling poor women to become economically independent and to avoid vulnerable social and economic situations. For Islamic women, this is achieved through women's access to education, employment and life skills, such as managing their own businesses. When Islamic women were asked about the difference between women's empowerment and charity, one of them replied: 'it is only physically and mentally disabled women and men who are equally entitled to Islamic charity. Islam urges able-bodied men and women to work and not to be reliant on others (*mutawakeleen*). Remember Khadija, the wife of Prophet Muhammad, she was a trader'.

Naeema is the president of Iethar (altruism), a charity-development organization in Kasserine. She does not deny that she belongs to Ennahda, but claims that her politics do not overlap with her civic institutional work. She is very much concerned to serve women from different political, social and geographical backgrounds. She said:

In the beginning, we all thought that institutional development work is easy and smooth because we did not experience such work during Ben-Ali's era. But we shortly discovered that supporting economic development projects, especially in the transitional period, takes a long time due to the bureaucracy of national and international organizations. During the period of waiting for funding, we have to provide vulnerable families with some support.

Interestingly, like Fatima, Naeema emphasizes the need to provide material support for those in need. She continues:

We have a large number of disabled people, vulnerable families who have no income earners, sick children, and many other social problems. We can't leave those people for months without support . . . these are immediate cases that the government has to provide them their basic needs. While we put pressure on the government, we have to rely on our local resources and good wealthy people to support those vulnerable people.

Regarding the issue of universal rights and CEDAW, secular women activists demonstrated considerable pragmatism. Fatima, speaking again in the FG interview with Islamic women, said:

We don't have to fear ideological encounters with people in Kasserine. It is true that some ordinary people would say 'why should we care about Doustourna network? They advocate for gay marriage and other issues that are not relevant to our culture'. This is not true, we believe in universal rights as a whole, but this does not mean that we are going to promote gay marriage because it is not relevant to our society. I am not saying that we don't need to have reservations on CEDAW, but our reservations have to be locally justified. Of course we don't need to get into an ideological clash with our local people because each society has its specificity. We need to negotiate our beliefs with people in order to persuade them and not impose our beliefs on them. What I ask for is to get rid of ideological fanaticism. We hate dividing our society into Islamist and non-Islamist. We are all Muslims and we have to accept each other.

Similarly, Naeema also demonstrated pragmatism in her discussion of
CEDAW:

> With regard to CEDAW, I think that we have to stop talking about
> this issue. We, Tunisian women, Islamic and secular, support
> CEDAW with reservations on some articles that are not compatible
> with our specific culture and religion. Secular women do not
> have to fear our reservations because these reservations would
> not undermine women's status, as long as together we educate
> women about their equal rights as they are stated in the CPS and in
> the constitution, whether based on Islam or on international laws.
> There is no contradiction between the two. The real threat against
> women's rights comes from the cultural heritage and how women
> are treated at home and in public. The real threat would also come
> from a dictator government that does not respond to women's
> needs and fails to protect women's rights.

Naeema ended her discussion by encouraging secular and Islamic
women to work together against the extremist interpretation of Islam
by some Salafist groups in Kasserine and other parts of Tunisia, who
distort the actual meaning of Islam and also threaten women's equal
participation in public life. For Naeema, the effective means for resisting this threat is to raise women's awareness of moderate Islam (al-
Islam al-mu'tadil), which does not contradict with modernity and gender equality, meaning that women have equal access to education and
employment, respect their families and live in peace in their local
communities.

The pragmatic discourse used by both Islamic women and feminist
activists shows that the two groups are learning from each other's
history and experiences. For example, Islamist women's organizations are learning from the history of secular women that their civic
institutional work must remain independent from state institutions.
Meanwhile, secular women are learning from Islamic women how to
avoid elitism in their feminist discourse. Similar to the experience of
Moroccan women, the mutual learning between Islamic and feminist
women has contributed to challenging the ideological binary between
feminism and Islam and the two groups of Islamic and feminist

women activists have succeeded in transforming one another through dialogue and political engagement (Salim 2011).

Moreover, in a relatively short period of time, moderate Islamic women have learned the language of secular feminism and used it in international fora to enhance their integration into the international community and to legitimize their politics.[11] Among several pioneering examples of agentive Islamic women is Ibtihal Abdellatif. She specializes in Islamic shariah and defines herself as an independent Islamic woman activist. She has succeeded in a short period of time since the Tunisian uprising to gain recognition at the local, national and international levels through her leading role in defending the rights of female victims of torture by the Ben-Ali regime. She has also participated in Islamic-feminist debates and developed a liberal understanding of Islam that is, from her point of view, not contradictory with universal women's rights. For Ibtihal, the incompatibility between Islam and universal women's rights is artificial, instrumentalized by different internal and external political and feminist forces for power interests. She believes that there is nothing in Islam that prohibits her from acting on an equal basis with men in public, as long as her participation does not compromise the ethics of Islam. Ibtihal is one of a considerable number of Islamic women activists interviewed who, like their secular feminist counterparts, were critical of the lack of women's representation in the post-uprising governments. She also advocates for gender equitable policies, especially with regard to women's equal access to education and employment. Ibtihal was selected in the first week of May 2014 as a member of the National Supreme Committee of Truth and Dignity, which is responsible for overseeing the implementation of transitional justice in Tunisia.

Through their political engagement in Islamist political parties and in CSOs, Islamic women activists have gained critical distance from the status quo and imagined alternatives to it (Karim 2009). Against the radical feminists' expectations, the interviewed Islamic women activists have developed a pragmatic narrative of women's rights, using religious and cultural values to mediate universal values. Moreover, they use this discourse to criticize patriarchal culture and advocate against patriarchal readings of Islam (Bona 2013: 247). Islamic women advocate for the ideology of Islam and its ideal gender norms, whilst simultaneously resisting normative patriarchal gender norms through their gendered bodily performance in social and political domains. Arguably, the multiple and contradictory practices of Islamic women's agency in Tunisia creates the potential to deconstruct gender norms in social life and in political institutions (Butler 2004: 42).

Conclusion

In this chapter, I argue that the Islamic/feminist binary is constructed for political reasons and does not reflect the reality of Islamic and secular women's activism. Despite the different ideological frameworks of Islamic and feminist women's groups on the ground, the two groups work towards common objectives, emphasizing issues of social justice and equality such as women's equal access to education, employment and political participation and the struggle against violence against women. The Islamic/secular feminist convergence has increased due to the pragmatic trend among secular feminists. Pragmatic feminists realize that the Islamic–secular feminist binary endangers the legitimacy of their feminist discourse. Consequently, they are open to mutual learning and dialogue with Islamic women activists in order to reach common ground.

Tunisian Islamic women activists, like secular feminists, do not speak with one voice or reflect a homogeneous experience of activism. They shape their forms of activism in accordance with their diverse historical and contextual experiences. Moderate Islamic women have learned from their political engagement and social activism that in order to achieve justice and equality for all women, they must go beyond both the conservative interpretations of Islam and the universal understanding of women's rights to reflect the actual experiences of Tunisian women. Secular feminists have also learned from Islamic women activists to contextualize their feminist approach, considering the cultural specificity of Tunisian society and its effect on gender and gender relations.

This research illustrates that women's rights cannot be standardized, but rather should be localized and contextualized so that a

multidimensional understanding of rights is articulated and accepted
by the majority of women (Abu-Lughod 2013). Thus, it is the home-
work of women's/feminist organizations, particularly pragmatic
democratic feminists and moderate Islamic women activists, to understand the context of poor Tunisian women and to rethink and restrategize women's empowerment based on local gender knowledge
and on the actual dynamics of actions and interactions undertaken by
women in a certain time and place. This would constitute a strong
base for dismantling the Islamic–secular feminist binary. Otherwise,
women's quest for justice and equality – whether it is based upon
Islamic or feminist ideology – will remain hostage to different political forces and tendencies (Mir-Hosseini 2011) and distanced from the
reality of women's life experiences.

Notes

1. Funding for this research was provided jointly by SIDA and Oxfam. The views
   expressed in this chapter are solely the views of the author and do not in
   any way represent the views of SIDA, Oxfam or its partner organizations. The
   findings presented in this chapter should not be interpreted as being those
   of SIDA, Oxfam or its partners. Any errors are the responsibility of the author
   alone. SIDA, Oxfam and its partners do not accept any liability for any errors
   in the research.
2. The term 'Islamic' refers to Muslim women activists in Tunisia who use Islam
   as the major source of reference to shape their social and political activism,
   whether they represent Islamist political agendas or are independent social
   and political activists. I avoid using the term 'Islamic feminism' to describe
   moderate Islamic women activists in Tunisia because they repeatedly emphasize that they reject feminism as a Western phenomenon.
3. Khalid al-Anani argues that the Arab uprisings have contributed to changing
   the Islamist parties' discourses, ideologies and tactics. Secular terms such as
   'democracy', 'civil rights' and 'political rights' have become central in their
   everyday political discourses. Al-Anani suggests that this is the starting point
   for the secularization of Islam, albeit subtly (2012: 468). Some Islamic female
   participants in this research represent Ennahda's pragmatic understanding that
   Islam is compatible with democracy and with secularism, mentioning the
   Turkish model.
4. This information is collected from the different publications and booklets
   produced by ATFD after the revolution, accessed from the ATFD office in Tunis
   in March 2013.

5. Quoted from an interview conducted with Ahlem Belhadj in March 2013.
6. In an interview conducted in April 2013, Farida Labidi, a human rights lawyer who sits on Ennahda's Shura Council, stated that the CPS does not contradict the shariah and that it is the baseline for women's rights and builds a common ground for the Tunisian women's movement to discuss and negotiate issues of women's rights in the future.
7. Centre de Recherche, d'Études, de Documentation et d'Information sur la Femme (CREDIF) is a semi-governmental institution working under the supervision of the Ministry of Women's Affairs.
8. In interviews with some Salafist women activists, they criticize the CPS for violating key tenets of shariah and do not see it as legitimate.
9. Responding to feminist critiques that the Islamic view of sexuality implies discrimination against sexual minorities, such as homosexuals, some of the interviewed Islamic women argued that the Tunisian society, with its traditions and values, would not produce homosexuals if its people were better educated on the moral virtues of Islam, unless some feminists want to advocate for an alien culture.
10. The Tunisian National Statistics of 2009 show that the divorce rate in Tunisia is the highest in the Arab world and second in the entire world. The national statistics of 2008 also show that the rate of divorced and widowed women is six times greater than that of men and the number of divorcees increased from 12,035 in 2008 to 12,871 in 2011.
11. For example, Mehrezia Labidi, the deputy president of the Tunisian National Constituent Assembly and a representative for Ennahda, attended a panel organized by Chatham House in London on 30 April 2013, entitled 'Women and Power in the Middle East – Social Justice, Democracy and Gender Equality'. She argued that the real challenge facing Tunisian women is to assure that all women (the elite, the educated, the poor, and urban and rural women) are protected by the national constitution and that their rights are secured by establishing the rule of the law. See the details of her speech, available at: www.chathamhouse.org/sites/default/files/public/Meetings/Meeting%20Transcripts/3004201 3panel1.pdf.

References

Abu-Lughod, L. (2013) *Do Muslim Women Need Saving?*, Harvard University Press, Cambridge, MA, and London.

Al-Anani, K. (2012) 'Islamist Parties Post-Arab Spring', *Mediterranean Politics*, 17 (3), pp. 466–72.

Arfaoui, K. (2007) 'The Development of the Feminist Movement in Tunisia 1920s–2000s', *The International Journal of the Humanities*, 4 (8), pp. 53–60.

Badran, M. (2009) *Feminism in Islam: Secular and Religious Convergences*, OneWorld Publications, Oxford.

Bona, M. (2013) 'Arab Women/Arab Culture(s): Reflections on Feminist Multicultural Discourse in the Wake of Mona Eltahawy's "Why Do They Hate Us?"', *Trans-Scripts*, 3. Available at: http://sites.uci.edu/transscripts/files/2014/10/2013_03_17.pdf (accessed on 6 January 2015).

Boulby, M. (1998) 'The Islamic Challenge: Tunisia Since Independence', *Third World Quarterly*, 10 (2), pp. 590–614.

Bucar, M. E. (2010) 'Dianomy: Understanding Religious Women's Moral Agency as Creative Conformity', *Journal of the American Academy of Religion*, 78 (3), pp. 662–86.

Butler, J. (2004) *Undoing Gender*, Routledge, New York.

Cavallaro, D. (2003) *French Feminist Theory*, Continuum Collection, London.

Charrad, M. (2001) *States and Women's Rights: The Making of Postcolonial Tunisia, Algeria, and Morocco*, California University Press, Berkeley.

Fitoussi, E., and A. Baron (2012) 'Tunisia: "The Fight against the Exploitation of Women can be an Engine for Social Change"' (Tunisie: «La lutte contre l'exploitation des femmes peut être un moteur de changement social global»), Interview with Ahlem Belhadj, President of the Tunisian Association of Democratic Women (TANF), *Europe Solidaire San Frontieres*, January. Available at: www.europe-solidaire.org/spip.php?article24731 (accessed on 22 July 2014).

Gataa, R. (2009) 'Tunisia: Women's Empowerment and Reproductive Health', in *Experiences in Addressing Population and Reproductive Health Challenges*, Vol. 19, pp. 211–28. Available at: http://tcdc2.undp.org/GSSDAcademy/SIE/Docs/Vol19/SIE.v19_CH9.pdf (accessed on 5 January 2015).

Gilman, S. (2007) 'Feminist Organizing in Tunisia: Negotiating Transnational Linkages and the State', in V. M. Moghadam, ed., *From Patriarchy to Empowerment: Women's Participation, Movement, and Rights in the Middle East, North Africa and South Asia*, Syracuse University Press, Syracuse.

Goulding, K. (2009) 'Unjustifiable Means to Unjustifiable Ends: Delegitimizing Parliamentary Gender Quotas in Tunisia', *Al-Raida*, Issue 126–27, pp. 71–78.

Gray, D. (2013) *Beyond Feminism and Islamism: Gender and Equality in North Africa*, I. B. Tauris, London.

Hopmann, P. T., and I. W. Zartman (2012) 'Tunisia: Understanding Conflict 2012', Conflict Management Program, Johns Hopkins University School for Advanced International Studies (SAIS).

Kandiyoti, D. (1998) 'Gender Power and Contestation: Rethinking "Bargaining with Patriarchy"', in C. Jackson and R. Pearson, eds, *Feminist Visions of Development: Gender Analysis and Policy*, Routledge, London, pp. 135–52.

Kandiyoti D., A. Maha, L. Mehrezia and K. Fatemah (2013) 'Women and Power in the Middle East: Social Justice, Democracy and Gender Equality', Transcript, Chatham House: London. Available at: http://www.chathamhouse.org/sites/files/chathamhouse/public/Meetings/Meeting%20Transcripts/30042013panel1.pdf (accessed on 26 February 2015).

Karim, J. (2009) *American Muslim Women: Negotiating Race, Class and Gender within the Ummah*, New York University Press, New York.

Labidi, L. (2012) 'Tunisia: Policies and Practices for Promoting Social Justice for Rural Women during a Democratic Transition', in *Is The Arab Awakening Marginalizing Women?*, Middle East Program Occasional Paper Series, Wilson Center, Washington, DC.

Mahmood, S. (2005) *Politics of Piety: The Islamic Revival and the Feminist Subject*, Princeton University Press, Princeton.

Mezran, K. (2007) *Negotiation and Construction of National Identities*, Martinus Nijhoff Publishers, Leiden.

Mir-Hosseini, Z. (2011) 'Beyond "Islam" vs. "Feminism"', Institute of Development Studies, *IDS Bulletin*, 42 (1), pp. 67–77.

Molyneux, M., and S. Razavi (2003) 'Gender Justice, Development and Rights', Governance and Human Rights Programme Paper Number 10, United Nations Research Institute for Social Development.

Moore, H. (2007) *The Subject of Anthropology: Gender, Symbolism and Psychoanalysis*, Polity Press, Cambridge.

Murphy, E. C. (2003) 'Women in Tunisia: Between State Feminism and Economic Reform', in E. Doumato and M. Pripstein Posusney, eds, *Women and Globalization in the Arab Middle East: Gender, Economy, and Society*, Lynne Rienner, Boulder.

Salim, Z. (2011) *Between Feminism and Islam: Human Rights and Sharia Law in Morocco*, University of Minnesota Press, Minnesota.

Taymoumi, H. (2008) *Tunis 1956–1987*, Dar Muhammad Ali Publishing, Tunis. (Arabic).

Taymoumi, H. (2013) *Khida' al-istabdad al-na'im fi Tunis, 23 sanna min hukm Bin 'Ali*, Dar Muhammad Ali Publishing, Tunis. (Arabic).

Towards New Epistemologies and Ontologies of Gender and Socio-Political Transformation in the Arab World

Maha El Said, Lena Meari and Nicola Pratt

This chapter aims to discuss the implications of the findings of the chapters presented here and to revisit the questions that we posed at the beginning of this volume. We asked, what are the epistemological and ontological implications of considering gender and sexualities in socio-political transformations in the Arab world? To what degree do socio-political transformations and other moments of women's resistance activities represent significant ruptures in gender identities, relations and norms? How do acts of resistance affect existing perceptions of gender and sexed bodies? How do women's various modalities of agency and their gendered experiences disrupt the secular/religious dichotomy? And, what does the case of the Arab world bring to theorizing about gender in revolutions and resistance? We present some reflections on these questions, particularly through the prism of rethinking epistemologies and ontologies for the study of gender and socio-political transformation in the Arab world. Finally, we suggest some further lines of research into the gendered dimensions of socio-political transformations.

In the Introduction, we began by arguing for the need to go beyond dichotomous discourses regarding women's experiences in socio-political transformations, that is, of women as either heroines or victims. Such discourses are constituted through a Eurocentric/Orientalist epistemological distinction between the 'West' and the 'Orient', or Arab world (Said 1978). Within such thinking, a whole set of oppositional characteristics is established. First and foremost, the (secular) West is posited as the source and model of progress and civilization, whilst the Arab-Muslim world is treated as the source of 'backwardness' and 'barbarity', particularly with regard to the treatment of women. Within such a framework, the subject is assumed to be either an agent or a victim (Asad 2003) and women's only form of agency is assumed to embody the secular-liberal desire for freedom and emancipation from cultural-religious patriarchal norms (Mahmood 2005). In other words, the West is posited as the model for women's agency and women's interests are conflated with Western secular-rational ideas. Meanwhile, local cultures and beliefs are assumed to be an obstacle to women's agency and women's interests. In addition, many commentators and some scholars have used the degree to which the Arab Spring has revolutionized gender (or not) as a marker for the success of the uprisings, thereby reducing complex questions of socio-political transformation to a measurement of women's freedom. Not only does such an epistemological approach fail to explain the gendered dimensions of the upheavals witnessed since the end of 2010, but, in line with Edward Said, we believe that such commentary and scholarship is part of the discursive apparatus or 'corporate institution for dealing with the Orient . . . by making statements about it, authorizing views of it, describing it, by teaching it, settling it, ruling over it: in short, Orientalism as Western style for dominating, restructuring, and having authority over the Orient' (Said 1978: 3).

Several of the chapters in this volume challenge such an epistemological approach in their study of women's agency and resistance. Rather than positing emancipation in opposition to culture, chapters by Meari, Sami, El Said and Alnaas and Pratt in particular have illustrated how women draw on national cultures, heritage and religion in making their demands for equal citizenship, resisting violence and securing their presence in the public space. In other words, women seek emancipation through critical engagement with rather than repudiation of their cultures. This challenges not only a Eurocentric/Orientalist epistemology, but also the practices of those women activists within the Arab world that continue to regard local religion and culture as an absolute obstacle to women's rights and to hold up CEDAW and other universal rights frameworks as the only means by which to guarantee women's interests, as Muhanna's chapter on Tunisia highlights.

However, in challenging an orientalist epistemology towards gender, we should also be careful not to merely reverse the binary. The advocacy of CEDAW by some activists should not always be assumed merely to reflect a desire on their part to reproduce the binary between the local and the universal. The adoption of CEDAW as a frame of reference for women's rights could be seen as an attempt by women's rights activists to escape local nationalist and/or Islamist discourses that have historically sought to control 'their' women as part of resistance to colonialism and Western hegemony. For example, in India under the British, nationalist elites supported Sati as an 'authentic' form of women's agency in the face of colonial efforts to outlaw it, under the banner of 'liberating' women and 'civilizing' the country (for example, see Chatterjee 1986; 1989; Mani 1987). The use of women's bodies in discursive battles between local nationalists and foreign colonizers is not a relic of history but continues into the colonial/post-colonial present of the Arab world (where post-colonial refers to continuities with as well as ruptures from colonialism and the colonial present continues in Palestine). The construction of such a binary as a fixed, hegemonic discourse leaves almost no position for Arab/Muslim women from which to be simultaneously critical of Western-imperialist-secular-liberal assumptions, on the one hand, or local-cultural-national-religious gender formations, on the other. This predicament led Gayatri Chakravorty Spivak to pose her famous question: 'can the subaltern speak?' (1988). Whilst the subjects of this book do not meet Spivak's definition of 'subaltern', nevertheless the signifying practices of colonialism, nationalism and Islamism greatly circumscribe the ways in which scholars and commentators interpret women's agency and interests in the Arab world, particularly since the end of 2010, when women's involvement in socio-political transformations has been highly visible.

We can see how the signifying practices of colonialism, nationalism and Islamism come into play in shaping interpretations of women's agency with regards to the cases of Aliaa Elmahdy, Amina Sboui and Sama El-Masry, as discussed by El Said and Al-Najjar and Abusalim. In particular, there is a noticeable difference in how local audiences interpreted the bodily performances of Aliaa and Amina, as opposed to those of Sama El-Masry. Whilst resisting nationalist/Islamist patriarchal discourses that control women's bodies, Aliaa and Amina simultaneously reproduce Orientalist notions about Arab/Muslim societies (see also Muhanna, Chapter 8, this volume). In particular, acts of veiling/unveiling; dressing/undressing are not culturally neutral against a backdrop of colonial feminism in North Africa, where colonial authorities sought to remove women's veils as symbolic of their 'civilizing mission' and to justify colonial subjugation. There were very few people who understood or attempted to interpret women's agency in relation to ideas of feminist/individual emancipation and self-expression. Meanwhile, Sama El-Masry's parody of belly dancing, in which she subverted gendered, sexualized and racialized structures of power reproduced through Orientalist discourse about Muslim women's bodies, was widely acclaimed. In other words, local audiences generally understood these women's bodily performances in relation to the colonial past and post-colonial present. This is not to reify or homogenize experiences of colonialism/post-colonialism, but rather to bring in the colonial/post-colonial in identifying and understanding the gender politics of socio-political transformations in the Arab world.

Similarly, the signifying practices of colonialism, nationalism and Islamism come into play in shaping the construction and regulation of gender by different political actors since the end of 2010. As Ashis Nandy argues (1983), colonial authorities have depicted those they seek to colonize and subjugate as 'feminine' (irrational, passive and incapable of governing themselves) and, in response, post-independence political elites have sought to re-masculinize the nation state. This has had implications for the regulation and legislation of gender relations, with gender hierarchies often being 'naturalized' on the basis of (locally 'authentic') religious texts. In other words, gender norms and relations have been a central site for asserting sovereignty in the post-colonial era, especially because post-colonial sovereignty is continuously undermined through globalization and geopolitical interests. In the case of Libya (Alnaas and Pratt, Chapter 6, this volume), the opposition of Islamists in Libya to CEDAW should not be interpreted merely as a reflection of their conservative ideology but also as a response to ongoing Western intervention in the country. Unable to resist Western intervention in the economic and military spheres, Islamists as well as non-Islamist nationalist leaders put their efforts into resisting Western intervention in the sphere of gender norms and relations.

In response to the construction of oppositional, fixed and essentialized identities (Butler 1999: 183–84), Judith Butler suggests that, 'The shift from an *epistemological* account of identity to one which locates the problematic within practices of *signification* permits an analysis that takes the epistemological mode itself as one possible and contingent signifying practice' (1999: 184, emphasis in the original). Indeed, Muhanna's examination of secular and Islamic Tunisian women's activism begins with an acknowledgement that the binary of 'secular' and 'Islamic' is itself a signifying practice contingent upon the competition for political power within post Ben-Ali Tunisia. Judith Butler goes on to propose that, 'the question of *agency* is reformulated as a question of how signification and resignification work' (1999: 184, emphasis in the original). Indeed, the chapters by Abouelnaga, Meari, Sami, El Said and Alnaas and Pratt have all illustrated that the resignification of gender norms and the malleability of gender and sexual identities have been a central feature of women's agency in socio-political transformations.

However, practices of signification/resignification cannot be understood merely in relation to gender. Gender, as a relation of power, does not fully explain the subject's lived experience. As many chapters in this volume illustrate, gender is articulated with other social relations such as class, nation and colonial power structures. Employing gender as a frame of analysis brings new insights to understanding socio-political transformations; yet, unless gender is articulated with other relations of power, there is a danger that we overlook or misinterpret significant dynamics, leading to de-contextualized and abstract analyses. For example, the modality of resistance of Palestinian women prisoners, as discussed by Meari, is only legible in relation to the struggle against Zionist settler colonialism. Fixed notions of culture are deployed by Israeli security agents to subjugate women and men and deter their resistance. The acts of resistance by Palestinian women against colonialism resignify cultural conceptions of gender and sexualities and destabilize the ontological conception of the body. In other words, women's resistance cannot be reduced to a universal modality of subversion of/subordination to patriarchy. The meanings and means of resistance are historically constituted.

In reformulating agency as a process of (re)signification (in line with Butler), women's resistance should be conceptualized as constituting socio-political transformations, rather than as an instrument towards socio-political transformation, as some liberal/feminist scholarship has tended to do. This has implications for an ontology of the study of gender in revolutions and resistance. Women's agency and gender politics cannot be reduced to what occurs within formal institutions such as parliaments, elections, constitutions and the judiciary. Formal political participation and legal frameworks can be important parts of a feminist strategy. However, by only examining women and gender in relation to formal institutions and procedural politics, we miss a significant part of the picture of gender dynamics and women's agency. This is particularly important when formal institutions continue to marginalize women and to operate as 'décor', rather than as serious sites of decision making (as is the case in many Arab countries, despite the holding of free elections since 2010).

Whilst the resignification and subversion of gender norms may be occurring in parliaments, nevertheless, this volume illustrates that the most creative processes of resignification are occurring in other spaces, such as public squares and streets, prisons as well as cyber-space. Women's bodily performances (dancing, riding bicycles, dress-ing/undressing) as well as aesthetics (graffiti, cartoons, posters) are some of the modalities of women's agency that we believe must be taken seriously in the study of gender in socio-political transforma-tions. Arguably, the most significant 'unit' in the study of gender in socio-political transformations is the gendered body, which is both an object of control by counter-revolutionary and authoritarian actors as well as a vehicle of resistance.

Lest we be accused of romanticizing women's agency and resist-ance, we should take heed of Abou-Bakr's call for an ethical politics. The resignification of gendered norms (in and through nation, class and coloniality), do not, in and of themselves, constitute an ethical project of socio-political transformation. As Abou-Bakr argued in this volume:

> If feminism developed out of exposing and rejecting exclusionary practices, it ought not to yield to a moral complacency that justifies concern for women's conditions only and ignores the larger frameworks of monopoly, state violence and despotism. As a conscionable movement, it can thus be distinguished from a history of institutional patriarchal practices of political opportunism and authoritarianism. Furthermore, ethical feminism in that sense should also consider class issues and the needs of poor, marginalized and disempowered women.

Such a paradigm shift would, as Shereen Abouelnaga noted here, contribute to creating a new discourse that puzzles the old patriarch and forces a 'rethinking of all forms of femininity and masculinity equally'.

We hope that this volume opens up further lines of enquiry and research. In particular, there is a need to further understand the emerg-ing subjectivities and agency of women beyond those who are highly visible in the public sphere and have formed the core subjects of our volume. These are amongst the women who were not previously mobilized before the end of 2010 or those who are involved in activities in their local communities or away from the urban centres that are often the focus of media as well as researchers.

In relation to this, there is a need to introduce the lens of class as both an identity and power structure into our discussions of gender and socio-political transformation. For the most part, the subjects of our volume have tended to be middle-class women, largely concerned with their rights and security. This is not to delegitimize their concerns or to essentialize working-class women as only concerned with issues specific to their class positions. Nevertheless, it is necessary to further problematize the intersections of gender, class and nation. For example, we should ask whether the politics of resignification and subversion of gender norms, of groups such as Baheya Ya Masr, Women On Walls or Friday's Bike, even whilst these resignify the nation, operate to accommodate neo-liberal politics and to marginalize socio-economic concerns of poverty, employment, housing and education or to ignore the plight of non-nationals, including the millions of refugees that have been displaced by the conflict in Syria since 2011 and are vulnerable to harassment and violence.

In addition, there is a need to further understand men and masculinities in socio-political transformations. Several of the chapters here have alluded to the increasing presence of men in campaigns and protests for women's rights and against violence against women. What norms of masculinity inform such agency? And do such notions of masculinity challenge or subvert the norms of masculinity underpinning counter-revolutionary projects as well as conservative nationalist and Islamist projects?

Undoubtedly, the political upheavals since the end of 2010 have created new subjectivities amongst women and men, opened up new opportunities for challenging fixed identities and subverting previously hegemonic gendered norms, as well as contributing towards the dismantling of some epistemological and ontological binaries. Yet, events since 2010 have also demonstrated the power of 'epistemological models' (Butler 1999: 184), which are wielded by those who seek to (re-)assert their authority. Counter-revolutionary actors have discredited revolutionary agency by positing an essentialized epistemological difference between women protesters and 'proper' Egyptian woman (see El Said, Chapter 4). Islamist actors, who have come to power through elections, have formulated their conservative gender agendas on the basis of a posited epistemological difference between the Arab-Muslim world and the West. The Egyptian military has ousted the Muslim Brotherhood on the basis of an epistemological difference between the 'modern' Egyptian Muslim and the 'backward' and 'alien' Muslim. The challenge for those women and men who seek socio-political transformation is not only to overthrow a regime but to continue to subvert epistemological models and the fixed identities that they produce. In light of armed conflicts and growing militarism as well as neo-liberal economic policies and continuing impoverishment across the region, we must also be attentive to the changing and complex ways in which women and men perform their agency and resist.

References

Asad, T. (2003) *Formations of the Secular: Christianity, Islam, Modernity*, Stanford University Press, Stanford.

Butler, J. (1999) *Gender Trouble: Feminism and the Subversion of Identity*, Routledge, New York and London.

Chatterjee, P. (1986) *Nationalist Thought and the Colonial World*, Zed Books, London.

Chatterjee, P. (1989) 'Colonialism, Nationalism, and the Colonized Women: The Contest in India', *American Ethnologist*, 16 (4), pp. 622–33.

Mahmood, S. (2005) *Politics of Piety: The Islamic Revival and the Feminist Subject*, Princeton University Press, Princeton.

Mani, L. (1987) 'Contentious Traditions: The Debate on Sati in Colonial India', *Cultural Critique*, 7, pp. 119–56.

Nandy, A. (1983) *The Intimate Enemy: Loss and Recovery of Self under Colonialism*, Oxford University Press, Oxford.

Said, E. (1978) *Orientalism*, Routledge and Kegan Paul, London.

Spivak, G. C. (1988) 'Can the Subaltern Speak?', in C. Nelson and L. Grossberg, eds, *Marxism and the Interpretation of Culture*, University of Illinois Press, Urbana.

About the Contributors

Omaima Abou-Bakr is professor of English and comparative literature at Cairo University. Her scholarly interests include women's mysticism and female spirituality in Christianity and Islam, feminist theology, Muslim women's history and gender issues in Islamic discourses and cultural history. She has published a number of articles in both English and Arabic on poetry and medieval literary texts, on historical representations of women in pre-modern Muslim societies, women and gender issues in religious discourses and Islamic feminism. She is also author of *Al-mar'ah wa-al-jindar* (Woman and Gender); editor of *Al-niswiyyah wa-al-dirasat al-diniyah* (Feminism and Religious Studies); and editor of *Feminist and Islamic Perspectives: New Horizons of Knowledge and Reform*.

Shereen Abouelnaga is a professor at the English Department, Cairo University. She writes in English and Arabic in the fields of gender, literary criticism and cultural studies. She is the author of *The Veil, Between the Local and Global: A Religious or a Political Identity?*; *Concepts of Home as Depicted by Arab Women Writers*; a novel, *Betrayal of Cairo*; and several articles in peer-reviewed journals, amongst other publications. Her forthcoming book, *Intellectuals in the Interregnum*, documents the role of intellectuals in the transitional period

(March 2011–July 2012). She is a member of the jury of the Naguib Mahfouz Medal for Literature (American University in Cairo); the editorial board of *New Perspectives on Theory/Culture/Politics*; the board of *Al-thaqafa al-jadida* (New Culture); and, from 2010 to 2012, the jury of the Mahmoud Darwish Prize. In October 2012, she was a visiting professor at the Centre for Critical and Cultural Theory at Cardiff University.

Anoud Abusalim is a senior instructor, teaching rhetoric and composition at the American University of Sharjah, United Arab Emirates. Her research interests are in excellence in teaching, composition and ideology, and composition pedagogical theories. Her work includes several books on rhetoric and composition that are being taught in the Department of Writing Studies in the American University of Sharjah. She also serves as the associate director of the Department of Writing Studies.

Sahar Mediha Alnaas completed an MA in gender and identity in the Middle East at the University of Exeter in 2013. Born and educated in Libya, she moved to the UK in 1995, where she has worked with various women's organizations, including ADVA (Against Domestic Violence and Abuse), Intercome, the Devon Rape Crisis Centre, and Forward. Her specialist area is gender-based violence within black ethnic minorities in the UK. Sahar has also worked with the women's organization Sout El-Haq and the Libyan Civil Society Forum, both based in Tripoli.

Abeer Al-Najjar has been assistant professor at the Department of Mass Communication, American University of Sharjah, United Arab Emirates, since 2005 and was the dean of Jordan Media Institute, Amman, from 2011 to 2012. Her research interests include journalism in Arab countries, popular culture, religious media and women and new media. Abeer has spoken at many regional and international conferences, both academic and professional, in addition to being interviewed by news media outlets, including Al Jazeera, Al Arabiya and SkyNews Arabia. She has also published journal articles and book chapters about Arab media, including 'Patriotism and Popularity in News: Tough Choices Facing Arab Journalists' in *Journal of Journalism Studies*, and 'Framing Political Islam in the Arab Popular Culture' in *Middle East Journal of Culture & Communication*.

Aitemad Muhanna is a visiting fellow at the Middle East Centre at the London School of Economics, where she researches gender, religion and sustainable human development in the Gaza Strip. In 2013, Aitemad led the centre's research on 'Women's Political Participation across the Arab region', funded by Oxfam GB. Originally from the Gaza Strip, Aitemad has worked for the last 20 years on numerous policy-orientated research programmes and publications for Oxfam GB, Sida, UNIFEM, UNDP and the World Bank. For several years, she conducted research and contributed to the Palestinian Human Development Report, as part of the Arab Human Development Report. She has written dozens of research papers and consultancy reports on the crisis of development under Israeli occupation, poverty and coping strategies, participation and community development approaches, and gender analysis. She is author of *Agency and Gender in Gaza: Masculinity, Femininity and Family during the Second Intifada*.

Hala G. Sami is associate professor in the English Department, Cairo University. Her current research interests include Middle Eastern studies, women's studies, Gothic studies, comparative literature, contemporary literary theory, history and politics. She is a member of the International Comparative Literature Association.

Index

Abaida, Magdulien 166
Abbas, Ramez 147
Abdellatif, Ibtihal 226
Abdo, Nahla. 67, 68–9
Abou-Bakr, O. 24
Abou El Fadl, K 200
Abouelnaga, S. 15, 19
Abu Ghraib prison 64–6
Abu-Lughod, L. 113, 120, 213
actions of women, interpretations of
    138–9
active citizenship, women in Egypt 95
activism of women: and agency 11–
    12; and capitalist market economies
    24; Egypt 16, 49, 101, 109, 187,
    190; and ethics 201; feminist agency
    of 215; framing of 22, 140; and
    historical/contextual experiences
    227; Islamic 211, 218–22, 226;
    Islamist women's 186; Libya 166;
    and political engagement 199–200;
    political of Baheya Ya Masr 49,

53n.4, 88–95, 101, 239; and rights
of women 218, 226; against sexual
harassment 49; and sexuality 140;
and state feminism 182; Tunisia
211–22, 226
activist discourse 49
activists: division between Islamic/
    secular 206; and femocrats 183–4;
    sexual violence against 15–16;
    women and NGOs 37, 188
African women, use of dance 123
agency, discrediting of revolutionary
    239–40
agency of women: and activism
    11–12; and bodily performances
    238; and colonialism 234–5;
    and context/political dimensions
    141; and culture 120, 121, 128,
    129; as doing 12–13; as dynamic
    222; effectiveness of 111, 127–8,
    129; Egypt 40, 42, 43; embodied
    12; erasure of 137; failure of

discourses: activist 49; on appearance/
behaviour of women 17; autocratic
in Egypt 95; conservative Islam 14,
168, 189, 196; excluding women
from public sphere 99; Islamist
conservative 92; moderate Islamic
194; of Muslim Brotherhood 14,
189, 196; new/of identity 45;
new spaces of 102; political 20;
power of marginal 48; pragmatic
215; pseudo-feminist 40–1;
reform/renewal of religious 194;
resignification of 168, 172;
resignification of national 15; rights
of women/Tunisia 211–22; secular/
Islamic on gender 87; shariah
frame of 208; state in Egypt 37; of
subjectivity 49; subversion of 102,
170, 172; women's experiences
in socio-political transformations
232–3; of women's sisterhood 81
disempowerment of women, Tunisia
210
dissent, popular culture as voice of 87
divorce, Tunisia 219–20, 229n.10
docile body, and power 112
documentation, of sexual harassment
in Egypt 50
domestic violence, Egypt 38, 39, 47
domination: and sexual torture 63;
strategies of 9
Doustourna 223, 224
Dreamer, The (painting) 116
dress of women: cultural significance
of 235; Islamic 167, 170–1; Libya
14–15, 19–20, 158, 164–5, 166–7,
170–1, 173, 175n.25; Tunisia 208,
221–2; the veil 21, 113, 137–8,
235
Dying Colonialism, A 59

economic change, and gender 7
education, Tunisia 208, 225, 226, 227

Egypt *see also* Egyptian Revolution: 1990s
36–41; April 6 Youth Movement
17; Eighteen Days 35–6, 42, 53n.2,
89, 139; post-revolutionary 86, 95;
protests 2013 3, 22; Supreme Council
of the Armed Forces (SCAF) *see*
Supreme Council of the Armed Forces
(SCAF)
Egypt as a Woman 89
Egyptian army, coup 3
Egyptian Revolution 14, 87, 90, 101,
109, 115, 117, 135, 139 *see also*
Eighteen Days
Egyptian women, prominent 96, 99
Egyptian women's movement 47, 49
Eighteen Days, Egypt 35–6, 42, 53n.2,
89, 139 *see also* Egyptian Revolution
Eladl, Doaa 88, 95–8, 100, 101
Elghali, Houd 168
elitism, in Tunisia 210, 213, 214
elitist-secular state feminism 23
Elmahdy, Aliaa 17, 18–19, 110, 111,
114–21, 127, 128, 129, 135,
136–7, 142–51, 235
Elmesallati, Sara 160
Elsadda, Hoda 37, 53, 87, 187, 188
el-sitt 91–2, 95, 102
emancipation, through critical
engagement 234
embodied agency 12
emotional responses, female protest
as 138–9
employment, access of women to 208,
225, 226
empowerment of women 52, 223,
228
engendered violence, and resistance in
Egypt 43
Ennahda 211, 214–15, 217, 218, 219,
228n.3
entertainment industry, and moral
decadence 137
epistemological models, power of 239

identity(ies): and class 239; and
culture 38, 39, 120, 128,
219; Egypt 40, 45, 86, 89;
epistemological account of 236;
gender/and parody 97–8; Islamic
157, 160, 173, 221; Islamic of
Tunisian women 239; national
see national identity; and national
costume 170; new discourse of 45;
new gendered 9; newly resignified
92; religious 120, 221, 222;
Shabak perceptions of 82; use of/
resignification of national 23
identity politics, and women's bodies
37
Idris, Wafa 138
Iethar 223
Al-Ifta, Dar 161, 163
illiberal democracy, Egypt 191
Imam, Sheikh 89
inheritance law, Islamic 209, 212, 213
injustice, patriarchal 201
International Conference on
Population and Development
(ICPD) 36, 186
international image, and Egypt 37
International Islamic Committee of
Women and Children 195
International Union for Muslim
Scholars 190
International Women's Day, Egypt 42,
54n.9, 90
internet: and nude images 150;
publicising women's participation
in sport 168; sharing testimonies
of women to violence 50; as site of
resistance 110
interrogation techniques see also
Supreme Council of the Armed
Forces (SCAF): becoming ineffective
80; failure of repetitive sexual
73–5; Israeli colonial state 62; on
Palestinian men 72–3; rape as 70,

71, 75–6, 78; resignification of
77–8; sexual 82; sexual in colonial
contexts 64–6; of the Shabak
60, 61, 66, 67, 69, 73–9, 80–2;
subversion of 69–73; use of family
in 79; women's sisterhood as 80–1
intimidation, sexual proximity as 75
invisibility, of women in public sphere
91
Iran, gender policies 185
Iraq, torture in Abu Ghraib prison 64–6
Islam see also political Islam: and
agency of women 234–5; and
CEDAW 162–3; counter-discourses
against conservative 168; different
perceptions/interpretations of 22,
222; and gender regulation 235;
moderate and modernity 225; and
modernism 113; and morality 219;
and nationalism 21–2; and rights
of women 210, 212, 214, 215;
secularization of 228n.3; and single
mothers 218–19; and subordination
of women 213; women's issues in
195
Islamic culture, and female bodies
112–13
Islamic discourse: moderate 194;
resisting conservative 92
Islamic dress 167, 170–1 see also dress
of women
Islamic feminism 24, 181–2,
194–201
Islamic/feminist binary, Tunisia 227
Islamic identity 157, 160, 173, 221
Islamic knowledge, alternative
gendered 194
Islamic law 140, 208
Islamic organizations in Tunisia,
charity work of 223–4
Islamic/secular binary 10, 20–4, 236
Islamic–secular feminist binary 205–6,
207, 211, 228

national heritage, use/resignification
of 23
national identity *see also* identity(ies):
and culture 23, 86, 89, 113, 119–20,
123, 128; and dance 123; Egypt 86,
89, 119–20; use/resignification of
23; and veils 113
nationalism: and agency of women
234–5; Egypt 38; and gender
regulation 235; and Islam 21–2;
as unifying force 21; and women's
bodies 113
nationalist discourse, resignifying of
15
national struggle movements, and state
building 185
National Supreme Committee of Truth
and Dignity, Tunisia 226
National Transitional Council (NTC),
Libya 156, 159, 164
nation-building, and position of
women 185–6
nation states, re-masculinization of
236
neo-liberal socio-economic policies 213
networks, of resistance/solidarity in
Egypt 46
New Woman Research Centre, Egypt
38
Nicaragua, practical v. strategic gender
interests 10
Nidaa Tunis 215
van Nieuwkerk, K. 123
Nijm, Ahmed Fuad 38, 89
niqab, Tunisia 208, 221–2 *see also* dress
of women
non-governmental organizations:
as alternative civil organizations
186; feminist agenda of 54n.9;
and human rights 194; and
independence of women 191;
NGO-ized women's movement 11;
and women activists 37, 188

normative femininity 16
nude art 115–17
'nude blogger', the *see* Elmahdy, Aliaa
nudity: cultural meaning of 121,
235; framing of 143; and
fundamentalism 117; and internet
150; liberal responses to 145–8;
and the media 137, 150; as
method of protest 136, 141–2;
and political action 117, 118;
and power relations 114, 116;
public understanding of 145;
regulation of 114; as resistance
144–5; as social action 118; and
social concern 145; Tunisia 147,
148, 149; women disowning nude
images 149

Al-Obeidi, Eman 141, 150
objectification: of dance 123; of
female body 114; of the gaze 115
occupation: practices of in Palestine
67; of spaces/significance of 93;
torture as technique of 65
Olympia (painting) 115
OpAntiSH collective 49
Operation Cast Lead 3
opposition, women's bodies as site
for 111
oppression: and gender equality 212;
in Palestine 82; reinforcing defiance
71; and sexual torture 63; and veils
21; and women's bodies 114
Orientalism: and naked women 149;
sexual 65
Orientalist/Eurocentric epistemology
233, 234
Orientalist perceptions: of Arab
masculinity 72–3; of Arab/Muslim
societies 235; of Palestinian
sexuality 69; of Palestinian society
78
Orientalist stereotypes 123

the interrogation encounter 62; malleability of in revolution/ resistance 8–15; as means of torture/control 69; Orientalist notions of 65; and power 63, 112; regulation of 61, 113, 124; Shabak perceptions of Palestinian 82; and women's activism 140

'Sexuality and Power' 124

sexualized violence: breaking silence over 18; Egypt/SCAF 15

sexual norms, and Arab Spring 136

sexual politics, of colonial rule 61

sexual power techniques 63; failure of repetitious 73–5

sexual propriety, notions of female 13–14

sexual proximity, as intimidation 75

sexual terrorism: on Egyptian female protesters 51; against Palestinian women prisoners 67

sexual, the/as political 63

sexual torture: in Abu Ghraib prison 64–6; colonial techniques of 62–3, 64–6; and domination/oppression 63; on Palestinian men 72–3; of Palestinian women 14, 67; of the Shabak 62–3

sexual violence: Egypt 15, 39, 51; against female activists 15, 16; and Palestinian society 67–8; against Palestinian women prisoners 67; popular indictment of the victim 39; refusal to remain silent about 14, 18; and subversion of hegemonic norms 9

Shabak: interrogation techniques of 60, 61, 66, 67, 69, 73–9, 80–2; Orientalist knowledge production of 65–6; torture of the 61, 62–3, 64, 66

Shadia 93

shame, and control of women's bodies 50, 113

Al-Sharqawi, Pakinam 189

Shay' min al-khawf 94

Sheehan, Donna 121

Shotwell, A. 127

signification, practices of 236 see also resignification

silence, of women in Egypt 41, 49–50, 191

silencing, of women in Libya 171–2, 173

single mothers 212, 218–19

El-Sisi, Abdel Fattah 3, 193, 196, 197

sisterhood 80–1, 141, 148

Sleeping Venus (painting) 115, 116

social action, nudity as 118

social concern, and nudity 145

social construction, of gender 9

social control, over women's bodies 110

social ethics 198, 199

social issues, framing of 143

socialist/liberal ideologies 212

social justice, and Islamic/feminist women's groups 227

social media see also internet; YouTube videos: and nude photos 136; sharing testimonies of violence by women 50

social order, bodies of women resisting 151

social power, of marginal discourses 48

social relations, and gender 237

social statement, of naked bodies 144

social status, women in Egypt 90

socio-cultural values, post-revolutionary Egypt 86

socio-economic inequalities, Tunisia 23, 209

socio-economic policies, neo-liberal 213

socio-political change: prior to 2010 4; since 2010 2

Tahrir Square 22, 41–2, 47, 89, 90, 92, 135, 139
Tahrir Square, Benghazi 170, 171
tamkeen 223
Tawhidic paradigm 201
'Technology of Gender, The' 87
Al-Tellawi, Mervat 189–90, 191, 192
terrorism, Israel's colonial state 64
testimonies, as technique of resistance 50, 55n.16
Tétreault, M. A. 65
threat(s): against female MPs 17; naked pictures as 147; of reversed gaze 117; to women in politics in Libya 171–2
'Thugs' 124
Tigar 223
torture *see also* atrocities; coercion; violence: culture/family/sexuality as means of 69; Egypt 43; and occupation/subjugation 64, 65; sexual and oppression 63; sexual in Abu Ghraib prison 64–6; of the Shabak 61, 62–3, 64, 66; and subjugation 64; testifying to inhumanity of occupiers 72; Tunisia 226
transformation, of Palestinian women prisoners 80
transitional justice, Tunisia 226
transversality 51
treason, protest as 141
Tripp, C. 93
Tunisia: post-revolutionary 23–4; revolution 35
Tunisian General Labour Union (UGTT) 212
Tunisian League for the Defence of Human Rights (LTDH) 212
Turkey, gender policies 185

Ukrainian women's group, naked demonstrations 114
Umm Kulthum (*el-Sitt*) 92, 95, 102

United Nations: Commission on the Status of Women (CSW) 189, 190, 191, 193; Convention on the Elimination of All Forms of Discrimination against Women (CEDAW) *see* Convention on the Elimination of All Forms of Discrimination against Women (CEDAW); declaration on violence against women 189; International Conference on Population and Development 36, 186
United States: colonization of Iraq 64; project of Empire 65
universal human rights, and cultural particularity 213–14
universality, of rights of women 212, 213, 214, 224
universal rights, and women's interests 10
'Uprising of Women in the Arab World, The' 51

values: cultural and subordination 120; destabilizing cultural 82; Egypt 40, 86, 110; and femininity 125; transformation of self/societies 77–80
veils, wearing of 21, 113, 137–8, 235 *see also* dress of women
victims, becoming warriors 49–52
violations of women, Egypt 17, 37, 119
violence *see also* atrocities; coercion; sexual violence; torture: domestic in Egypt 38, 39, 47; gendered 43, 44–5, 46, 50, 52; and Muslim Brotherhood 17, 190, 191; political Islam justifying 17; of SCAF 15, 139, 189, 190; socially justified against women 143; against women in Egypt 37–8, 47–8, 110, 190, 193; against women in public